LANGUAGE AWARENESS

LANGUAGE AWARENESS

EDITORS
Paul A. Eschholz
Alfred F. Rosa
Virginia P. Clark
UNIVERSITY OF VERMONT

ST. MARTIN'S PRESS · NEW YORK

Library of Congress Catalog Card Number: 74-75772

Manufactured in the United States of America.
For information, write:
St. Martin's Press, Inc., 175 Fifth Avenue, New York, N.Y. 10010

AFFILIATED PUBLISHERS:
Macmillan Limited, London—
also at Bombay, Calcutta, Madras, and Melbourne

ACKNOWLEDGMENTS

p. 49 "Occupational Euphemisms," from *The American Language,* Fourth Edition, by H. L. Mencken. Copyright 1919, 1921, 1936 by Alfred A. Knopf, Inc. and renewed 1964 by August Mencken and Mercantile-Safe Deposit & Trust Co. Reprinted by permission of Alfred A. Knopf, Inc.

p. 56 "The Traveler's Guide to Hash-House Greek," by Dan Carlinsky, *The New York Times,* September 5, 1971. © 1971 by the New York Times Company. Reprinted by permission.

p. 58 Cartoon by M. Norman, from *The New York Times,* September 5, 1971. © 1971 by The New York Times Company. Reprinted by permission.

p. 61 "Burger Heaven," by Charles Kuralt from the CBS News series *On The Road.* Reprinted by permission.

p. 65 "The Language of the Law," from Chapter 15 of *The Language of the Law,* by David Mellinkoff. Copyright © 1963 by Little, Brown & Company (Inc.). Reprinted by permission.

p. 71 "Football Verbiage," by William Eben Schultz, reprinted from *American Speech,* XXVI (October 1951), by permission of Columbia University Press and June Schultz. Mr. Schultz died April 16, 1964 in Bloomington, Illinois, at the age of 77. At that time he was teaching English at Illinois Wesleyan University and was also college historian.

p. 75 "Fast as an Elephant, Strong as an Ant," by Bil Gilbert, *Sports Illustrated* (April 25, 1966). Copyright © 1966 Time Inc. Reprinted by permission.

p. 82 "Police Have a Slanguage of Their Own," by David Burnham, *The New York Times,* February 15, 1970. © 1970 by the New York Times Company. Reprinted by permission.

p. 86 "The Semantics of Patient-Dentist Relations," by Samuel H. Stein, *ETC: A Review of General Semantics,* Vol. XVII, No. 4 (1960). Reprinted by permission of the International Society for General Semantics.

p. 89 "Gobbledygook," by Stuart Chase, from *The Power of Words,* copyright 1953, 1954 by Stuart Chase. Reprinted by permission of Harcourt Brace Jovanovich, Inc.

p. 101 "Little Miss Muffet," from *Poor Russell's Almanac,* by Russell Baker. Copyright © 1972 by Russell Baker, © 1962, 1965, 1966, 1967, 1968, 1969, 1970, 1971 by The New York Times Company. Reprinted by permission of Doubleday & Company, Inc.

III PRISONERS OF LANGUAGE

p. 107 "Linguistic Factors in Prejudice," by Gordon Allport. Reprinted from Chapter 11 of *The Nature of Prejudice,* by Gordon Allport. Copyright 1954 by Addison-Wesley Publishing Company, Reading, Mass. Used by permission.

p. 118 From *Knots,* by R. D. Laing. Copyright © 1970 by The R. D. Laing Trust. Reprinted by permission of Pantheon Books/A Division of Random House, Inc.

p. 120 "The English Language Is My Enemy!" by Ossie Davis, from *The Negro History Bulletin.* Copyright © by The Association for the Study of Negro Life and History, Inc. Reprinted by permission.

p. 122 "The Language of Sexism," by Haig A. Bosmajian, *ETC: A Review of General Semantics,* Vol XXIX, No. 3 (1972). Reprinted by permission of the International Society for General Semantics.

p. 131 "Does Language Libel the Left-Handed?" from *English Highlights,* Vol. XXV, No. 3 (March–April 1968). Copyright © 1968 by Scott, Foresman and Company. Reprinted by permission of the publisher.

p. 133 "The Language of the Hospital and Its Effects on the Patient," by Anna Teresa Baziak and Robert Knox Dentan, *ETC: A Review of General Semantics,* Vol. XVII, No. 3 (1960). Reprinted by permission of the International Society for General Semantics.

p. 139 From "Semantic Systems of Children: Some Assessments of Social Class and Ethnic Differences," by Doris R. Entwisle, in *Language and Poverty: Perspectives on a Theme,* ed. Frederick Williams, Chicago: Markham Publishing Company, 1970, pp. 123–124. Reprinted by permission of Rand McNally College Publishing Company.

p. 140 From "The Invisible Minority: Report of the NEA-Tucson Survey of the Teaching of Spanish to the Spanish Speaking," Department of Rural Education, National Education Association, Washington, D.C., 1966. Reprinted by permission.

p. 143 From "Language, Poverty, and the North American Indian," by Lynn R. Osborn, in *Language and Poverty: Perspectives on a Theme,* ed. Frederick Williams, Chicago: Markham Publishing Company, 1970, pp. 229–230, 237, 240–241. Reprinted by permission of Rand McNally College Publishing Company.

p. 145 From "On Communication with Children," by S. I. Hayakawa, *ETC: A Review of General Semantics,* Vol. XXIII, No. 2 (1966). Reprinted by permission of the author and the International Society for General Semantics.

p. 146 From *The Lore and Language of Schoolchildren,* by Iona and Peter Opie. © 1959 by Iona and Peter Opie. Reprinted by permission of The Clarendon Press, Oxford.

p. 147 From "Greetings from the Lonely Crowd," by Catherine M. Norris, *Nursing Forum* (Winter 1961–62), Nursing Publications, Inc. Reprinted by permission of the publisher.

p. 147 From "Who Needs the Aged Anyhow?" by Terri Schultz, *Today's Health* (June 1973). Published by the American Medical Association. Reprinted by permission.

p. 148 From *Nobody Ever Died of Old Age,* by Sharon R. Curtin. Copyright © 1972 by Sharon Curtin. Reprinted by permission of Little, Brown and Co. in association with the *Atlantic* Monthly Press.

p. 151 "UN Group Urges Dropping of Words with Racist Tinge," *The New York Times,* December 13, 1968. © 1968 by The New York Times Company. Reprinted by permission.

IV INFLUENCING LANGUAGE

p. 155 "Weasel Words: God's Little Helpers," by Paul Stevens (pseudonym, Carl P. Wrighter), from *I Can Sell You Anything,* by Carl P. Wrighter, Copyright © 1972 by Ballantine Books, Inc. Reprinted by permission of Ballantine Books, Inc./A Division of Random House, Inc.

p. 173 "The Corporate Censor," by Nicholas Johnson, *TV Guide* (July 5, 1969). Mr. Johnson is also the author of *How to Talk Back to Your Television Set* (Boston: Atlantic-Little, Brown & Co., 1970; New York: Bantam, 1970) and *Test Pattern for Living* (New York: Bantam, 1972).

p. 183 "Bunkerisms: Archie's Suppository Remarks in 'All in the Family,'" by Alfred F. Rosa and Paul A. Eschholz, *Journal of Popular Culture* (Winter 1972). Reprinted with permission of the editor of the *Journal of Popular Culture.*

p. 190 "Politigabble," from *Poor Russell's Almanac,* by Russell Baker. Copyright © 1972 by Russell Baker, © 1962, 1965, 1966, 1967, 1968, 1969, 1970, 1971 by The New York Times Company. Reprinted by permission of Doubleday & Company, Inc.

p. 193 "A Vivacious Blonde Was Fatally Shot Today or How to Read a Tabloid," by Otto Friedrich, *American Scholar,* XXVIII (Autumn 1959). Copyright © 1959 by Otto Friedrich. Reprinted by permission of William Morris Agency, Inc.

p. 200 "Dullness and Dishonesty: The Rhetoric of Newswriting," from *Tough, Sweet and Stuffy: An Essay on Modern Prose Style,* by Walker Gibson (1966). Reprinted by permission of Indiana University Press.

V PROSPECTS

p. 217 "The Computer's First Christmas Card," by Edwin Morgan, *ETC: A Review of General Semantics* (December 1970). Reprinted by permission of Edinburgh University Press.

p. 219 "The Dream of a World Language," by Jacob Ornstein and William W. Gage, from *The ABC's of Language and Linguistics* (1964). Reprinted by permission of Rand McNally & Company.

p. 228 From *A Clockwork Orange,* by Anthony Burgess. Copyright © 1962 by Anthony Burgess, © 1963 by W. W. Norton & Company, Inc. Reprinted by permission of W. W. Norton & Company, Inc. and William Heinemann Ltd.

p. 230 "The Limitations of Language," by Melvin Maddocks, *Time* (March 8, 1971). Reprinted by permission of *Time,* The Weekly Newsmagazine; Copyright Time Inc.

p. 235 "The Semi-Literate Shakespeare," from *Future Shock,* by Alvin Toffler. Copyright © 1970 by Alvin Toffler. Reprinted by permission of Random House, Inc.

p. 239 "Hot Language and Cool Lives," by Arthur Berger, *ETC: A Review of General Semantics,* Vol. XXVIII (1971). Reprinted by permission of the International Society for General Semantics.

p. 243 "The Principles of Newspeak," from *1984,* by George Orwell. Reprinted by permission of A. M. Heath & Company Ltd. on behalf of Sonia Brownell Orwell and Secker & Warburg.

p. 254 "The Linguistic Wonder of the Modern World," from *The Treasure of Our Tongue,* by Lincoln Barnett. Copyright © 1962, 1963, 1964 by Lincoln Barnett. Reprinted by permission of Alfred A. Knopf, Inc.

On the Relation of Language to Public Policy

Resolved, That the National Council of Teachers of English find means to study the relation of language to public policy, to keep track of, publicize, and combat semantic distortion by public officials, candidates for office, political commentators, and all those who transmit through the mass media.

On Dishonest and Inhumane Uses of Language

Resolved, That the National Council of Teachers of English find means to study dishonest and inhumane uses of language and literature by advertisers, to bring offenses to public attention, and to propose classroom techniques for preparing children to cope with commercial propaganda.

Resolutions Passed by the National Council of Teachers of English at the Sixty-First Annual Meeting, 1971

To Billy, Sarah, Ricky, Elizabeth, Debbie, Dave, and Susie

PREFACE

MOST OF US ACCEPT LANGUAGE AS WE ACCEPT THE AIR WE BREATHE: we cannot get along without it, and we take it for granted almost all of the time. Few people are aware of the extent to which language is used dishonestly to mislead and manipulate them. Few are fully conscious of the ways, subtle or not so subtle, in which their own use of language may affect the lives of others. Still fewer recognize that their very perceptions of the world in which they live are influenced, and their thoughts at least partially shaped, by language.

These would be reasons enough, we believe, for a book such as *Language Awareness;* for if it is true that we are all in some sense prisoners of language, it is equally true that liberation begins with an awareness of that fact. To foster such an awareness is one of the goals of this book.

But we are, of course, the beneficiaries of language far more than we are its victims. Language is in fact one of mankind's greatest achievements and most important resources, and it is a subject endlessly fascinating in itself. We very much hope that the readers of *Language Awareness* will gain a heightened appreciation of the richness, flexibility, and vitality of their language and will wish to explore it further.

Above all, our purpose in *Language Awareness* is to encourage its readers to use language more responsibly and effectively themselves. Although the book might appropriately be used in any of several courses, we have developed it with writing courses particularly in mind. It seems to us that the study of language is the best possible basis for courses in writing, for the one common denominator of all good writing is the writer's conscious concern for language. That concern is emphasized, in different ways, by all of the selections here, as well as by the questions for discussion and the suggestions for writing that we have added.

All of our aims in *Language Awareness* are serious ones, but a serious book need not be humorless. Readers may rightly be appalled by examples here of the ways in which language is used to classify, dehumanize, deceive, and control human beings; but Charles Kuralt's catalog of American hamburgers not only teaches us a number of things about language and something about our culture but is funny besides. So, we think, are Lamar's "Does a Finger Fing?" Buchwald's "All-Purpose Press Release," and Gilbert's "Fast as an Elephant, Strong as an Ant"—among others. Indeed, we would like to think that the readers of *Language Awareness* will have as much fun in using the book as we have had in preparing it.

It is impossible to acknowledge here all of our indebtedness, but for helpful advice and criticism we wish to express our special appreciation to Robert Bashore, Jr., Janet Kay Houston Clinton, Dick Friedrich, Mark Hall, and Frank Weir.

Paul A. Eschholz
Alfred F. Rosa
Virginia P. Clark

Burlington, Vermont
January 1974

CONTENTS

II LANGUAGE AND OCCUPATION 47

III PRISONERS OF LANGUAGE 105

LANGUAGE AWARENESS

PERSPECTIVES I

To concepts like suicide, homicide, and genocide, we should add "semanticide"—the murder of language. The deliberate (or quasi-deliberate) misuse of language through hidden metaphor and professional mystification, breaks the basic contract between people, namely the tacit agreement on the proper use of words. Thus it is that the "great" philosophers and politicians whose aim was to control man, from Rousseau to Stalin and Hitler, have preached and practiced semanticide; whereas those who have tried to set man free to be his own master, from Emerson to Kraus and Orwell, have preached and practiced respect for language.

Thomas Szasz, *The Second Sin*

BERGEN EVANS 1

Words: Our Most Important Tools

"Words are the tools for the job of saying what you want to say," begins Bergen Evans, well-known writer and lexicographer and Professor of English at Northwestern University. With this sentence he introduces both the central point of his article and a theme that will recur in each of the five sections of this book: the importance of the word. In this selection, taken from Evans' book The Word-a-Day Vocabulary Builder, *he develops the analogy of words as tools and shows how many qualities, in addition to size, vocabulary must possess if it is to be effective.*

WORDS ARE THE TOOLS FOR THE JOB OF SAYING WHAT YOU WANT to say. And what you want to say are your thoughts and feelings, your desires and your dislikes, your hopes and your fears, your business and your pleasure—almost everything, indeed, that makes up *you.* Except for our vegetablelike growth and our animallike impulses, almost all that we are is related to our use of words. Man has been defined as a tool-using animal, but his most important tool, the one that distinguishes him from all other animals, is his speech.

As with other tools, the number and variety of the words we know should meet all our needs. Not that any man has ever had a vocabulary exactly fitted to his every need at all times. The greatest writers —those who have shown the rest of us how *in*adequate our own command of words is—have agonized over their verbal shortcomings. But we can approach our needs. The more words we know, the closer we can come to expressing precisely what we want to.

We can, for instance, give clear instructions, and reduce misunderstandings. If we say, "See that he does it," we should make sure that the person spoken to knows what he is to do when he *sees,* that it is clear to him who *he* is and what *it* is and what must be accomplished to *do* it.

Some of history's great disasters have been caused by misunderstood directions. The heroic but futile charge of the Light Brigade at Balaclava in the Crimean War is a striking example. "Someone had blundered," Tennyson wrote. That was true, and the blunder consisted of the confusion over one word, which meant one thing to the person speaking but another to the persons spoken to.

The brigade was ordered to charge "the guns." The man who gave the order was on a hilltop and had in mind a small battery which was very plain to him but was concealed from the soldiers in the valley by a slight rise. The only guns *they* could see were the main Russian batteries at the far end of the valley. Therefore they assumed that "the guns" referred to the batteries *they* saw. The command seemed utter madness, but it was a command and the leader of the Brigade, after filing a protest, carried it out.

Fortunately, most misunderstandings don't have such disastrous consequences. But the continual confusion about such general terms as *thing, deal, it, fix,* and the like, certainly can be frustrating. Taken as a whole, the exasperation, humiliation, disappointment and quarreling caused by misunderstandings probably produce a thousand times the misery and suffering that the Light Brigade endured.

So the wise man, who wants peace of mind, and the efficient man, who wants to get on with the job, will take the trouble to use specific terms instead of doubtful ones.

Besides clarity, a large vocabulary provides variety. And that is useful; it is the basis for discrimination, since it provides a larger number of tools to choose from. A hammer won't do when a file is called for. Furthermore a large and varied vocabulary makes the speaker or writer more interesting. It allows him to avoid the dullness of repetition and to provoke attention. The interesting man is much more likely to be persuasive than the dull one. Dull people bore us. We don't listen to them. We hear them, but with a secret distaste. Instead of listening to them, we think only about getting away from them. Therefore a varied vocabulary is very useful for winning others to our point of view.

Thomas Wolfe reveled in words with more glory and gusto than perhaps any man since Shakespeare or Rabelais. On seeing a shabby little man lying dead on a subway bench, Wolfe was struck with the thought of the dull and miserable existence such a man must have had because of the sterility of his speech. "Poor, dismal, ugly, sterile, shabby little man," Wolfe wrote in his essay, "Death the Proud Brother," "with your little scrabble of harsh oaths, and cries, and stale constricted words, your pitiful little designs and feeble purposes. . . . Joy, glory, and magnificence were here for you upon this earth, but you scrabbled along the pavements rattling a few stale words like gravel in your throat, and would have none of them."

When Caliban, the half-human monster in Shakespeare's last play, *The Tempest,* furiously denies that he owes any gratitude to his master, the magician Prospero, he demands to know what Prospero has ever done for him. The magician passes over all the many benefits he has conferred on the wretched creature, to stress only one: he has taught him to speak.

I . . . took pains to make thee speak.
When thou didst not, savage,
Know thine own meaning, but wouldst gabble like
A thing most brutish, I endow'd thy purposes
With words that made them known.

The simple fact is that we all begin as Calibans—and do not know even our own purposes until we endow them with words. Do not, indeed, know ourselves. The pleasure you will feel as you develop your vocabulary is not solely the pleasure that comes with increased power; it is also the greater pleasure that comes with increased knowledge, especially of yourself. You will begin to appreciate expression as an art and to feel not only the advantage of commanding words but the satisfaction. You will notice that this or that phrase which someone utters in your hearing or which you see in the newspapers is very good.

And you will be pleased that it *is* good, just as you are pleased to see a forward pass completed, or a long putt holed, or a dance step gracefully executed. For words are to the mind what such actions are to the body.

You will see that the rightness of a well-chosen word is not merely a source of pleasure; it may provoke the most serious consequences or avoid the gravest danger. When, for example, America and

Russia confronted each other during the Cuban crisis in 1962, and the world hovered for a few days on the brink of disaster, the use of the word *quarantine* instead of *blockade* was extremely important. A *blockade* is an act of war. No one knew quite what a *quarantine* meant, under the circumstances. But the very use of the word indicated that, while we were determined to protect ourselves, we wanted to avoid war. It was all a part of giving Russia some possibility of saving face. We wanted her missiles and planes out of Cuba and were prepared to fight even a nuclear war to get them out. But we certainly preferred to have them removed peacefully. We did not want to back Russia into a corner from which there could have been no escape except by violence.

Thus the use of *quarantine,* a purposefully vague word, was part of our strategy. Furthermore, it had other advantages over *blockade.* It is commonly associated with a restriction imposed by all civilized nations on people with certain communicable diseases to prevent them from spreading their disease throughout the community. It is a public health measure which, for all the inconvenience that it may impose on the afflicted individual, serves the public welfare. Thus, whereas a blockade would have been an announcement that we were proceeding aggressively to further our own interests, regardless of the rights of others, quarantine suggested a concern for the general welfare. In addition, it suggested that what was going on in Cuba was a dangerous disease which might spread.

So, as you develop a larger vocabulary you will be increasingly aware of what is going on. You will enjoy what you read more. New pleasures will be opened to you.

You will understand more. Difficult books whose meaning has been uncertain will become readable. The great poets who have enlarged our experience, the philosophers who have shaped our thoughts, the historians who have sought for patterns in the human story, the essayists whose observations have delighted men for centuries—all these and more will be available to you. And in sharing their thoughts your own world will expand. This particular benefit of an increased vocabulary is dramatically apparent in the strides that children make in comprehension as they progress in their use of language. Increased learning increases the child's word stock and the increased word stock makes learning easier. The National Conference on Research in English says "a child's ability to read, to speak, to write, and to think is inevitably conditioned by his vocabulary."

This goes for an adult too. Words cannot be separated from ideas. They interact. The words we use are so associated with our experiences and what the experiences mean to us that they cannot be separated. The idea comes up from our subconscious clothed in words. It can't come any other way.

We don't know how words are stored in our minds, but there does seem to be a sort of filing system. The filing system appears to be controlled by a perverse if not downright wacky filing clerk. Everyone has tried to remember a word and been unable to. Sometimes it is a common word, one that we *know* we know. Yet it won't come when we want it. It can be almost a form of torture trying to recall it, but no amount of fuming or fretting helps. Then suddenly, usually some time later when it is no longer useful to us, it will come to mind readily. When we are searching for one of these words—often for a person's name—we will come up with others words or names that we know are close to but not exactly the one we want. This is curious in itself. For if we can't remember the word we want, how do we know the other word is very much like it? It's as though the filing clerk had seen the word we actually wanted or was even holding it in his hand but wouldn't give it to us.

Often we know that the unacceptable word has the same sound or begins with the same letter as the word we can't remember. And when we finally recall the word we wanted, we find this is so. It seems as though our mental filing systems were arranged alphabetically and cross-indexed for similarity of internal sound. If we are well-read, we can call up a host of synonyms (words that mean the same thing) for many words, which suggests more crossfiling. Furthermore, words have subtle and complex associations. The speech and writing of some people who have sustained brain injuries or suffered strokes indicate a curious kind of damage. Some injured people seem to lose all proper names, some all adjectives, and many mix up capitals and small letters. This indicates that the interlocking connections of words in our minds are more complex than we can imagine. The chances are that the most spectacular computer is a simple gadget compared to the human mind.

For our purposes, our ignorance of how this intricate filing system works does not matter. What matters to a person trying to enlarge his vocabulary is the many connections among the words he knows. Once we master a word, it is connected in our mind with scores of other words in what appears to be an infinite number of relationships and shades of meaning. A new word does not drop as a single addition into our word stock. Each new word learned enlarges a whole complex of thinking and is itself enlarged in meaning and significance.

A vocabulary is a tool which one uses in formulating the important questions of life, the questions which must be asked before they can be answered. To a large extent, vocabulary shapes all the decisions we make. Most decisions, of course, are shaped by our emotions, by circumstances, and by the forces which may hold us back or urge us on. These circumstances and forces are largely beyond our control. But our speech is a sort of searchlight that helps us to see these things more clearly and to see ourselves in relation to them. At least it helps us call things by their right names.

To a great extent our speech affects our judgments. We don't always—sometimes we can't—distinguish between words and things. A slogan, for example, especially if it rhymes, or is alliterative (that is, has a number of words that begin with the same sound), or has a strong rhythm, will move us to action. It convinces us that the action is necessary. "Motorists wise Simonize" is far more effective in promoting sales than "Simonize, wise motorists" or "Wise motorists, Simonize" would have been. It's the witchery of rhythm, one of the most subtle and dangerous of unseen forces that move and muddle our minds. Seduced by "Fifty-four forty or fight," our great-grandfathers almost went to war in 1844. And there are historians who trace much of the misery of the modern world to the fascination that Grant's "Unconditional surrender" held for four generations of Americans.

Certainly anyone who develops the valuable habit of examining his own prejudices will find that many of them are, at bottom, verbal. A situation automatically calls forth a single word. The word is bathed in emotion. So whenever the situation is repeated, it produces the same emotional response. There is no effort to be rational, to see what is actually going on. The word triggers the response. But the more words one has at his command, the greater the possibility that he may be his own master. It takes words to free us from words. Removing an emotionally charged word from a phrase and substituting a neutral synonym often gives us an insight that nothing else can.

Speech is the means of relating our separate experiences and emotions, of combining them, reliving them and, as far as we can, understanding them. If we did not have the words *justice, equal, radiation*—and a thousand others like them—our minds and our whole lives would be much narrower. Each new word of this kind increases the scope of thought and adds its bit to humanity. Once we have the word, of course, it seems natural and it is an effort to imagine being without it.

Consider that remarkable British phrase which Lord Broughton invented during the reign of George IV (1820–1830): "His Majesty's opposition." Political parties rose in seventeenth-century England during a period of limited civil war and they behaved as if parliamentary victories were military ones. When one party gained power it immediately proceeded to impeach the leaders of the other party, demanding their very heads. But after a hundred and fifty years of peace and prosperity, men's tempers began to cool. A sense of fairness compelled them to grant their neighbor the right to a different opinion and even to grant that men who opposed them might still be loyal and honorable. But the atmosphere Lord Broughton described had to precede his phrase, just as the invention of the wheel had to precede the medieval concept of Fortune's wheel.

Once uttered, the phrase helped to further the idea it described. Men saw that criticism of an administration can be as much a part of good government as the government itself and that a man was not necessarily a traitor because he disagreed with the party in power.

Many studies have established the fact that there is a high correlation between vocabulary and intelligence and that the ability to increase one's vocabulary throughout life is a sure reflection of intellectual progress.

It is hard to stretch a small vocabulary to make it do all the things that intelligent people require of words. It's like trying to plan a series of menus from the limited resources of a poverty-stricken, war-torn country compared to planning such a series in a prosperous, stable country. Words are one of our chief means of adjusting to all the situations of life. The better control we have over words, the more successful our adjustment is likely to be.

FOR DISCUSSION AND REVIEW

1. Consider the central metaphor of Evans' essay: speech, more specifically words, as a tool. In what ways do you consider vocabulary a tool?

2. Many newspapers carry regular "vocabulary building" columns, and the *Reader's Digest* has had for years a section called "It Pays to Enrich Your Word Power." What does the continuing popularity of these features suggest about the attitudes of many Americans toward language?

3. Semantics teaches us that there is an important distinction between symbols and the things they stand for, that is, their referents. For example, a person should not confuse an actual chair (physical object) with the word "chair" (symbol). Evans points out, however, that "We don't always—sometimes we can't—distinguish between words and things." In this connection, discuss the following episode

in which a small child is talking to her mother: "Mommy! I'm scared of *death.* I don't like to hear that word. It frightens me! If only it were called something else, like *looma.*"

4. As Evans points out, many of our prejudices are basically verbal —that is, some situation makes us think of an emotionally loaded word and we respond to the word and the emotions it arouses rather than to the actual situation. What connection do you see between our tendency to confuse word and object and our attitudes toward "four-letter words"?

5. Evans writes: "Words cannot be separated from ideas. . . . The idea comes up from our subconscious clothed in words. It can't come any other way." He is suggesting that in order to think man must use words. Is this always true, or are there some kinds of "thinking" that take place without the use of words? Consider, for example, your own experiences with music, dreams, and philosophy.

NEDRA NEWKIRK LAMAR 2

Does a Finger Fing?

Children unconsciously learn how to form new words in many different ways. They add-ment *to some verbs, for example, to form nouns like* excitement *and* development. *These rules for word formation are not, of course, altogether consistent. In this article free-lance writer Nedra Newkirk Lamar reveals the incongruities that result when the "rules" are applied mechanically.*

EVERYBODY KNOWS THAT A TONGUE-TWISTER IS SOMETHING THAT twists the tongue, and a skyscraper is something that scrapes the sky, but is an eavesdropper someone who drops eaves? A thinker is someone who thinks but is a tinker someone who tinks? Is [a] clabber something that goes around clabbing?

Somewhere along the way we all must have had an English teacher who gave us the fascinating information that words that end in ER mean something or somebody who *does* something, like trapper, designer, or stopper.

A stinger is something that stings, but is a finger something that fings? Fing fang fung. Today I fing. Yesterday I fang. Day before yesterday I had already fung.

You'd expect eyes, then, to be called seers and ears to be hearers. We'd wear our shoes on our walkers and our sleeves on our reachers. But we don't. The only parts of the body that sound as if they might indicate what they're supposed to do are our fingers, which we've already counted out, our livers, and our shoulders. And they don't do what they sound as if they might. At least, I've never seen anyone use his shoulders for shoulding. You shoulder your way through a crowd, but you don't should your way. It's only in slang that we follow the pattern, when we smell with our smellers and kiss with our kissers.

The animal pattern seems to have more of a feeling for this formation than people do, because insects actually do feel with their feelers. But do cats use their whiskers for whisking?

I've seen people mend socks and knit socks, but I've never seen anyone dolage a sock. Yet there must be people who do, else how could we have sock-dolagers?

Is a humdinger one who dings hums? And what is a hum anyway, and how would one go about dinging it? Maybe Winnie the Pooh could have told us. He was always humming hums, but A. A. Milne never tells us whether he also was fond of dinging them. He sang them but do you suppose he ever dang them?

Sometimes occupational names do reveal what the worker does, though. Manufacturers manufacture, miners mine, adjusters adjust—or at least try to. But does a grocer groce? Does a fruiterer fruiter? Does a butler buttle?

No, you just can't trust the English language. You can love it because it's your mother tongue. You can take pride in it because it's the language Shakespeare was dramatic in. You can thrill to it because it's the language Browning and Tennyson were poetic in. You can have fun with it because it's the language Dickens and Mark Twain and Lewis Carroll were funny in. You can revere it because it's the language Milton was majestic in. You can be grateful to it because it's the language the Magna Carta and the Declaration of Independence were expressed in.

But you just can't trust it!

FOR DISCUSSION AND REVIEW

1. What point is Lamar trying to make? How does she support it?

2. What is her attitude toward her subject? What evidence of this attitude can you cite?

3. What are some examples of words ending in *er* in which the suffix means something other than "one who does"?

4. A person learning English as a second language might have difficulty with the irregularities in our processes of word formation. Give some examples of the kinds of errors such a person might make.

CHARLES OSGOOD 3

WCBS Radio Report

In this radio script, CBS news commentator Charles Osgood examines the way in which the propagandist uses labels to dehumanize people. Osgood reminds us that "To call somebody a nigger or a kike or a spick or wop is to rob a person of his humanity" and that such labeling has often been the first step toward even more serious forms of victimization.

TO HATE SOMEBODY, TO HATE THEM ENOUGH TO KILL THEM, YOU must first dehumanize them in your mind. Remember the cartoons of the Japanese and the Germans during World War II? Outrageous. Racist. But effective war propaganda means painting the enemy as something other than human. That way I can hate him. That is why racial and religious epithets are so evil. To call somebody a nigger or a kike or a spic or wop is to rob a human being of his humanity. It is a frame of hate, a form of murder.

GI's in Vietnam don't like to think about killing fathers, mothers, children. They talk about killing gooks. Yes they do.

We are in trouble these days and part of it, anyway, is our willingness to despise people by reducing them to non-humans. Peace protesters who deplore that process when they see it in Vietnam do it themselves when they call policemen pigs. No person there inside that uniform. Just a pig. Campus demonstrators acting in the name of love and peace and humanity bait the authorities, the police, the administrations of their schools with their insults, their cutting, accusing *up against the wall* masters of the four letter word. Oh how satisfying to curl one's lip and through clenched teeth let them have it. Tell them how you feel. Oh how wonderfully self-righteous. And how pleasing to stand before some dinner and talk about punks and hippies to write *off* protesting students that way. How comfortable to think that everything would be fine if it weren't for the bums or the effete snobs or whatever other dehumanizing name you want to use. . . .

The word is the father of the act. If we are going to avoid blood then we must learn soon to curb our tongues, to end this orgy of self-indulgence in words with warheads.

Carl Sandburg said it. "Look out how you use proud words. When you let proud words go, it is not easy to call them back. They wear long boots, hard boots. Look out how you use proud words."

FOR DISCUSSION AND REVIEW

1. What does Osgood mean when he says "The word is the father of the act"?

2. Is the Sandburg quotation apt? What does "proud words" mean?

3. Osgood presents a negative view of the labeling process. Are there any instances in which labels are beneficial?

4. Explain Osgood's phrase "a frame of hate."

5. Define each of the following:
   a) hippie
   b) straight
   c) women's libber
   d) "the system"

TIME 4

The Euphemism: Telling It Like It Isn't

Many Americans feel that nothing is taboo anymore—that anything that can be imagined can be said or filmed or printed. The editors of Time, *however, make clear in this essay that the euphemism is alive and well in America precisely because people often do not want to "tell it like it is." The euphemisms themselves and the aspects of life to which they are applied may change, but the euphemism as a phenomenon shows no signs of disappearing.*

MODERN AMERICAN SPEECH, WHILE NOT ALWAYS CLEAR OR CORRECT or turned with much style, is supposed to be uncommonly frank. Witness the current explosion of four-letter words and the explicit discussion of sexual topics. In fact, gobbledygook and nice-Nellyism still extend as far as the ear can hear. Housewives on television may chat about their sex lives in terms that a decade ago would have made gynecologists blush; more often than not, these emancipated women still speak about their children's "going to the potty." Government spokesmen talk about "redeployment" of American troops; they mean withdrawal. When sociologists refer to blacks living in slums, they are likely to mumble about "nonwhites" in a "culturally deprived environment." The CIA may never have used the expression "to terminate with extreme prejudice" when it wanted a spy rubbed out. But in the context of a war in which "pacification of the enemy infrastructure" is the military mode of reference to blasting the Viet Cong out of a village, the phrase sounded so plausible that millions readily accepted it as accurate.

The image of a generation blessed with a swinging, liberated language is largely an illusion. Despite its swaggering sexual candor, much contemporary speech still hides behind that traditional enemy of plain talk, the euphemism.

From a Greek word meaning "to use words of good omen," euphemism is the substitution of a pleasant term for a blunt one—telling it like it isn't. Euphemism has probably existed since the beginning of language. As long as there have been things of which men thought the less said the better, there have been better ways of saying less. In everyday conversation the euphemism is, at worst, a necessary evil; at its best, it is a handy verbal tool to avoid making enemies needlessly, or shocking friends. Language purists and the blunt-spoken may wince when a young woman at a party coyly asks for direction to "the powder room," but to most people this kind of familiar euphemism is probably no more harmful or annoying than, say, a split infinitive.

On a larger scale, though, the persistent growth of euphemism in a language represents a danger to thought and action, since its fundamental intent is to deceive. As Linguist Benjamin Lee Whorf has pointed out, the structure of a given language determines, in part, how the society that speaks it views reality. If "substandard housing" makes rotting slums appear more livable or inevitable to some people, then their view of American cities has been distorted and their ability to assess the significance of poverty has been reduced. Perhaps the most chilling example of euphemism's destructive power took place in Hitler's Germany. The wholesale corruption of the language under Nazism, notes Critic George Steiner, is symbolized by the phrase *endgültige Lösung* (final solution), which "came to signify the death of 6,000,000 human beings in gas ovens."

No one could argue that American English is under siege from linguistic falsehood, but euphemisms today have the nagging persistence of a headache. Despite the increasing use of nudity and sexual innuendo in advertising, Madison Avenue is still the great exponent of talking to "the average person of good upbringing"—as one TV executive has euphemistically described the ordinary American—in ways that won't offend him. Although this is like fooling half the people none of the time, it has produced a handsome bouquet of roses by other names. Thus there is "facial-quality tissue" that is not intended for use on faces, and "rinses" or "tints" for women who might be unsettled to think they dye their hair. In the world of deodorants, people never sweat or smell; they simply "offend." False teeth sound truer when known as "dentures."

Admen and packagers, of course, are not the only euphemizers. Almost any way of earning a salary above the level of ditchdigging is known as a profession rather than a job. Janitors for several years have been elevated by image-conscious unions to the status of "custodians"; nowadays, a teen-age rock guitarist with three chords to his credit can class himself with Horowitz as a "recording artist." Cadillac dealers refer to autos as "preowned" rather than "secondhand." Government researchers concerned with old people call them "senior citizens." Ads for bank credit cards and department stores refer to "convenient terms"— meaning 18% annual interest rates payable at the convenience of the creditor.

Jargon, the sublanguage peculiar to any trade, contributes to euphemism when its terms seep into general use. The student New Left, which shares a taste for six-syllable words with Government bureaucracy, has concocted a collection of substitute terms for use in politics. To "liberate," in the context of campus uproars, means to capture and occupy. Four people in agreement form a "coalition." In addition to "participatory democracy," which in practice is often a description of anarchy, the university radicals have half seriously given the world "anticipatory Communism," which means to steal. The New Left, though, still has a long way to go before it can equal the euphemism-creating ability of Government officials. Who else but a Washington economist would invent the phrase "negative saver" to describe someone who spends more money than he makes?

A persistent source of modern euphemisms is the feeling, inspired by the prestige of science, that certain words contain implicit subjective judgments, and thus ought to be replaced with more "objective" terms. To speak of "morals" sounds both superior and arbitrary, as though the speaker were indirectly questioning those of the listener. By substituting "values," the concept is miraculously turned into a condition, like humidity or mass, that can be safely measured from a distance. To call someone "poor," in the modern way of thinking, is to speak pejoratively of his condition, while the substitution of "disadvantaged" or "underprivileged," indicates that poverty wasn't his fault. Indeed, says Linguist Mario Pei, by using "underprivileged," we are "made to feel that it is all our fault." The modern reluctance to judge makes it more offensive than ever before to call a man a liar; thus there is a "credibility gap" instead.

The liberalization of language in regard to sex involves the use of perhaps a dozen words. The fact of their currency in what was once known as polite conversation raises some unanswered linguistic questions. Which, really, is the rose, and which the other name? Are the old forbidden obscenities really the crude bedrock on which softer and shyer expressions have been built? Or are they simply coarser ways of expressing physical actions and parts of the human anatomy that are more accurately described in less explicit terms? It remains to be seen whether the so-called forbidden words will contribute anything to the honesty and openness of sexual discussion. Perhaps their real value lies in the power to shock, which is inevitably diminished by overexposure. Perhaps the Victorians, who preferred these words unspoken and unprinted, will prove to have had a point after all.

For all their prudery, the Victorians were considerably more willing than modern men to discuss ideas—such as social distinctions, morality and death—that have become almost unmentionable. Nineteenth century gentlewomen whose daughters had "limbs" instead of suggestive "legs" did not find it necessary to call their maids "housekeepers," nor did they bridle at referring to "upper" or "lower" classes within society. Rightly or wrongly, the Victorian could talk without embarrassment about "sin," a word that today few but clerics use with frequency or ease. It is even becoming difficult to find a doctor, clergyman or undertaker (known as a "mortician") who will admit that a man has died rather than "expired" or "passed away." Death has not lost its sting; the words for it have.

There is little if any hope that euphemisms will ever be excised from mankind's endless struggle with words that, as T. S. Eliot lamented, bend, break and crack under pressure. For one thing, certain kinds of everyday euphemisms have proved their psychological necessity. The uncertain morale of an awkward teen-ager may be momentarily buoyed if he thinks of himself as being afflicted by facial "blemishes" rather than "pimples." The label "For motion discomfort" that airlines place on paper containers undoubtedly helps the squeamish passenger keep control of his stomach in bumpy weather better than if they were called "vomit bags." Other forms of self-deception may not be beneficial, but may still be emotionally necessary. A girl may tolerate herself more readily if she thinks of herself as a "swinger" rather than as "promiscuous." Voyeurs can salve their guilt feelings when they buy tickets for certain "adult entertainments" on the ground that they are implicitly supporting "freedom of artistic expression."

Lexicographer Bergen Evans of Northwestern University believes that euphemisms persist because "lying is an indispensable part of making life tolerable." It is virtuous, but a bit beside the point, to contend that lies are deplorable. So they are; but they cannot be moralized or legislated away, any more than euphemisms can be. Verbal miasma, when it deliberately obscures truth, is an offense to reason. But the inclination to speak of certain things in uncertain terms is a reminder that there will always be areas of life that humanity considers too private, or too close to feelings of guilt, to speak about directly. Like stammers or tears, euphemisms will be created whenever men doubt, or fear, or do not know. The instinct is not wholly unhealthy; there is a measure of wisdom in the familiar saying that a man who calls a spade a spade is fit only to use one.

FOR DISCUSSION AND REVIEW

1. People use euphemisms, defined by *Time* as "the substitution of a pleasant term for a blunt one," when they want to avoid talking directly about subjects that make them uncomfortable, although what makes people uncomfortable changes. For example, we have been able to talk about "legs" and "breasts" for quite a while, and "venereal disease" for a shorter time; but many people still avoid the words "die" and "death." Identify some other subjects for which euphemisms are still prevalent and list several euphemisms for each. Do you use the same euphemisms as your parents? As your grandparents?

2. Explain how our tendency to confuse words and things (mentioned by Evans) can combine with our use of euphemisms and affect both our behavior and our opinion of our behavior. Consider, for example, the following expressions used during the Vietnam war:

refugee camp	new life hamlet
air raid	limited duration protective reaction strike
defoliation	resources control program

List other euphemisms used by government and big business. How do they attempt to influence behavior?

3. What does *Time* mean by the "psychological necessity" of euphemisms?

GEORGE ORWELL 5

Politics and the English Language

Occasionally an essay becomes a classic, usually because it makes an important statement about some subject with unusual effectiveness. Such is the case with this essay, written in the 1940s. Here Orwell discusses the condition of the English language and the ways in which it has seriously deteriorated. He concludes by suggesting a number of remedies to help restore the language to a more healthy state.

MOST PEOPLE WHO BOTHER WITH THE MATTER AT ALL WOULD admit that the English language is in a bad way, but it is generally assumed that we cannot by conscious action do anything about it. Our civilization is decadent and our language—so the argument runs—must inevitably share in the general collapse. It follows that any struggle against the abuse of language is a sentimental archaism, like preferring candles to electric light or hansom cabs to aeroplanes. Underneath this lies the half-conscious belief that language is a natural growth and not an instrument which we shape for our own purposes.

Now, it is clear that the decline of a language must ultimately have political and economic causes: it is not due simply to the bad influence of this or that individual writer. But an effect can become a cause, reinforcing the original cause and producing the same effect in an intensified form, and so on indefinitely. A man may take to drink because he feels himself to be a failure, and then fail all the more completely because he drinks. It is rather the same thing that is happening to the English language. It becomes ugly and inaccurate because our thoughts are foolish, but the slovenliness of our language makes it easier for us to have foolish thoughts. The point is that the process is reversible. Modern English, especially written English, is full of bad habits which spread by imitation and which can be avoided if one is willing to take the necessary trouble. If one gets rid of these habits one can think more clearly, and to think clearly is a necessary first step towards political regeneration: so that the fight against bad English is not frivolous and is not the exclusive concern of professional writers. I will come back to this presently, and I hope that by that time the meaning of what I have said here will have become clearer. Meanwhile here are five specimens of the English language as it is now habitually written.

These five passages have not been picked out because they are especially bad—I could have quoted far worse if I had chosen—but because they illustrate various of the mental vices from which we now suffer. They are a little below the average, but are fairly representative samples. I number them so that I can refer back to them when necessary:

> (1) I am not, indeed, sure whether it is not true to say that the Milton who once seemed not unlike a seventeenth-century Shelley had not become, out of an experience ever more bitter in each year, more alien [*sic*] to the founder of that Jesuit sect which nothing could induce him to tolerate.
>
> Professor Harold Laski (Essay in *Freedom of Expression*).

> (2) Above all, we cannot play ducks and drakes with a native battery of idioms which prescribes such egregious collocations of vocables as the Basic *put up with* for *tolerate* or *put at a loss* for *bewilder*.
>
> Professor Lancelot Hogben (*Interglossa*).

> (3) On the one side we have the free personality: by definition it is not neurotic, for it has neither conflict nor dream. Its desires, such as they are, are transparent, for they are just what institutional approval keeps in the forefront of consciousness; another institutional pattern would alter their number and intensity; there is little in them that is natural, irreducible, or culturally dangerous. But *on the other side,* the social bond itself is nothing but the mutual reflection of these self-secure integrities. Recall the definition of love. Is not this the very picture of a small academic? Where is there a place in this hall of mirrors for either personality or fraternity?
>
> Essay on psychology in *Politics* (New York).

(4) All the "best people" from the gentlemen's clubs, and all the frantic fascist captains, united in common hatred of Socialism and bestial horror of the rising tide of the mass revolutionary movement, have turned to acts of provocation, to foul incendiarism, to medieval legends of poisoned wells, to legalize their own destruction of proletarian organizations, and rouse the agitated petty-bourgeoisie to chauvinistic fervor on behalf of the fight against the revolutionary way out of the crisis.

Communist pamphlet.

(5) If a new spirit *is* to be infused into this old country, there is one thorny and contentious reform which must be tackled, and that is the humanization and galvanization of the B.B.C. Timidity here will bespeak canker and atrophy of the soul. The heart of Britain may be sound and of strong beat, for instance, but the British lion's roar at present is like that of Bottom in Shakespeare's *Midsummer Night's Dream*—as gentle as any sucking dove. A virile new Britain cannot continue indefinitely to be traduced in the eyes or rather ears, of the world by the effete languors of Langham Place, brazenly masquerading as "standard English." When the voice of Britain is heard at nine o'clock, better far and infinitely less ludicrous to hear aitches honestly dropped than the present priggish, inflated, inhibited, school-ma'amish arch braying of blameless bashful mewing maidens!

Letter in *Tribune*.

Each of these passages has faults of its own, but, quite apart from avoidable ugliness, two qualities are common to all of them. The first is staleness of imagery; the other is lack of precision. The writer either has a meaning and cannot express it, or he inadvertently says something else, or he is almost indifferent as to whether his words mean anything or not. This mixture of vagueness and sheer incompetence is the most marked characteristic of modern English prose, and especially of any kind of political writing. As soon as certain topics are raised, the concrete melts into the abstract and no one seems able to think of turns of speech that are not hackneyed: prose consists less and less of *words* chosen for the sake of their meaning, and more and more of *phrases* tacked together like the sections of a prefabricated hen-house. I list below, with notes and examples, various of the tricks by means of which the work of prose-construction is habitually dodged:

Dying Metaphors

A newly invented metaphor assists thought by evoking a visual image, while on the other hand a metaphor which is technically "dead" (e.g., *iron resolution*) has in effect reverted to being an ordinary word and can generally be used without loss of vividness. But in between these two classes there is a huge dump of worn-out metaphors which have lost all evocative power and are merely used because they save people the trouble of inventing phrases for themselves. Examples are: *Ring the changes on, take up the cudgels for, toe the line, ride roughshod over, stand shoulder to shoulder with, play into the hands of, no axe to grind, grist to the mill, fishing in troubled waters, on the order of the day, Achilles' heel, swan song, hotbed.* Many of these are used without knowledge of their meaning (what is a "rift," for instance?), and incompatible metaphors are frequently mixed, a sure sign that the writer is not interested in what he is saying. Some metaphors now current have been twisted out of their original meaning without those who use them even being aware of the fact. For example, *toe the line* is sometimes written *tow the line.* Another example is the *hammer and the anvil,* now always used with the implication that the anvil gets the worst of it. In real life it is always the anvil that breaks the hammer, never the other way about: a writer who stopped to think what he was saying would be aware of this, and would avoid perverting the original phrase.

Operators or Verbal False Limbs

These save the trouble of picking out appropriate verbs and nouns, and at the same time pad each sentence with extra syllables which give it an appearance of symmetry. Characteristic phrases are *render inoperative, militate against, make contact with, be subjected to, give rise to, give grounds for, have the effect of, play a leading part* (*role*) *in, make itself felt, take effect, exhibit a tendency to, serve the purpose of, etc., etc.* The keynote is the elimination of simple verbs. Instead of being a single word, such as *break, stop, spoil, mend, kill,* a verb becomes a *phrase,* made up of a noun or adjective tacked on to some general-purposes verb such as *prove, serve, form, play, render.* In addition, the passive voice is wherever possible used in preference to the active, and noun constructions are used instead of gerunds (*by examination of* instead of *by examining*). The range of verbs is further cut down by means of the *-ize* and *de-* formations, and the banal statements are given an appearance of profundity by means of the *not un-* formation. Simple conjunctions and prepositions are replaced by such phrases as *with respect to, having regard to, the fact that, by dint of, in view of, in the interests of, on the hypothesis that;* and the ends of sentences are saved from anticlimax by such resounding common-places as *greatly to be desired, cannot be* *left out of account, a development to be expected in the near future, deserving of serious consideration, brought to a satisfactory conclusion,* and so on and so forth.

Pretentious Diction

Words like *phenomenon, element, individual* (as noun), *objective, categorical, effective, virtual, basic, primary, promote, constitute, exhibit, exploit, utilize, eliminate, liquidate,* are used to dress up simple statements and give an air of scientific impartiality to biased judgments. Adjectives like *epoch-making, epic, historic, unforgettable, triumphant, age-old, inevitable, inexorable, veritable,* are used to dignify the sordid processes of international politics, while writing that aims at glorifying war usually takes on an archaic color, its characteristic words being: *realm, throne, chariot, mailed fist, trident, sword, shield, buckler, banner, jackboot, clarion.* Foreign words and expressions such as *cul de sac, ancien régime, deus ex machina, mutatis mutandis, status quo, gleichschaltung, weltanschauung,* are used to give an air of culture and elegance. Except for the useful abbreviations *i.e., e.g.,* and *etc.,* there is no real need for any of the hundreds of foreign phrases now current in English. Bad writers, and especially scientific, political and sociological writers, are nearly always haunted by the notion that Latin or Greek words are grander than Saxon ones, and unnecessary words like *expedite, ameliorate, predict, extraneous, deracinated, clandestine, subaqueous* and hundreds of others constantly gain ground from their Anglo-Saxon opposite numbers.[1] The jargon peculiar to Marxist writing (*hyena, hangman, cannibal, petty bourgeois, these gentry, lacquey, flunkey, mad dog, White Guard,* etc.) consists largely of words and phrases translated from Russian, German or French; but the normal way of coining a new word is to use a Latin or Greek root with the appropriate affix and, where necessary, the *-ize* formation. It is often easier to make up words of this kind (*deregionalize, impermissible, extramarital, non-fragmentary* and so forth) than to think up the English words that will cover one's meaning. The result, in general, is an increase in slovenliness and vagueness.

[1] An interesting illustration of this is the way in which the English flower names which were in use till very recently are being ousted by Greek ones, *snapdragon* becoming *antirrhinum, forget-me-not* becoming *myosotis,* etc. It is hard to see any practical reason for this change of fashion: it is probably due to an instinctive turning-away from the more homely word and a vague feeling that the Greek word is scientific.

Meaningless Words

In certain kinds of writing, particularly in art criticism and literary criticism, it is normal to come across long passages which are almost completely lacking in meaning.[2] Words like *romantic, plastic, values, human, dead, sentimental, natural, vitality,* as used in art criticism, are strictly meaningless, in the sense that they not only do not point to any discoverable object, but are hardly ever expected to do so by the reader. When one critic writes, "The outstanding feature of Mr. X's work is its living quality," while another writes, "The immediately striking thing about Mr. X's work is its peculiar deadness," the reader accepts this as a simple difference of opinion. If words like *black* and *white* were involved, instead of the jargon words *dead* and *living,* he would see at once that language was being used in an improper way. Many political words are similarly abused. The word *Fascism* has now no meaning except in so far as it signifies "something not desirable." The words *democracy, freedom, patriotic, realistic, justice,* have each of them several different meanings which cannot be reconciled with one another. In the case of a word like *democracy,* not only is there no agreed definition, but the attempt to make one is resisted from all sides. It is almost universally felt that when we call a country democratic we are praising it: consequently the defenders of every kind of régime claim that it is a democracy, and fear that they might have to stop using the word if it were tied down to any one meaning. Words of this kind are often used in a consciously dishonest way. That is, the person who uses them has his own private definition, but allows his hearer to think he means something quite different. Statements like *Marshal Pétain was a true patriot, The Soviet Press is the freest in the world, The Catholic Church is opposed to persecution,* are almost always made with intent to deceive. Other words used in variable meanings, in most cases more or less dishonestly, are: *class, totalitarian, science, progressive, reactionary, bourgeois, equality.*

Now that I have made this catalogue of swindles and perversions, let me give another example of the kind of writing that they lead to. This time it must of its nature be an imaginary one. I am going to

[2] Example: "Comfort's catholicity of perception and image, strangely Whitmanesque in range, almost the exact opposite in aesthetic compulsion, continues to evoke that trembling atmospheric accumulative hinting at a cruel, an inexorably serene timelessness. . . . Wrey Gardiner scores by aiming at simple bull's-eyes with precision. Only they are not so simple, and through this contented sadness runs more than the surface bittersweet of resignation." (*Poetry Quarterly.*)

translate a passage of good English into modern English of the worst sort. Here is a well-known verse from *Ecclesiastes:*

"I returned and saw under the sun, that the race is not to the swift, nor the battle to the strong, neither yet bread to the wise, nor yet riches to men of understanding, nor yet favour to men of skill; but time and chance happeneth to them all."

Here it is in modern English:

"Objective consideration of contemporary phenomena compels the conclusion that success or failure in competitive activities exhibits no tendency to be commensurate with innate capacity, but that a considerable element of the unpredictable must invariably be taken into account."

This is a parody, but not a very gross one. Exhibit (3), above, for instance, contains several patches of the same kind of English. It will be seen that I have not made a full translation. The beginning and ending of the sentence follow the original meaning fairly closely, but in the middle the concrete illustrations—race, battle, bread—dissolve into the vague phrase "success or failure in competitive activities." This had to be so, because no modern writer of the kind I am discussing—no one capable of using phrases like "objective consideration of contemporary phenomena"—would ever tabulate his thoughts in that precise and detailed way. The whole tendency of modern prose is away from concreteness. Now analyse these two sentences a little more closely. The first contains forty-nine words but only sixty syllables, and all its words are those of everyday life. The second contains thirty-eight words of ninety syllables: eighteen of its words are from Latin roots, and one from Greek. The first sentence contains six vivid images, and only one phrase ("time and chance") that could be called vague. The second contains not a single fresh, arresting phrase, and in spite of its ninety syllables it gives only a shortened version of the meaning contained in the first. Yet without a doubt it is the second kind of sentence that is gaining ground in modern English. I do not want to exaggerate. This kind of writing is not yet universal, and outcrops of simplicity will occur here and there in the worst-written page. Still, if you or I were told to write a few lines on the uncertainty of human fortunes, we should probably come much nearer to my imaginary sentence than to the one from *Ecclesiastes.*

As I have tried to show, modern writing at its worst does not consist in picking out words for the sake of their meaning and inventing images in order to make the meaning clearer. It consists in gumming together long strips of words which have already been set in order by someone else, and making the results presentable by sheer humbug. The attraction of this way of writing is that it is easy. It is easier —even quicker, once you have the habit—to say *In my opinion it is not an unjustifiable assumption that* than to say *I think*. If you use ready-made phrases, you not only don't have to hunt about for words; you also don't have to bother with the rhythms of your sentences, since these phrases are generally so arranged as to be more or less euphonious. When you are composing in a hurry—when you are dictating to a stenographer, for instance, or making a public speech—it is natural to fall into a pretentious, Latinized style. Tags like *a consideration which we should do well to bear in mind* or *a conclusion to which all of us would readily assent* will save many a sentence from coming down with a bump. By using stale metaphors, similes and idioms, you save much mental effort, at the cost of leaving your meaning vague, not only for your reader but for yourself. This is the significance of mixed metaphors. The sole aim of a metaphor is to call up a visual image. When these images clash—as in *The Fascist octopus has sung its swan song, the jackboot is thrown into the melting pot*—it can be taken as certain that the writer is not seeing a mental image of the objects he is naming; in other words he is not really thinking. Look again at the examples I gave at the beginning of this essay. Professor Laski (1) uses five negatives in fifty-three words. One of these is superfluous, making nonsense of the whole passage, and in addition there is the slip *alien* for akin, making further nonsense, and several avoidable pieces of clumsiness which increase the general vagueness. Professor Hogben (2) plays ducks and drakes with a battery which is able to write prescriptions, and, while disapproving of the everyday phrase *put up with,* is unwilling to look *egregious* up in the dictionary and see what it means; (3), if one takes an uncharitable attitude towards it, is simply meaningless: probably one could work out its intended meaning by reading the whole of the article in which it occurs. In (4), the writer knows more or less what he wants to say, but an accumulation of stale phrases chokes him like tea leaves blocking a sink. In (5), words and meaning have almost parted company. People who write in this manner usually have a general emotional meaning—they dislike one thing and want to express solidarity with another—but they are not interested in the detail of what they are saying. A scrupulous writer, in every sentence that he writes, will ask himself at least four questions, thus: What am I trying to say? What words will express it? What image or idiom will make it clearer? Is this image fresh enough to have an effect? And he will probably ask himself two more: Could I put it more shortly? Have I said anything that is avoidably ugly? But you are not obliged to go to all this trouble. You can shirk it by simply throwing your mind open and letting the ready-made phrases come crowding in. They will construct your sentences for you—even think your thoughts for you, to a certain extent—and at need they will perform the important service of partially concealing your meaning even from yourself. It is at this point that the special connection between politics and the debasement of language becomes clear.

In our time it is broadly true that political writing is bad writing. Where it is not true, it will generally be found that the writer is some kind of rebel, expressing his private opinions and not a "party line." Orthodoxy, of whatever color, seems to demand a lifeless, imitative style. The political dialects to be found in pamphlets, leading articles, manifestos, White Papers and the speeches of under-secretaries do, of course, vary from party to party, but they are all alike in that one almost never finds in them a fresh, vivid, home-made turn of speech. When one watches some tired hack on the platform mechanically repeating the familiar phrases—*bestial atrocities, iron heel, blood-stained tyranny, free peoples of the world, stand shoulder to shoulder* —one often has a curious feeling that one is not watching a live human being but some kind of dummy: a feeling which suddenly becomes stronger at moments when the light catches the speaker's spectacles and turns them into blank discs which seem to have no eyes behind them. And this is not altogether fanciful. A speaker who uses that kind of phraseology has gone some distance towards turning himself into a machine. The appropriate noises are coming out of his larynx, but his brain is not involved as it would be if he were choosing his words for himself. If the speech he is making is one that he is accustomed to make over and over again, he may be almost unconscious of what he is saying, as one is when one utters the responses in church. And this reduced state of consciousness, if not indispensable, is at any rate favorable to political conformity.

In our time, political speech and writing are largely the defence of the indefensible. Things like the continuance of British rule in India, the Russian purges and deportations, the dropping of the atom bombs on Japan, can indeed be defended, but only by arguments which are too brutal for most people to face, and which do not square with the professed aims of political parties. Thus political language has to consist largely of euphemism, question-begging and sheer cloudy vagueness. Defenceless villages are bombarded from the air, the inhabitants driven out into the countryside, the cattle machine-gunned, the huts set on fire with incendiary bullets: this is called *pacification.* Millions of peasants are robbed of their farms and sent trudging along the roads with no more than they can carry: this is called *transfer of population* or *rectification of frontiers.* People are imprisoned for years without trial, or shot in the back of the neck or sent to die of scurvy in Arctic lumber camps: this is called *elimination of unreliable elements.* Such phraseology is needed if one wants to name things without calling up mental pictures of them. Consider for instance some comfortable English professor defending Russian totalitarianism. He cannot say outright, "I believe in killing off your opponents when you can get good results by doing so." Probably, therefore, he will say something like this:

"While freely conceding that the Soviet régime exhibits certain features which the humanitarian may be inclined to deplore, we must, I think, agree that a certain curtailment of the right to political opposition is an unavoidable concomitant of transitional periods, and that the rigors which the Russian people have been called upon to undergo have been amply justified in the sphere of concrete achievement."

The inflated style is itself a kind of euphemism. A mass of Latin words falls upon the facts like soft snow, blurring the outlines and covering up all the details. The great enemy of clear language is insincerity. When there is a gap between one's real and one's declared aims, one turns as it were instinctively to long words and exhausted idioms, like a cuttlefish squirting out ink. In our age there is no such thing as "keeping out of politics." All issues are political issues, and politics itself is a mass of lies, evasions, folly, hatred and schizophrenia. When the general atmosphere is bad, language must suffer. I should expect to find—this is a guess which I have not sufficient knowledge to verify—that the German, Russian and Italian languages have all deteriorated in the last ten or fifteen years, as a result of dictatorship.

But if thought corrupts language, language can also corrupt thought. A bad usage can spread by tradition and imitation, even among people who should and do know better. The debased language that I have been discussing is in some ways very convenient. Phrases like *a not unjustifiable assumption, leaves much to be desired, would serve no good purpose, a consideration which we should do well to bear in mind,* are a continuous temptation, a packet of aspirins always at one's elbow. Look back through this essay, and for certain you will find that I have again and again committed the very faults I am protesting against. By this morning's post I have received a pamphlet dealing with conditions in Germany. The author tells me that he "felt impelled" to write it. I open it at random, and here is almost the first sentence that I see: "[The Allies] have an opportunity not only of achieving a radical transformation of Germany's social and political structure in such a way as to avoid a nationalistic reaction in Germany itself, but at the same time of laying the foundations of a cooperative and unified Europe." You see, he "feels impelled" to write—feels, presumably, that he has something new to say—and yet his words, like cavalry horses answering the bugle, group themselves automatically into the familiar dreary pattern. The invasion of one's mind by ready-made phrases (*lay the foundations, achieve a radical transformation*) can only be prevented if one is constantly on guard against them, and every such phrase anaesthetizes a portion of one's brain.

I said earlier that the decadence of our language is probably curable. Those who deny this would argue, if they produced an argument at all, that language merely reflects existing social conditions, and that we cannot influence its development by any direct tinkering with words and constructions. So far as the general tone or spirit of a language goes, this may be true, but it is not true in detail. Silly words and expressions have often disappeared, not through any evolutionary process but owing to the conscious action of a minority. Two recent examples were *explore every avenue* and *leave no stone unturned,* which were killed by the jeers of a few journalists. There is a long list of flyblown metaphors which could similarly be got rid of if enough people would interest themselves in the job; and it should also be possible to laugh the *not un-* formation out of existence,[3] to reduce the amount of Latin and Greek in the average sentence, to drive out foreign phrases and strayed scientific words, and, in general, to make pretentiousness unfashionable. But all these are minor points. The defence of the English language implies more than this, and perhaps it is best to start by saying what it does *not* imply.

To begin with, it has nothing to do with archaism, with the salvaging of obsolete words and turns of speech, or with the setting up of a "standard English" which must never be departed from. On the contrary, it is especially concerned with the scrapping of every word or idiom which has outworn its usefulness. It has nothing to do with correct grammar and syntax, which are of no importance so long as one makes one's meaning clear, or with the avoidance of Americanisms, or with having what is called a "good prose style." On the other hand it is not concerned with fake simplicity and the attempt to make written English colloquial. Nor does it even imply in every case preferring the Saxon word to the Latin one, though it does imply using the fewest and shortest words that will cover one's meaning. What is above all needed is to let the meaning choose the word, and not the other

[3] One can cure oneself of the *not un-* formation by memorizing this sentence: *A not unblack dog was chasing a not unsmall rabbit across a not ungreen field.*

way about. In prose, the worst thing one can do with words is to surrender to them. When you think of a concrete object, you think wordlessly, and then, if you want to describe the thing you have been visualizing you probably hunt about till you find the exact words that seem to fit it. When you think of something abstract you are more inclined to use words from the start, and unless you make a conscious effort to prevent it, the existing dialect will come rushing in and do the job for you, at the expense of blurring or even changing your meaning. Probably it is better to put off using words as long as possible and get one's meaning as clear as one can through pictures or sensations. Afterwards one can choose—not simply *accept*—the phrases that will best cover the meaning, and then switch round and decide what impression one's words are likely to make on another person. This last effort of the mind cuts out all stale or mixed images, all prefabricated phrases, needless repetitions, and humbug and vagueness generally. But one can often be in doubt about the effect of a word or a phrase, and one needs rules that one can rely on when instinct fails. I think the following rules will cover most cases:

(i) Never use a metaphor, simile, or other figure of speech which you are used to seeing in print.
(ii) Never use a long word where a short one will do.
(iii) If it is possible to cut a word out, always cut it out.
(iv) Never use the passive where you can use the active.
(v) Never use a foreign phrase, a scientific word or a jargon word if you can think of an everyday English equivalent.
(vi) Break any of these rules sooner than say anything outright barbarous.

These rules sound elementary, and so they are, but they demand a deep change of attitude in anyone who has grown used to writing in the style now fashionable. One could keep all of them and still write bad English, but one could not write the kind of stuff that I quoted in those five specimens at the beginning of this article.

I have not here been considering the literary use of language, but merely language as an instrument for expressing and not for concealing or preventing thought. Stuart Chase and others have come near to claiming that all abstract words are meaningless, and have used this as a pretext for advocating a kind of political quietism. Since you don't know what Fascism is, how can you struggle against Fascism? One need not swallow such absurdities as this, but one ought to recognize that the present political chaos is connected with the decay of language, and that one can probably bring about some improvement by starting at the verbal end. If you simplify your English, you are freed from the worst follies of orthodoxy. You cannot speak any of the necessary dialects, and when you make a stupid remark its stupidity will be obvious, even to yourself. Political language—and with variations this is true of all political parties, from Conservatives to Anarchists—is designed to make lies sound truthful and murder respectable, and to give an appearance of solidity to pure wind. One cannot change this all in a moment, but one can at least change one's own habits, and from time to time one can even, if one jeers loudly enough, send some worn-out and useless phrase—some *jackboot, Achilles' heel, hotbed, melting pot, acid test, veritable inferno* or other lump of verbal refuse—into the dustbin where it belongs.

FOR DISCUSSION AND REVIEW

1. It is often said that "mixed metaphors" (e.g., "politicians are leading the country over the precipice with their heads in the sand") are undesirable in either speech or writing because they are inaccurate. For Orwell, a mixed metaphor is symptomatic of a greater problem. What is it?

2. Give some other examples of what Orwell calls "operators or verbal false limbs." How can you avoid such devices?

3. Our world seems to be becoming increasingly prefabricated. What does the concept of prefabrication have to do with Orwell's argument concerning the prevalence of the habitual and hackneyed phrase?

4. Orwell states that he himself in this essay is guilty of some of the errors he is pointing out. Can you detect any of them?

5. According to Orwell, what are the four important pre-writing questions a scrupulous writer will ask himself?

6. What are Orwell's six rules for composition? Can you add a seventh?

7. Orwell says that one of the evils of political language is "begging the question." What does he mean? (Consult your dictionary if you are unsure of your definition.)

8. Why, according to Orwell, has political language deteriorated? Do you agree with him that "the decadence of our language is probably curable"? Explain.

ART BUCHWALD 6
All-Purpose Press Release

For centuries satirists have recognized that ridicule is often the most effective form of criticism. It is employed effectively in this mock-serious press release by one of the country's most popular columnists and lecturers, noted for his satirical jabs at the foibles of contemporary life.

THINGS HAPPEN SO FAST THESE DAYS THAT THE STATE DEPARTMENT no longer has time to put out a statement for each crisis. To solve the problem a friend of mine has devised an all-purpose press release which is being sent out to newspapers, magazines and television stations throughout the country.

It goes like this:

DEPARTMENT OF STATE

ALL-PURPOSE PRESS STATEMENT

(Date)

For Release _____.

The United States government welcomes the progress, during the past 12 hours, toward freedom and increased stability in _____. While reluctant to condone any resort to violence, we regard the events in

_____ as a significant step toward more orderly democracy and the strengthening of the _____ world. We pledge our firm support to Gen. _____ of the _____ party, and are encouraged by his promise to return _____ in due course to civilian rule.

His actions have spelled defeat for the tyrannical forces of (a) General (b) Colonel (c) President (d) Premier (e) Prince _____ of the badly split _____ party, and have given new hope for the free people of _____.

Our support of Gen. _____'s government represents no change in United States policy toward _____.

Nor does it change the United States posture vis-à-vis _____ or _____ or _____.

To help the people of _____ get back on their feet, the President has authorized a special fund of _____ dollars to pay for the salaries of the army and new government officials. The President has also promised _____ dollars in loans to _____ and has promised military aid and advisers to prevent another _____.

The _____ U.S. Fleet has been dispatched to _____ the capital of _____ to prevent further bloodshed and to protect American _____ there.

. . .

The President and the National Security Council met today to discuss the _____ situation and the President is sending _____ as his personal representative to give him a firsthand report and to make future recommendations. This in no way shows his lack of confidence in Ambassador _____ _____, who has been called back to Washington for consultation.

Gen. _____ is considered a friend of the United States, having studied at the _____ War College, in Washington, and he has promised strong, forceful leadership for _____, something that has been lacking in the past under the weak regime of _____ and his so-called democratic government.

(a) General (b) Colonel (c) President (d) Premier (e) Prince _____ has sought political asylum in the _____ embassy and will probably be allowed to leave the country.

FOR DISCUSSION AND REVIEW

1. What specific points in Orwell's essay does this press release illustrate?

2. What is Buchwald satirizing in this selection?

3. Is Buchwald serious when he says that "the State Department no longer has time to put out a statement for each crisis"? Can you account for the sameness of tone and attitude characteristic of most government pronouncements?

4. One student reacted to Buchwald's press release by writing this "Carbon Stop-a-Carbon Letter."

Dear ___________:

I am sure you are sick and tired of hearing "Buy this! Buy our product!" and don't appreciate constantly being the victim of "junk mail." Well, ________________________, we feel we owe it to you to tell you about our fantastic new invention to stop junk mail and form letters from coming into your home. It is called "STOP-A-CARBON." The way it works is, it simply rejects any letter with a *hint* of carbon in it. This is wonderful for stopping chain letters, advertisements, and best of all, for stopping those terrible letters from people who pretend to call you by your name, by leaving a blank in the carbon, and filling in your name later. I am sure, ________________________, that you hate those terrible things as much as I do. Wouldn't it be nice to be able to stop them from entering your house in the first place? Write now, before it's too late! Just send $98.99—sorry, no c.o.d.'s—to

Joe (Pal) Moocher
P.O. Box 198
Los Angeles, Calif. 90000

P. S. Don't forget, ________________________________, write soon!

Comment on the effectiveness of this letter as satire.

THOMAS SZASZ 7
Language

Thomas Szasz, psychiatrist and prolific author, is one of our most provocative and original thinkers. His book The Second Sin, *from which this selection is excerpted, takes its title from a Biblical allusion. If man's first sin was the knowledge of good and evil, then his second sin, Szasz suggests, was speaking clearly. "Knowing and doing good and evil, thinking and speaking clearly—," he writes, "these are man's fundamental affronts against God, the child's against the parent, the citizen's against the state."*

[1] IT WOULD SEEM LIKELY THAT ABORIGINAL MAN FIRST VOCALIZED idiosyncratically; that is, each man made noise rather than spoke a language. When two or more individuals adapted their noisemaking to a common pattern, language was born. Language may thus constitute the original social contract, out of which grew all the others.

[2] Language separates men from other animals. It also reduces them to the level of animals—as in calling Jews "vermin" or policemen "pigs."

[3] In the animal kingdom, the rule is, eat or be eaten; in the human kingdom, define or be defined.

[4] Mystification is the principal semantic tool of the would-be leader; demystification, of the man who wants to be his own master. Rousseau, Marx, Freud mystified; Emerson, Mill, Adler demystified. It is perhaps one of the immutable tragedies of the human condition that while the demystifier influences individuals, the mystifier moves multitudes.

[5] A Hungarian proverb warns: "Tell the truth, and you will get your head bashed in." Only in free and egalitarian situations can people be truthful. Because such situations are rare, speaking the truth is a luxury few people can afford.

[6] When we couch behavior in the language of religion, we legitimize it; when we couch it in the language of psychiatry, we illegitimize it.

We say that Catholics who do not eat meat on Fridays and Jews who do not eat pork at all are devoutly religious; we do not say that Catholics suffer from recurrent attacks of meat phobia, or that Jews are afflicted with a fixed phobia of pork.

. . .

[7] The struggle for definition is veritably the struggle for life itself. In the typical Western two men fight desperately for the possession of a gun that has been thrown to the ground: whoever reaches the weapon first, shoots and lives; his adversary is shot and dies. In ordinary life, the struggle is not for guns but for words: whoever first defines the situation is the victor; his adversary, the victim. For example, in the family, husband and wife, mother and child do not get along; who defines whom as troublesome or mentally sick? Or, in the apocryphal story about Emerson visiting Thoreau in jail; Emerson asks: "Henry, what are you doing over there?" Thoreau replies: "Ralph, what are you doing over there?" In short, he who first seizes the word imposes reality on the other: he who defines thus dominates and lives; and he who is defined is subjugated and may be killed.

[8] Definers (that is, persons who insist on defining others) are like pathogenic microorganisms: each invades, parasitizes, and often destroys his victim; and, in each case, those whose resistance is low are the most susceptible to attack. Hence, those whose immunological defenses are weak are most likely to contract infectious diseases; and those whose social defenses are weak—that is, the young and the old, the sick and the poor, and so forth—are most likely to contract invidious definitions of themselves.

[9] If the essence of conversion hysteria is that it is an indirect, ambiguous sort of communication, then professional jargon may be regarded as semantic hysteria. When a person speaks or writes in political, psychiatric, or sociological jargon, he expresses himself with a certain indirectness and ambiguity; and like the hysteric, he dramatizes what he says as something profound, although it may be trivial. This indirection also allows the speaker to express dangerous and forbidden ideas without fear of retribution by censor or colleagues. Compare the articles in contemporary psychoanalytic journals with Freud's early case histories; or sociological studies on war with Hemingway's stories. In short, if you want to learn about psychology or psychiatry, do not read psychology or psychiatry, but great literature, and especially biography. In the professional literature, for every sentence that clarifies (if, indeed, there are any such), there are two that obscure and mystify. Were a novelist or playwright to write like that, he would never get published.

[10] Medical mendacities:
The prevention of parenthood is called "planned parenthood."
Homicide by physicians is called "euthanasia."
Imprisonment by psychiatrists is called "mental hospitalization."

[11] *Quod licet Jovi, non licet bovi* (What is permitted to Jove, is not permitted to the cow):

Policemen receive bribes; politicians receive campaign contributions.

Marijuana and heroin are sold by pushers; cigarettes and alcohol are sold by businessmen.

Mental patients who use the courts to regain their liberty are troublemakers; psychiatrists who use the courts to deprive patients of their liberty are therapists.

If General Motors sells cars, it's called advertising; if the National Institute of Mental Health sells psychiatry, it's called education; if a streetwalker sells sex, it's called soliciting; if a street urchin sells heroin, it's called pushing dope.

FOR DISCUSSION AND REVIEW

1. Szasz states his belief that language may constitute the first social contract [1]. Is his conclusion that all subsequent social contracts are based on language valid? Explain.

2. What does Szasz mean by mystification as an important semantic tool [4] and why does he consider it significant? Cite contemporary examples of the use of mystification by leaders or would-be leaders.

3. When Szasz writes "speaking the truth is a luxury few people can afford" [5], he is condoning lying for practical purposes. Drawing upon your own experiences, support or refute Szasz's position.

4. Szasz sees the struggle to define as a struggle for one's very existence [7]. Is this an overstatement? Explain.

5. What is "semantic hysteria" [9]? Can you argue with Szasz's belief that technical jargon constitutes "semantic hysteria"? Does Szasz himself manifest such hyteria?

6. Is a campaign contribution really a "bribe" called by another name [11]? Does the size of the contribution make any difference? How do words shape our perceptions of reality?

WRITING

1. Many product names are chosen because of their connotative or suggestive value. For example, the name *Tide* for the detergent suggests the power of the ocean tides and the rhythmic surge of cleansing waters. Write a paragraph explaining how the connotations of one of the following brand names enhance the product's appeal: Atlas tires, Mercury Cougar, Pride, Axion, Downy, Arrid, Love cosmetics, Ajax.

2. Thomas Szasz argues in one of his statements on language that he who can define is master, that the struggle to define is the struggle for existence itself. As a writer you will often need to define, and the more precise your definitions, the more clearly you will communicate. One way of defining a term is to place it in a class of similar items and then to show how it is different from the other items in that class. For example,

WORD	CLASS	CHARACTERISTICS
a *watch*	is a *mechanical device*	*for telling time and is usually carried or worn.*
semantics	is an *area of linguistics*	*concerned with the study of the meanings of words.*

Certainly such definitions are not complete, and one could write an entire paragraph, essay, or book to more fully define these terms. This process, however, is useful for both thinking and writing.

Place each of the following terms in a class and then write a statement differentiating each term:

paper clip
pamphlet
anxiety
freedom

3. A variety of sentence patterns can often be achieved by embedding one sentence within another. For example, "The boys are big" can be combined with "The boys play football" to produce "The big boys play football." In addition, embedding usually eliminates unnecessary verbiage. Without changing important words or the overall meaning, rewrite the following paragraph to eliminate the dull, repetitive nature of the short, choppy sentences:

> The hunter crept through the leaves. The leaves had fallen. The leaves were dry. The hunter was tired. The hunter had a gun. The gun was new. The hunter saw a deer. The deer had antlers. A tree partly hid the antlers. The deer was beautiful. The hunter shot at the deer. The hunter missed. The shot frightened the deer. The deer bounded away.

4. Osgood says, "Remember the cartoons of the Japanese and Germans during World War II? Outrageous. Racist. But effective war propaganda. . . ." In some current cartoons look for groups of people who are frequently stereotyped—for example, middle-aged women, big businessmen, politicians. Both the way in which the drawings depict these people and the language attributed to them contribute to the stereotype. In a paragraph, describe the image of one such stereotyped group and explain how the language of the cartoons helps create this image.

5. The order of the following six sentences has been changed. As originally written, they are the second paragraph of an article by C. P. Idyll, "The Anchovy Crisis," which appeared in *Scientific American* (June, 1973). Place the sentences in what seems to you a logical sequence.

a. During the lifetime of some generations, however, their world may be put out of joint.
b. Finding their world poorer, the little anchovies scatter; many may die prematurely and many in the successor generation may not be born at all.
c. In the brief life-span of the anchovy, rarely longer than three years, its cold-current environment usually changes only within narrow limits.

d. The slow northward drift of the current, only two-tenths to three-tenths of a knot (compared with the six knots of the Gulf Stream off Florida), becomes still slower and may even reverse itself.
e. The sea change known as El Niño has arrived.
f. The water grows warmer and less salty; the makeup of its populations changes and many of the usually abundant microscopic plants and animals dwindle in number.

Explain your reasons for the placement of each sentence in terms of the language signals on which you relied. For example, the word "however" in (a) is a transition word and refers back to an earlier statement. Therefore this sentence is not the opening sentence of the paragraph.

6. Study the following diagrams:

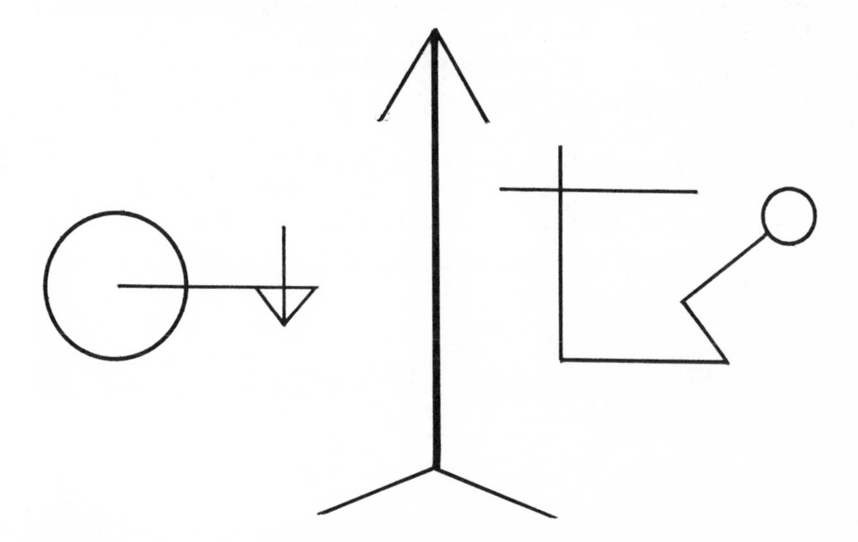

Next, produce a diagram of your own of comparable difficulty. Write a description of your diagram. Give your description (but not your diagram) to another member of your class and ask him to draw the figure you have described. Compare your original drawing with your classmate's drawing based on your description. Discuss the reasons for any discrepancies that exist.

7. One of the purposes of the Buchwald "All-Purpose Press Release" is to emphasize the need of officials for a facade of objectivity in acknowledging world events before their full implication can be assessed. Create your own "All-Purpose Press Release" to report the visits of foreign dignitaries to the United States. Compare your press release with those written by other members of the class.

8. The following excerpt from Benjamin Lee Whorf's *Language, Thought and Reality* suggests that language acts as a filter for our experience and as such helps shape reality for us:

> We have the same word for falling snow, snow on the ground, snow packed hard like ice, slushy snow, wind-driven flying snow—whatever the situation may be. To an Eskimo, this all-inclusive word would be almost unthinkable; he would say that falling snow, slushy snow, and so on, are sensually and operationally different, different things to contend with; he uses different words for them and for other kinds of snow. The Aztecs go even farther than we in the opposite direction with "cold," "ice," and "snow" all represented by the same basic word. . . .

Using "Language Shapes Reality" as the thesis and title of a short paper, describe several incidents from your own experience that clearly exemplify the shaping power of language. For example, consider some of the recent purchases you have made. Have any of them been influenced by brand names, advertisements, or language used by salesmen? Did you ever find yourself taking or avoiding a course primarily because of its name?

NOTABLE QUOTATIONS

The following quotations are drawn from articles in this section. They are presented as possible topics for additional writing assignments.

"Words are one of our chief means of adjusting to all the situations of life." *Evans*

"A vocabulary is a tool which one uses in formulating the important questions of life, the questions which must be asked before they can be answered." *Evans*

"Man has been defined as a tool-using animal, but his most important tool, the one that distinguishes him from all other animals, is his speech." *Evans*

"No, you just can't trust the English language." *Lamar*

"The image of a generation blessed with a swinging, liberated language is largely an illusion." *Time*

"Verbal miasma, when it deliberately obscures truth, is an offense to reason." *Time*

"Like stammers or tears, euphemisms will be created whenever men doubt, fear, or do not know." *Time*

"But if thought corrupts language, language can also corrupt thought." *Orwell*

"The inflated style is itself a kind of euphemism." *Orwell*

"In our time, political speech and writing are largely the defense of the indefensible." *Orwell*

"Most people who bother with the matter at all would admit that the English language is in a bad way, but it is generally assumed that we cannot by conscious action do anything about it." *Orwell*

LANGUAGE AND OCCUPATION

II

MECHANIX Illustrated

π R SQUARE
PLUMBER'S WRENCH, N.C.

Dear Fellow Craftsman,

With your current subscription to *Mechanix Illustrated* due to expire in three months, it's high time you were getting down to your basement shop to start work on a renewal application. A professional-looking job can be done with a minimum of power tools merely by following these step-by-step directions:

1. Detach subscription coupon (A) from this letter (B) along perforated line (C). A linoleum knife or tinsmith shears will do the trick, although any tool sharp enough to cut paper (such as No. 8 household scissors) may also be used.

2. With a strong, dependable marking instrument, such as a pencil (D) or pen (E), fill out subscription coupon (A) as follows: On blank line opposite the printed word "NAME" (F), print your name. Taking care not to smudge, follow similar procedure for inserting your address (G) and zip code (H).

3. Before returning marking instrument to its drawer or holder (I or J), utilize it to make out check for $8.50 (K). Your local banker (L) probably can show you how to do this.

4. Place completed coupon (A) and signed check (K) *inside* envelope (M) and affix stamp (N) to upper-right-hand corner of *outside* of envelope. Making stamp adhere to envelope can be simplified by first wetting sticky side of stamp with a liquid-base compound, such as household water or spit.

5. Drop completed project in corner mailbox (O) after making sure you have not committed common error of placing stamp *inside* while leaving check and coupon *outside*. Should this mistake occur, it can easily be rectified merely by starting all over.

Anxiously awaiting your handiwork,

Phillips S. Driver
Editorial Putterer

H. L. MENCKEN 1
Occupational Euphemisms

In a recent article in Time, *the editors reported on an attempt in Germany to merchandise and make more respectable the "oldest profession in the world." Large, comfortable hotels used for prostitution are now called "Eros-centers" and the girls who work in them are called "Erostesses." This amusing use of euphemisms is only the latest in a long history of attempts by man to elevate himself by retitling his occupation. In this selection, H. L. Mencken, outspoken journalist, social critic, and commentator on American English during the 1920's and 1930's, has provided us with what has now become a classic discussion of this topic.*

THE AMERICAN, PROBABLY MORE THAN ANY OTHER MAN, IS PRONE to be apologetic about the trade he follows. He seldom believes that it is quite worthy of his virtues and talents; almost always he thinks that he would have adorned something far gaudier. Unfortunately, it is not always possible for him to escape, or even for him to dream plausibly of escaping, so he soothes himself by assuring himself that he belongs to a superior section of his craft, and very often he invents a sonorous name to set himself off from the herd. Here we glimpse the origin of a multitude of characteristic American euphemisms, *e.g., mortician* for *undertaker, realtor* for *real-estate agent, electragist* for *electrical contractor, aisle manager* for *floor-walker, beautician* for *hairdresser, exterminating engineer* for *rat-catcher,* and so on. *Realtor* was devised by a high-toned real-estate agent of Minneapolis, Charles N. Chadbourn by name. He thus describes its genesis:

> It was in November, 1915, on my way to a meeting of the Minneapolis Real Estate Board, that I was annoyed by the strident peddling of a scandal sheet: "All About the Robbery of a Poor Widow by a Real Estate Man." The "real estate man" thus exposed turned out to be an obscure hombre with desk-room in a back office in a rookery, but the incident set me to thinking. "Every member of our board," I thought, "is besmirched by this scandal article. Anyone, however unworthy or disreputable, may call himself a real estate man. Why do not the members of our board deserve a distinctive title? Each member is vouched for by the board, subscribes to its Code of Ethics, and must behave himself or get out." So the idea incubated for three or four weeks, and was then sprung on the local brethren.

As to the etymology of the term, Mr. Chadbourn says:

> Real estate originally meant a royal grant. It is so connected with land in the public mind that *realtor* is easily understood, even at a first hearing. The suffix *-or* means a doer, one who performs an act, as in *grantor, executor, sponsor, administrator.*

The Minneapolis brethren were so pleased with their new name that Mr. Chadbourn was moved to dedicate it to the whole profession. In March, 1916, he went to the convention of the National Association of Real Estate Boards at New Orleans, and made a formal offer of it. It was accepted gratefully, and is now defined by the association as follows:

> A person engaged in the real estate business who is an active member of a member board of the National Association of Real Estate Boards, and as such, an affiliated member of the National Association, who is subject to its rules and regulations, who observes its standards of conduct, and is entitled to its benefits.

In 1920 the Minneapolis Real Estate Board and the National Association of Real Estate Boards applied to Judge Joseph W. Molyneaux of Minneapolis for an injunction restraining the Northwestern Telephone Exchange Company from using *realtor* to designate some of its hirelings, and on September 10 the learned judge duly granted this relief. Since then the National Association has obtained similar injunctions in Virginia, Utah and other States. Its general counsel is heard from every time *realtor* is taken in vain, and when, in 1922, Sinclair Lewis applied it to George F. Babbitt, there was an uproar.

But when Mr. Chadbourn was appealed to he decided that Babbitt was "fairly well described," for he was "a prominent member of the local board and of the State association," and one could scarcely look for anything better in "a book written in the ironic vein of the author of 'Main Street.' " Mr. Chadbourn believes that *realtor* should be capitalized, "like *Methodist* or *American,*" but so far it has not been generally done. In June, 1925, at a meeting of the National Association of Real Estate Boards in Detroit, the past presidents of the body presented him with a gold watch as a token of their gratitude for his contribution to the uplift of their profession. On May 30, 1934, the following letter from Nathan William MacChesney, general counsel of the National Association, appeared in the *New Republic:*

> [*Realtor*] is not a word, but a trade right, coined and protected by law by the National Association of Real Estate Boards, and the term is a part of the trade-mark as registered in some forty-four States and Canada. Something over $200,000 has been spent in its protection by the National Association of Real Estate Boards in attempting to confine its use to those real estate men who are members of the National Association of Real Estate Boards, subject to its code of ethics and to its discipline for violation. It has been a factor in making the standards of the business generally during the past twenty years, and the exclusive right of the National Association of Real Estate Boards has been sustained in a series of court decisions, a large number of injunctions having been issued, restraining its improper use.

In 1924 the *Realtor's Bulletin* of Baltimore reported that certain enemies of realtric science were trying to show that *realtor* was derived from the English word *real* and the Spanish word *toro,* a bull, and to argue that it thus meant *real bull.* But this obscenity apparently did not go far; probably a hint from the alert general counsel was enough to stop it. During the same year I was informed by Herbert U. Nelson, executive secretary of the National Association, that "the real-estate men of London, through the Institute of Estate Agents and Auctioneers, after studying our experience in this respect, are planning to coin the world *estator* and to protect it by legal steps." This plan, I believe, came to fruition, but *estator* never caught on, and I can't find it in the Supplement to the Oxford Dictionary. *Realtor,* however, is there—and the first illustrative quotation is from *Babbitt!* In March, 1927, J. Foster Hagan, of Ballston, Va., reported to *American Speech* that he had encountered *realtress* on the window of a real-estate office there, but this charming derivative seems to have died a-bornin'. In 1925 or thereabout certain ambitious insurance solicitors, inflamed by *realtor,* began to call themselves *insurors,* but it, too, failed to make any progress.

Electragist, like realtor, seems to be the monopoly of the lofty technicians who affect it: "it is copyrighted by the Association of Electragists International, whose members alone may use it." But *mortician* is in the public domain. It was proposed by a writer in the *Embalmers' Monthly* for February, 1895, but the undertakers, who were then *funeral-directors,* did not rise to it until some years later. On September 16, 1916, some of the more eminent of them met at Columbus O., to form a national association, on the lines of the American College of Surgeons, the American Association of University Professors, and the Society of the Cincinnati, and a year later they decided upon National Selected *Morticians* as its designation. To this day the association remains so exclusive that, of the 24,000 undertakers in the United States, only 200 belong to it. But any one of the remaining 23,800 is free to call himself a *mortician,* and to use all the other lovely words that the advance of human taxidermy has brought in. *Mortician,* of course, was suggested by *physician,* for undertakers naturally admire and like to pal with the resurrection men, and there was a time when some of them called themselves *embalming surgeons.* A *mortician* never handles a *corpse;* he *prepares* a *body* or *patient.* This business is carried on in a *preparation-room* or *operating-room,* and when it is achieved the patient is put into a *casket* and stored in the *reposing-room* or *slumber-room* of a *funeral-home.* On the day of the funeral he is moved to the *chapel* therein for the last exorcism, and then hauled to the cemetery in a *funeral-car* or *casket-coach.* The old-time shroud is now a *négligé* or *slumber-shirt* or *slumber-robe,* the mortician's worktruck is an *ambulance,* and the cemetery is fast becoming a *memorial-park.* In the West cemeteries are being supplanted by public mausoleums, which sometimes go under the names of *cloisters, burial-abbeys,* etc. To be laid away in one runs into money. The vehicle that morticians use for their expectant hauling of the ill is no longer an *ambulance,* but an *invalid-coach. Mortician* has been a favorite butt of the national wits, but they seem to have made no impression on it. In January, 1932, it was barred from the columns of the Chicago *Tribune.* "This decree goes forth," announced the *Tribune,* "not for lack of sympathy with the ambition of undertakers to be well regarded, but because of it. If they haven't the sense to save themselves from their own lexicographers, we shall not be guilty of abetting them in their folly." But *mortician* not only continues to flourish; it also begets progeny, e.g., *beautician, cosmetician, radiotrician* and *bootician.* The barbers, so far, have not devised a name for themselves in *-ician,* but they may be trusted to do so anon. In my youth they were *tonsorial artists,* but in recent years some of them have been calling themselves *chirotonsors.* Practically all American press-agents are now *public relations counsels, contact-managers or publicists,* all tree-trimmers are *tree-surgeons,* all milk-wagon and bakery-wagon drivers have become *salesmen,* nearly all janitors are *superintendents,* many gardeners have become *landscape-architects* (in England even the whales of the profession are simple *landscape-gardeners*), cobblers are beginning to call themselves *shoe-rebuilders,* and the corn-doctors, after a generation as *chiropodists,* have burst forth as *podiatrists.* The American fondness for such sonorous appellations arrested the interest of W. L. George, the English novelist, when he visited the United States in 1920. He said:

> Business titles are given in America more readily than in England. I know one *president* whose staff consists of two typists. Many firms have four *vice-presidents.* In the magazines you seldom find merely an *editor;* the others need their share of honor, so they are *associate* (not *assistant*) *editors.* A dentist is called a *doctor.* I wandered into a university, knowing nobody, and casually asked for the *dean.* I was asked, "Which *dean?*" In that building there were enough deans to stock all the English cathedrals. The master of a secret society is *royal supreme knight commander.* Perhaps I reached the extreme at a theatre in Boston, when I wanted something, I forgot what, and was told that I must apply to the *chief of the ushers.* He was a mild little man, who had something to do with people getting into their seats, rather a comedown from the pomp and circumstance of his title. Growing interested, I examined my programme, with the following result: It is not a large theatre, but it has a *press-representative,* a *treasurer* (box-office clerk), an *assistant treasurer* (box-office junior clerk), an *advertising-agent,* our old friend the *chief of the ushers,* a *stage-manager,* a *head-electrician,* a *master of properties* (in England called *props*), a *leader of the orchestra* (pity this—why not *president?*), and a *matron* (unknown.)

George might have unearthed some even stranger magnificoes in other playhouses. I once knew an ancient bill-sticker, attached to a Baltimore theatre, who boasted the sonorous title of *chief lithographer.* Today, in all probability, he would be called a *lithographic-engineer.* For a number of years the *Engineering News-Record,* the organ of the legitimate engineers, used to devote a column every week to just such uninvited invaders of the craft, and some of the species it unearthed were so fantastic that it was constrained to reproduce their business cards photographically in order to convince its readers that it was not spoofing. One of its favorite exhibits was a bedding manufacturer who first became a *mattress-engineer* and then promoted himself to the lofty dignity of *sleep-engineer.* No doubt he would have called himself a *morphician* if he had thought of it.

Another exhilarating specimen was a tractor-driver who advertised for a job as a *caterpillar-engineer*. A third was a beautician who burst out as an *appearance-engineer*. In an Atlanta department-store the *News-Record* found an *engineer of good taste*—a young woman employed to advise newly-married couples patronizing the furniture department, and elsewhere it unearthed *display-engineers* who had been lowly window-dressers until some visionary among them made the great leap, *demolition-engineers* who were once content to be house-wreckers, and *sanitary-engineers* who had an earlier incarnation as garbage-men. The *wedding-engineer* is a technician employed by florists to dress churches for hymeneal orgies. The *commence-ment-e.* arranges college and high-school commencements; he has lists of clergymen who may be trusted to pray briefly, and some sort of fire-alarm connection, I suppose, with the office of Dr. John H. Finley, the champion commencement orator of this or any other age. The *packing-e.* is a scientist who crates clocks, radios and chinaware for shipment. The *correspondence-e.* writes selling-letters guaranteed to pull. The *income-e.* is an insurance solicitor in a new false-face. The *dwelling-e.* replaces lost keys, repairs leaky roofs, and plugs up rat-holes in the cellar. The *vision-e.* supplies spectacles at cut rates. The *dehorning-e.* attends to bulls who grow too frisky. The *Engineering News-Record* also discovered a *printing-e.*, a *furniture-e.*, a *photographic-e.*, a *financial-e.* (a stock-market tipster), a *paint-e.*, a *clothing-e.*, a *wrapping-e.* (a dealer in wrapping-paper), a *matrimonial-e.* (a psychoanalyst specializing in advice to the lovelorn), a *box-e.* (the *packing-e.* under another name), an *automotive-painting-e.*, a *blasting-e.*, a *dry-cleaning-e.*, a *container-e.*, a *furnishing-e.*, a *socioreligious-e.* (an uplifter), a *social-e.* (the same), a *feed-plant-e.*, a *milk-e.*, a *surface-protection-e.*, an *analyzation-e.*, a *fiction-e.*, a *psychological-e.* (another kind of psychoanalyst), a *casement-window-e.*, a *shingle-e.*, a *fumigating-e.*, a *laminated-wood-e.*, a *package-e.* (the *packing-e.* again), a *horse-e.*, a *podiatric-e.* (a corn-doctor), an *ice-e.*, a *recreation-e.*, a *tire-e.*, a *paint-maintenance-e.*, a *space-saving-e.*, a *film-e.*, (or *film-gineer*), a *criminal-e.* (a criminologist), a *diet-kitchen-e.*, a *patent-e.*, an *equipment-e.*, a *floor-covering-e.*, a *society-e.*, a *window-cleaning-e.*, a *dust-e.*, a *hospitalization-e.*, a *baking-e.*, a *directory-e.*, an *advertising-e.*, a *golf-e.*, (a designer of golf courses), a *human-e.* (another variety of psychoanalyst), an *amusement-e.*, an *electric-sign-e.*, a *household-e.*, a *pageant-e.*, an *idea-e.*, a *ballistics-e.*, a *lace-e.* and a *sign-e.* Perhaps the prize should go to the *dansant-e.* (an agent supplying dancers and musicians to nightclubs), or to the *hot-dog-e.* The exterminating-engineers have a solemn national association and wear a distinguishing pin; whether or not they have tried to restrain non-member rat-catchers from calling themselves *engineers* I do not know. In 1923 the *Engineering News-Record* printed a final blast against all the pseudo-engineers then extant, and urged its engineer readers to boycott them. But this boycott apparently came to nothing, and soon thereafter it abated its indignation and resorted to laughter. Next to *engineer, expert* seems to be the favorite talisman of Americans eager to augment their estate and dignity in this world. Very often it is hitched to an explanatory prefix, e.g., *housing-, planning-, hog-, erosion-, marketing-, boll-weevil-,* or *sheep-dip-,* but sometimes the simple adjective *trained-* suffices. When the Brain Trust came into power in Washington, the town began to swarm with such quacks, most of them recent graduates of the far-flung colleges of the land. One day a humorous member of Congress printed an immense list of them in the *Congressional Record,* with their salaries and academic dignities. He found at least one whose expertness was acquired in a seminary for chiropractors. During the John Purroy Mitchel "reform" administration in New York City (1914–18) so many bogus *experts* were put upon the payroll that special designations for them ran out, and in prodding through the Mitchel records later on Bird S. Coler discovered that a number had been carried on the books as *general experts.*

FOR DISCUSSION AND REVIEW

1. As you have learned, euphemism is the substitution of a "pleasant term for a blunt one." Do you feel that there is a substantial difference between "real estate man" and "realtor"? Why do you think that Chadbourn was offended by "real estate man"?

2. If you worked as a writer for a newspaper, would you prefer to be called a commentator, journalist, reporter, or newspaperman? Why?

3. Specifically, how does Mencken reveal his attitude toward occupational euphemisms?

4. Usually it is those who are in the occupations themselves who call for occupational euphemisms. Do you feel that Mencken or anyone else is justified in criticizing such desires or euphemistic usages? Explain.

5. What are some occupational euphemisms that you have heard recently? Some will probably appear more acceptable to you than others. Why?

DAN CARLINSKY 2

The Traveler's Guide to Hash-House Greek

While only some of us may ever actually get to work in one of the nation's largest industries—the restaurant business—all of us have had considerable experience with this aspect of American life. We have all eaten in a number of restaurants of varying size, quality, and atmosphere. Dan Carlinsky, a contributor to Esquire, Look, *and the* Times, *takes us on a brief excursion into the language of one of America's unique eateries, the roadside diner.*

BEFORE YOU GO TO PARIS, YOU LEARN TO SAY "BONJOUR, MONSIEUR, *je voudrais bien avoir un Château-briand avec des pommes de terre et un grand verre de Bordeaux.*" On the plane to Frankfurt, you memorize "*Guten abend, wir möchten zweimal Sauerbraten, Erbsen, etwas Schwarzbrot, und eine kalte Flasche Zeller Schwarze Katz haben.*" So in your own country—where, if you expect to do any traveling, you run the risk of getting stuck in a diner at some time and place—you owe it to yourself to learn Hash-House Greek, the peculiar American lunch-counter cant.

How else will you comprehend "stretch one and let it bleed"? Or "hold the cow"? How else would you know that to order submarine sandwiches (those grand concoctions of onions, sandwich meat, cheese, lettuce, tomatoes, oregano and oil served on a long roll) you must ask for *hoagies* in Birmingham, *grinders* in Hartford, *heroes* in New York, *poor boys* in New Orleans, *rockets* in Cheyenne, *torpedoes* in San Diego, *Italian sandwiches* in Louisville, and *Cuban sandwiches* in Miami.

So, herewith, a glossary for beginners:

Adam and Eve on a raft Two poached eggs on toast.

All the way With a full complement of condiments; e.g., a burger *all the way* has catsup, onions, relish, salt and pepper. Can also mean well done.

—and Signifies the second half of a ham and eggs; coffee *and*—coffee and donut, etc.

apple Apple pie, as in a slice of *apple.*

black and white Chocolate soda with vanilla ice cream.

blood Cherry flavoring: stretch one, let it *bleed* (or make it *bloody*)—a cherry Coke. Also refers to rare meat: a *bloody* burger—a rare hamburger.

b.l.t. Bacon, lettuce and tomato sandwich.

bowl Bowl of soup, as in a *bowl* of chicken. In one-soup establishments, a *bowl* is a bowl of the soup du jour.

bowl of red; bowl of fire Bowl of chili.

bridge Four orders of an item. Derives from foursome at bridge game.

bucket of mud Dish of chocolate ice cream.

burn it; burned Well done.

burn one Make a malted milk shake.

c.b. Corned beef.

china Cup of tea. See spot.

cow Milk, as in a glass of *cow;* also cream, as in draw one, hold the *cow*—a cup of coffee, no cream. See **grade "a."**

crowd Three orders of an item. Derives from "two's company, three's a crowd."

down Toasted, as in b.l.t. *down;* also used as a noun; as in an order of *down,* smeared—buttered toast.

draw one Pour a cup of coffee. Derives from the motion of drawing the handle of the coffee-urn spigot.

drop Sundae. Derives from the action of dropping a scoop of ice cream into a dish.

eighty-six Unavailability of an item. Also used to signify an undesirable customer, suggesting that for him the restaurant is out of everything. Derives from rhyme with "nix."

g.j. Grapefruit juice.

grade "a" Milk. See **cow.**

DRAW ONE, HOLD THE COW—That means a cup of coffee, no cream.

hail Ice, as in hold the *hail*—without ice.
handful Five orders of an item. Derives from the number of fingers on a hand.
let it walk The order is to be taken out, to go. See **on wheels.**
nineteen Banana split.
ninety-five A customer who walks out without paying.
o.j. Orange juice.
on the hoof Very rare. Derives from vision of the meat still attached to the rest of the animal.
on wheels To go. See **let it walk**.
over Of an egg, fried on both sides, as in two *over*.
over easy Of an egg, fried on both sides, softly.

patch Strawberry. Derives from strawberry patch.
radio Tuna sandwich on toast. Derives from "tune 'er down."
r.b. Roast beef.
set-up Silverware and paper napkin on the table.
side A side order, which costs extra; e.g., a *side* of french—french-fried potatoes in addition.
smear Butter.
spot Cup of tea. Derives from English expression "spot of tea." Cold *spot*—iced tea.
stack Hot-cakes, as in a *stack* of wheat—wheatcakes; toast, as in a buttered *stack;* ice cream in a dish, as in a *stack* of van—a scoop of vanilla ice cream in a dish.
stretch Coca-Cola. Derives from shoot one and *stretch* it—take a shot of syrup, enough for a small (6-ounce) Coke, and stretch it with extra soda water to make a large (10-ounce) glass. used as verb (*stretch* a pair) and noun (gimme a crowd of *stretches*).
suds Root beer. Derives from bartenders' term for beer, coming from the foamy head. Sometimes refers to coffee, deriving from joking reference to the taste of dishwater.
thirteen The boss is around—watch out.
twist Slice of lemon; a spot with a *twist*—tea with lemon.
up Of an egg, fried on one side (sunny side up), as in two *up*.
with Used like—**and** (which see); burger *with*—hamburger with onion (or with french fries), etc.
working The order is being prepared, as in "Hey, cookie—I've got a burger on the hoof all the way *working!*" or, in answer to "Where's my milk shake, please?"—it's *working!*
wreck 'em Of eggs, scramble them, as in Adam and Eve on a raft, *wreck 'em;* a stack of wheat, smeared; a large g.j., give me hail; a large o.j., hold it; draw two and make one with extra cow.

FOR DISCUSSION AND REVIEW

1. Hash-House Greek is used more by countermen, waitresses, and cooks than by customers. Why did such terminology develop and what are its advantages?

2. As Carlinsky notes, submarine sandwiches go by various names depending on the region where they are sold. If you were to order a nonalcoholic carbonated beverage, by what name would you call it? What do such variations suggest about the American language?

3. Carlinsky does not explain how all the terms in his lexicon are derived. What are some possible explanations for "Adam and Eve on a raft," "down," and "china"?

4. Make as many additions to Carlinsky's list as you can. Are any of your terms likely to be used by customers as well as by waitresses and cooks?

5. Discuss some of the humorous and incongruous images that are brought to mind by particular Hash-House Greek terms. What else makes this jargon entertaining?

CHARLES KURALT 3

Burger Heaven

One of the most popular items on diner menus is the great American hamburger. Charles Kuralt became impressed by the variety of burgers available everywhere as he traveled throughout the United States filming episodes for his award-winning "On the Road" series for the CBS Evening News. This script is a catalog of colorful burger names. Obviously Americans are not satisfied with the notion that a hamburger is a hamburger is a hamburger.

Cronkite: My colleague Charles Kuralt must be having some troubles with his expense account. From the road he sends subtle, indirect words to the CBS NEWS business office that lately he has been keeping his meal tabs at least down.
Kuralt: It is truly said that America is an infinite and various country. The infinity shows up on our speedometer. As for the variety, well, we have found, for example, that at lunchtime On The Road, we have our choice, of all kinds of hamburgers.
Man: The tacoburger and island burger well, a side of fries, yes, sir.
Kuralt: Americans ate 40 billion hamburgers in the last year; give or take a few hundred million, and On The Road you tend to eat more than your share. You can find your way across this country using

burger joints the way a navigator uses stars. Where are we now? Oh, Missouri, of course, but there is mo—much mo. We have munched Bridge burgers in the shadow of the Brooklyn Bridge and Cable Car burgers hard by the Golden Gate, Dixie burgers in the sunny South and Yankee Doodle Dandy burgers in the North. The Civil War must be over—they taste exactly alike. And which lovely mountains are these? Count on it, a burger stand will tell you, and block your view of the Great Smoky Mountains. We had a Capitol burger—guess where. And, so help us, in the inner courtyard of the Pentagon, a Penta burger. The free world may be lost.

Waitress: Hippoburger with a bippieburger. Well on the bippie, Medium rare on the hippo.

Kuralt: Ernie Campbell, down there in Johnson City, Tennessee, couldn't resist naming his burger for himself. We have also consumed burgers from the grills of guys named Oliver, Buddy, Murray, Chuck, Ben and Juan. It begins to get to you after a while. In Tulsa we took note of a machine that turns out 12 burgers a minute, complete with a machine that mustards and catsups a burger in a tenth of a second.

We've had king burgers, queen burgers, mini burgers, maxi burgers, tuna burgers, Smithfield burgers, bacon burgers, wine burgers, heavenly burgers, and yum burgers. Yum. Yum.

In Independence, Kansas, we lunched on poppa burgers, momma burgers, and little teeny baby burgers.

And then there was the night in New Mexico when the lady was just closing up and we had to decide in a hurry. What'll it be, she said, a whoppa burger or a bitta burger? Hard to decide.

Waitress: I still have a French burger coming.

Kuralt: The Acropolis of burger joints is probably the Hippo in San Francisco, home of the nude burger, strip burger, hamburger de luxe, bippieburger, Italian burger, Joe's burger, mushroom burger, Bronx burger, Terry burger, Russian burger, Tahitian burger, onion burger, taco burger, smorgasburger, continental burger, French burger, and so on, ad infinitum, to hundreds of strains and mutations.

Waitress: Decided what you'd like.

Man: Myer burger for the two kids.

Waitress: One?

Man: One, right. I'm going to split it. And bippieburger for her, well done.

Waitress: One bippie well done.

Man: Right. And I'll have a mushroom burger.

Waitress: How would you like yours, sir?

Man: Medium rare, please.

Kuralt: But this is not merely a local phenomenon. The smell of fried onions is abroad in the land, and if the French chefs among us will avert their eyes, we will finish reciting our menu of the last few weeks on the highways of America. We've had grabba burgers, kinda burgers, lotta burgers, castle burgers, country burgers, bronco burgers. Broadway burgers, broiled burgers, beefnut burgers, bell burgers, plush burgers, prime burgers, flame burgers, lunch burgers, top burgers, Plaza burgers, tasty burgers, dude burgers, char burgers, tall boy burgers, golden burgers, 747 jet burgers, whiz burgers, nifty burgers, and thing burgers. One day in the desert I had a vision that the last ding dong of doom had sounded, that the land was empty and that the last American had left only one small monument to mark his passing.

Charles Kuralt, CBS NEWS, On The Road.

Cronkite: And that's the way it is, Monday, November 16th, 1970. This is Walter Cronkite, CBS NEWS. Good night.

"We've got some made with ham, too— but we don't know what to call them."

FOR DISCUSSION AND REVIEW

1. Kuralt's list of names for hamburgers is a brief study in what is known as product differentiation. Categorize the primary ways in which burgers are given names around the country.

2. Of the burgers that Kuralt mentions that you have never tasted, which appeal to you most and why? Have you eaten any burgers that Kuralt does not include?

3. Why is the cartoon on page 63 funny? What is the derivation of the word "hamburger"?

DAVID MELLINKOFF 4

The Language of the Law

Most of us find the language of the lawyer to be unintelligible and therefore boring. Legalese, however, is extremely influential and one might even argue that its power derives from its very obscurity. Not wishing to grant such an absurdity, David Mellinkoff, himself an attorney, claims in this excerpt from his book The Language of the Law *that there is no legitimate reason for our legal system to be a major dispenser of gobbledygook.*

INTELLIGIBLE AND UNINTELLIGIBLE HAVE AN OVERPOWERING SOUND of absoluteness that limits their usefulness in discussion of the language of the law. It is a very empty phrase that someone, somewhere, cannot squeeze a drop of sense from, yet some glittering nonsense discourages the effort. Take this specimen, spawned by a current vogue for legislation about emergency calls on party lines:

> In every telephone directory . . . there shall be printed in type not smaller than any other type appearing on the same page, a notice preceded by the word "warning" printed in type at least as large as the largest type on the same page, . . .

This is no misprint. It had models in the laws of sister states, and in turn has become a model for others. Take comfort that some draftsmen have refused to buy this pre-wrapped shoddy, stopping the word flow when they had had enough for law, for good English, and for people—after the word *warning.* Take comfort too that complete gibberish is not the typical instance of language mangling by lawyers.

It is still aiming too low to be satisfied with language that is only "capable of being understood," the standard definition of *intelligible.* The general antipathy to absolutes has for centuries split *intelligible* into degrees, and as used in this book it means "easily understood," what some mean by clear or plain. Its opposite—*unintelligible*—covers the full muddy spectrum available to lawyers. From the shortest nonsense—*ss.*[1] Through long rows of unnecessarily unclear words and constructions, variously distinguished as obscure, vague, ambiguous, and in other circles called doubletalk, officialese, gobbledygook, federal prose, etc, etc. Down into the scraps of language which at best are not easily understood, such as *and/or* and *or/and.*

This breadth of range is a further reminder that intelligibility is not synonymous with brevity, though verbosity does make it easier for the writer to lose himself while losing his reader.

Likewise, intelligibility is not dependent upon precision, which sometimes must be sacrificed for quick understanding, as in the traffic signs which tell pedestrians to WAIT (without saying for how long), and to WALK (without adding, "if you want to."). The sacrifice of precision for intelligibility needs mention, not to encourage sloppiness but appropriateness, and to offset the single-minded teaching which reverses the rites—making intelligibility always the goat. There are still times when magic words make a legal difference—e.g., *consideration for the lease* (instead of *prepaid rent*), or the weaker magic of *liquidated damages* (instead of *forfeiture* or *penalty*). Even so, there is little legal prose of any sort which cannot be made more intelligible than it usually is.

Once the draftsman starts with a clear understanding of what it is he wants to say, making himself understood is more a matter of how than of what. If the simplest truth goes in fuzzy, it will come out that way. And if complexity goes in clear, it can come out that way—gospel or not. Even ". . . Holmes was sometimes clearly wrong; but . . . when this was so he was always wrong clearly."

Any legal prose can be made more intelligible if the draftsman is striving for intelligibility, but even the careful draftsman sometimes finds more pressing concerns—some legitimate. There is, for example,

[1] Editors' note: *ss* abbreviates the Latin *scilicet* (to wit).

the deliberate use of language which everyone recognizes as being easily misunderstood, accepted for the sake of quick agreement. This sort of *calculated ambiguity* is left for later. Also left for later is the deliberate use of language which though not always easily understood is quickly felt, the language of ceremony and persuasion.

On the blacker side is the art of planned confusion, which has its advocates, its gray and off-white shadings, and above all its patterns for identification. The patterns are so strong that at times the "planned" aspect has dropped deep into the inner lawyer, to become merely habitual without taint of sinister purpose.

Planned confusion takes two major forms: (1) saying-nothing and making it look like something, and (2) saying-something and making it look like nothing, or like something else. The law has no monopoly on either form, but as wholesale dealers in words lawyers have found the patterns too useful.

At its mildest, nonprofessional saying-nothing takes the form of small talk, the polite lying that is the mark of civilized society. Thus,

we say	**instead of**
I find it stimulating	Absolute nonsense
Most interesting	What a bore
Very stately	Real ugly
We must get together soon	Thank God, you're leaving town

Related to this is the lawyer's

"progress" letter	**instead of**
Your matter is being given due consideration in the light of the pertinent statutes and case law, and you will be further advised in due course.	Right now it looks like you're stuck. But don't go shopping for another lawyer.

A more widespread malady of nothingness at the bar is the *one-legged subjunctive.* Its most prevalent forms are *it would seem* and *it may well be,* which make no more sense when joined together like this:

> It would seem also that a further and more far reaching effect of the instant judgment may well be to encourage other persons to breach their obligations . . .

Variants are *one might wish* and the emphatically spurious *it may very well be.*

Unlike the bald fraud of *yes and no,* these phrases equivocate even on being equivocal. *It would seem* (that is the appearance of things, says the writer)—and you wait in vain for the other shoe to drop. Not *it would seem to be, but the fact is,* just way up in the air, *it would seem.* So that the writer can never be called to account. Not what I thought or believed or what the fact was, just what it seemed to be. And then again, *it may well be* something completely different or *it may well not be.* I'm not sure or won't say; at least I haven't said.

The lawyer's addiction to *it would seem* is related to the old and continuing law use of French *semble* (it seems). But that is a technical expression of uncertainty and lack of authority which still has a place (in footnotes), and should be kept there. A more intelligible statement of guess is *one of the possibilities is,* and a candid *I don't know* would win the law some friends.

A more vicious way of saying-nothing is the lawyer's *agreement to agree,* or—as it frequently appears by design or accident—*subject to change by mutual consent.* Of course. It always is. Like the *whereas* recital, this phrase gives the hurried bargainer the false impression that something has been taken care of. It is eyewash or worse.

One step deeper into bad morals is saying-something calculated to mislead. This is a species of unintelligibility related to the practice of using fine print to make contracts illegible. The object of each is the same—to force law on the victim without arousing suspicion that it is there. Various paths lead to the same sinkhole.

One of them is using words so ordinary in appearance that the reader thinks he understands. Here is a sample. Without counsel, the citizen in the hurried sanctuary of the voting booth ponders "Yes" or "No" on a—

Ballot	**Meaning**
ASSESSMENT OF GOLF COURSES. Assembly Constitutional Amendment No. 29. Establishes manner in which non-profit golf-courses should be assessed for purposes of taxation.	Private golf courses shall be taxed less than other private property.

These ballot words are carefully designed to produce a "yes" vote (which they did). First, they speak of the "manner" of *doing something*—"assessment," "establishes," "assessed," "taxation." So that attention is diverted from the fact that the words are consistent with a way of *not doing something*—not assessing, not taxing. Second, they speak of *non-profit,* which (if it means anything to the voter) has a vaguely charitable sound, unconnected with expensive memberships. Yet on the statute books, the words will mean what they mean to lawyers—". . . not designed primarily to pay dividends . . ." If the ballot measure had said what it meant, the issue would have been clear and the vote in doubt.

Another form of saying-something is the disarmingly disingenuous letter agreement. Here boring repetition and amiable fairness combine to mask the one sharp tooth:

> We agree to pay all bills in full promptly as they come in, including without limitation of the generality of the foregoing all bills for labor, services, and materials, supplies, utilities, taxes, permits, fees, royalties, and everything else directly or indirectly for or used in connection with the construction of your building, you of course to reimburse us for everything spent for labor, services, and materials, supplies, utilities, taxes, permits, fees, royalties, overhead, and everything else directly or indirectly for or used in connection with the construction of your building.

FOR DISCUSSION AND REVIEW

1. Mellinkoff argues that legal prose should be "intelligible"—that is, "easily understood"—but that it does not necessarily need to be brief or precise. Explain this apparent paradox.

2. How does Mellinkoff defend "calculated ambiguity"? Give some examples of it.

3. What does Mellinkoff mean by "planned confusion"? Do you agree that it is justifiable?

4. What, according to Mellinkoff, is "the one-legged subjunctive"? Why does he object to it?

5. Identify and discuss "the one sharp tooth" in the letter agreement quoted by Mellinkoff.

6. The following item appeared in the San Francisco *Chronicle.*

State Makes It Perfectly Clear

> *Sacramento*
> For some time the public has wondered what to make of most bureaucratic twaddle—but a new State law has set the record straight at last.

From the revised State code of the Division of Consumer Services, Department of Consumer affairs, Title 4: subsection 2102, comes the official word:

"Tenses, Gender and Number: For the purpose of the rules and regulations contained in this chapter, the present tense includes the past and future tenses, and the future, the present; the masculine gender includes the feminine, and feminine, the masculine; and the singular includes the plural, and the plural the singular."

Our Correspondent

Comment on this example of legalese.

WILLIAM EBEN SCHULTZ 5

Football Verbiage

All of us at one time or another have tried to find fresh and more specific ways of describing commonplace events. Nowhere is this need more evident than on the sports pages of our newspapers. Here William Schultz presents an extensive list of the "action" verbs that sports writers use to avoid triteness and brighten their reporting.

AMERICAN SPEECH IS CONCEDED TO BE ENERGETIC AND PICTURESQUE, possibly as an expression or reflection of national activity and variety. The sports pages of our newspapers, while often filled with a jargon not too desirable, and sometimes affected, help to illustrate this idea. Aside from the graphic names of athletic teams (not studied in this article, but well known to the average reader—such as Titans, Trojans, and Tigers, along with a whole menagerie of other animals), there is no more outstanding characteristic of news stories rushed into print during the football season than the use of action verbs in the headlines. The following illustrations, arranged alphabetically, have been gathered from week-end editions of a miscellaneous assortment of daily papers, ranging from small publications to the metropolitan press. Only examples of the last three years [1948–1951] have been included, as language students who also cultivate the gridiron may recognize, and these are limited to the college field.

Duke *annexes* victory
Lake Forest *baffles* Augustana
Iowa State *bags* tie with Mississippi
Ohio State *beats* Badgers
Lawrence *belts* Monmouth
Michigan Normal *blanks* Ball State
Illini *blast* Indiana
Gophers *bounce* Indiana
Oklahoma *bowls* over Nebraska
Gophers *bruise* Iowa
Tulane *bumps* Mississippi
Michigan *buries* Northwestern
Illinois *clips* Purdue
Millikin *clouts* Illinois College
Duke *conquers* North Carolina
Baylor *cops* close one
California *cracks* Washington
Huskies *crown* S.I.U.
Ohio *crushes* Minnesota
Cornell *douses* Columbia
Case *downs* Western Reserve
Illinois Wesleyan *drops* tough game to DePauw
Tulane *drowns* Navy
Anderson *drubs* McKendree
Notre Dame *dumps* Nebraska
Oklahoma *edges* Texas
Northwestern *explodes* Illinois Title
Illinois *grinds* out win
Yale *handed* defeat by Dartmouth
Navy *hangs* up victory
Georgia *halters* Boston College
Florida *halts* Vanderbilt
Eureka *humbles* McKendree
Colorado *jars* Aggies
Northwestern *jolts* Illinois
Western *laces* Shurtleff
Stanford *licks* Washington
Notre Dame *mauls* Indiana
Northwestern *nicks* Ohio
Oregon *nips* St. Mary's
U.S.C. *noses* out Stanford
Texas *nudges* Baylor
Texas Christian *outscrambles* Mississippi

Army *overwhelms* Lions
Normal *plasters* Western
Shurtleff *pops* Principia
St. Joseph *pounds* Mansfield
Drake *pummels* New Mexico
California *quells* U.S.C.
Tulane *races* to win
State Normal *racks* up win
Penn. State *raps* Quakers
Oklahoma *rips* Colorado
Wesleyan *roars* to victory
Alabama *rolls* over Florida
Spartans *romp* over Cyclones
Ohio *routs* Northwestern
Tulane *shades* Auburn
Irish *shellack* Navy
Indiana *shocks* Pittsburgh
Pittsburgh *slaps* W. Virginia
Kansas State *smacks* Iowa
Yale *smashes* Harvard
Brown *smothers* Colgate
Michigan *snaps* Gopher streak
Wildcats *spank* Purdue
Flowers *sparks* Northwestern to victory
Cornell *spills* Navy
Wisconsin *squeezes* out decision over Illinois
Wake Forest *startles* Drake
Cyclones *stun* Illini
Texas *subdues* Oklahoma
Bucs *swamp* Pittsburgh
Notre Dame *tames* Iowa
Iowa *throttles* Wisconsin
Yale *thumps* Columbia
Washington *thwarts* Illinois Wesleyan
Iowa State *tips* Colorado
California *topples* Washington
Dartmouth *tops* Harvard
Wolverines *trample* Navy
Knox *trims* Beloit
Knox *trips* Monmouth
Mississippi *triumphs* over Tennessee
Princeton *tromps* Harvard
U.C.L.A. *trounces* Purdue

Louisiana State *upsets* North Carolina
Northwestern *wallops* Pittsburgh
Denver *whips* Wyoming
Iowa *yields* to Minnesota

There are many additional expressions for which I have saved no definite references, like these: *batters, bows to, deals defeat, lashes, outslickers, paces, shatters hopes, slashes, snares, squelches, swats, whales.* I have not included common terms like *wins, loses, beats, defeats, overcomes, outscores, takes game,* etc.

With such an expressive array of "verbiage," there seems to be no danger that the sports editors will become stagnant, or that football as a game will lose its numerous and enthusiastic artists in the field of athletic ballyhoo.

FOR DISCUSSION AND REVIEW

1. Some writers claim that there are no exact synonyms in English, no two words that have precisely the same meaning. The long list of action verbs offered by Schultz provides an opportunity to test this claim, since all these verbs describe a situation in which one team wins and another team loses. Sort the verbs into two groups: those for winners and those for losers. Then compare the verbs in each group—for example, what exactly is the difference between "crushes" and "downs" or between "halts" and "humbles"? Are there any exact synonyms?

2. All of these headlines involve the use of figurative language. Explain the figures of speech and how they work in several of the headlines.

3. Just as the sportswriter must repeatedly describe similar situations, so all of us talk about actions that we perform daily. If we were restricted to only the verbs "eat," "drink," "sleep," "work," for example, our conversations would be repetitive and monotonous. List as many verbs as you can to describe these four actions. What denotative and connotative differences do you find in your list of alternatives?

BIL GILBERT 6

Fast as an Elephant, Strong as an Ant

Bil Gilbert, a frequent contributor to Sports Illustrated, *feels that while the language of the sports page is vivid and energetic, its metaphors are inaccurate. He contends that tradition and haste of composition have forced the sportswriter and the rest of us into mindless habitual language patterns. His suggestion for improvement—"high-fidelity zoological metaphors," of course.*

ONE DAY RECENTLY I WAS READING A STORY ABOUT THE SAN DIEGO Chargers when I came across the following sentence describing Mr. Ernie Ladd, a tackle who is said to be 6 feet 9 inches tall and to weigh 300 pounds. Ladd, the report stated, has "a body that a grizzly bear could be proud of." Now, this is an example of the falsely anthropomorphic and the factually inaccurate natural-history metaphor, a literary device widely used by sportswriters and one that I have long thought should be reported to authorities and stamped out.

The description of Ernie Ladd is objectionable on two counts. First, there is no evidence that bears take pride in their personal appearance, physical prowess or muscular development. Among animals, only men seem susceptible to narcissism. And even if grizzlies did have the emotions of a beach boy and sat about the woods admiring their physiques, no bear would be proud of having a body like that of Mr. Ladd.

According to my copy of *Mammals of the World* (Ernest P. Walker, The Johns Hopkins Press, 1964, page 1173), "Grizzlies 2.5 meters [about 8 feet] in length and 360 kg. [800 pounds] in weight have been recorded. . . ." In brief, Mr. Ladd is simply too puny to impress a grizzly even if grizzlies were impressionable in these matters.

I have never been one to criticize without offering constructive alternatives. Additional reading of *Mammals of the World* has uncovered some statistics that may prove useful in the future. Should the need arise, one might accurately (though still anthropomorphically) write that Mr. Ernie Ladd has a body that a female gray seal (150 kg., 2 meters) or a pygmy hippopotamus (160 kg., 1.9 meters, counting tail) might be proud of.

It is not my purpose to embarrass or harass the man who wrote the story. Rather, it is to point out that he is the inheritor, the victim, of a bad journalistic tradition. Sportswriters have been comparing such and such an athlete to this or that animal since the dawn of sports. Many of these long-standing figures, metaphors, similes and tropes are even more wildly inaccurate and ridiculous than the comparison of Mr. Ladd to a grizzly bear.

An example that comes quickly to mind is the expression "wild as a hawk," used to describe either erratic performance (a baseball pitcher who cannot throw the ball across the plate) or untamable behavior (a fractious horse). In both senses the phrase is misleading. As far as control goes, the birds of prey are the antithesis of wildness (in the baseball use of the word). A duck hawk, for example, flying a mile high in the sky, can suddenly turn, dive earthward at 175 mph and strike a tiny sandpiper flying just a few feet above the ground. Sandy Koufax should be so accurate. As to being untamable, I, as a falconer, have often captured a feral adult hawk and in a month had the bird flying free, returning to my hand in response to a whistled command.

My own suggestion is that "wild as a heron" would better suggest the kind of behavior that wild as a hawk is supposed to describe. In many situations herons appear uncoordinated, almost spastic. Seeing a long-legged, gangly heron trying to land or take off from the ground is an experience. Furthermore, herons are far wilder (in the ferocious sense) than hawks. The most painful injury I ever received from an animal was given me by an American bittern (a heron type), who gouged a large hole in my wrist as I was attempting to free him from a fish trap.

"Loose as a goose" is an avian simile, supposedly suggesting extreme suppleness. Actually, geese have rigid pinions and are more or less bound like weight lifters by a heavy layer of pectoral muscle. Straight as a goose, stiff as a goose, pompous as a goose would be all right. But loose as a goose? Never. A better expression of the notion would be: "Though Slats Slattern has been a stellar NBA performer for 12 seasons, he remains young in spirit and loose as a mink." The slim-bodied minks, as well as weasels, ferrets and otters, are designed along the lines of a wet noodle. They look, and in fact are, far looser than a goose can possibly be.

Turning to mammals, an agility simile is "quick as a cat," often used in connection with such athletes as shortstops and goalies. It is true that cats are quicker than some things—turtles, mice, goldfish in bowls, for example—but they are much less quick than many other creatures. Any wheezing old dog worth its salt can catch a cat. I once had a crow so quick that it could fly down and deliver three pecks between the eyes of a cat (which the crow despised) before the feline could raise a paw in self-defense. Not long ago I was watching a tame baboon which had the run of a yard in which was caged an ocelot. The baboon, even though working through bars, would reach into the cage and, while the ocelot was trying to get her reflexes in order, grab the cat by both her handsome tail and pointed ears. Baboon-quick is accurate and has a nice exotic ring to it.

Cats may not be the quickest animals, but at least one of the family, the cheetah, is the swiftest mammal as far as straight-ahead sprinting goes. It would seem that "run like a cheetah" would be a natural simile for sportswriters, but what do we have? "Ziggy Zagowski, slashing left half for the Keokuk Kidneys, ran like a rabbit through the defending Sioux City Spleens." Now, for a few jumps a rabbit can move at a rate of 30 or 35 miles an hour, but 20 mph is its pace for a distance as great as 100 yards. This rate is about the same as—or a bit slower than—that of a journeyman human sprinter over the same course. The chances are that if old Zig could not outleg a bunny he would not have even made his high school team, If, however, he could run like a cheetah, it would be a different matter, since those cats can do the 440 at 71 mph.

Since an elephant can skip along as fast as 25 mph (a bit faster than Bob Hayes or the average cottontail), it would be highly complimentary to say of an athlete that he runs like an elephant. However, the expression "elephantine" is actually used in sports as a term of derision, to twit a ponderous, slow-moving, clumsy performer. Actually, elephants are not only swift beasts but graceful ones. Despite their size, they are almost as quick as a baboon or as loose as a mink.

They can slip quietly through the jungle, stand on a barrel or a ballerina at the behest of a ringmaster. "Horsine" would be a better term to designate a stumblebum. Horses are forever falling over small pebbles, ropes and their own feet. When a horse and rider start down even a gradual incline or up a path slightly narrower than the Pennsylvania Turnpike, the rider must dismount, and it is he who must lead, guide and, in general, prop up the horse.

Great strength has its place in sports, and it is traditional to describe the athlete who possesses it as being "strong as an ox." As in the case of quick cats and fast rabbits, the simile is not completely false, only inadequate. In proportion to their bulk, oxen are relatively strong but not overpoweringly so. A team of oxen weighing 3,400 pounds can move a dead weight, say a block of granite, equal to about three times its own weight. This is a fair feat when compared to a 150-pound weight lifter who can dead-lift 300 pounds. However, it is a feeble effort when one considers the ant, which can pick up a load 50 times heavier than itself. To speak of a fullback as being strong as an ant would be high praise indeed, since it would signify that the player could, without undue strain, carry the entire opposing team not only across the goal line, but right up into Row E.

Held in high regard by coaches, reporters and fans is the athlete who works incessantly at mastering the fundamentals of his game. Often such persevering types are admired as "beavers." This, of course, is a contraction of the folksy expressions "to work like a beaver" or "to be as busy as a beaver," both of which are based upon a misunderstanding of the beaver's nature and misobservation of the animal's customary behavior. Unlike some animals that must travel many miles a day just to rustle up a square meal, beavers seldom forage more than a hundred yards from their home. Beavers construct their well-publicized dams and lodges only when it is absolutely impossible to find a suitable natural waterscape. The lowly mole, on the other hand, may dig several hundred yards of tunnel in a day in an incessant effort to keep body and soul together. "I like that boy, all spring long he's been moling away," would be an apt way for a coach to describe and praise industriousness.

Canines have a strong attraction for scribes looking for a vivid, if fallacious, phrase. There is, for example, the veteran who is a "sly, foxy" competitor. (If foxes are so sly, how come they never run down the hounds? Who ever heard of a hunt catching a skunk?) Then there is the prizefighter about to addle the brains of his opponent or the fast-ball pitcher poised to stick one in a batter's ear. These violent men, we are often told, have a "wolfish grin" on their faces.

One of the few naturalists who have been close enough long enough to *au naturel* wolves to observe their facial expressions is Farley Mowat, who spent a summer camped virtually on the den step of a family of Arctic wolves. Mowat in his delightful book, *Never Cry Wolf,* claims that *his* wolves were kindly, affectionate, tolerant animals who looked and acted more like diplomats than thugs. This stands to reason. Many creatures besides man are predatory, but hardly any species except man tries to do real violence to its own kind in play while contemplating the prospect with a grin. If such a premayhem facial expression as a "wolfish grin" actually exists, it is probably unique to man. If this peculiar look of violence must be compared to that of some other animal, I recommend the short-tailed shrew.

The short-tailed shrew is one of the commonest animals of North America and one of the most perpetually predatory. Ounce for ounce (which is what a large shrew weighs), there is no busier killer in the world. Awake, the shrew is almost always preparing to kill, is killing or has just killed, and its victims include rodents, reptiles, birds and mammals several times its own size. The shrew, like almost all other mammals, does not kill out of capriciousness or playfulness, but rather because it has an extraordinarily high metabolic rate. It must daily consume the equivalent of its own body weight in order to keep the inner fires burning. (Eat like a shrew, rather than eat like a horse, would better describe the habits of a first baseman who is such a formidable trencherman that he can no longer bend down to scoop up low throws.) When a shrew closes in to kill something, say a white-footed mouse, it wears a really dreadful expression. A shrew is chinless, and its long mouth slashes across the underpart of its muzzle in a cruel, sharklike line. As the tiny killer closes in, its eyes glitter with excitement and two long brown fangs (which, incidentally, drip with a venomous saliva) are exposed. If Sonny Liston looked only half as wicked as a short-tailed shrew he might still be heavyweight champion of the world.

I fully realize that many of the criticisms and suggestions offered here do violence to some of the most cherished traditions of sports journalism, but there is no holding back literary and scientific progress. Consider, for example, the manner in which the style I advocate, high-fidelity zoological metaphor, injects color as well as accuracy into the following interview with Sig Schock of the Pardy Pumas:

"Sig Schock, a big horsine man, grizzled as a Norway rat, leaned back against the plywood bench, taking up a position so that the hot sun beat down on his ant-like shoulders. The eyes, old but still sharp as a barn owl's, flicked over the practice field, where the young Pumas cavorted as quick as so many baboons. 'I'll tell you,' Sig confided in his disconcertingly high, spring-peeperlike voice. 'These kids has got it. The most of them can run like elephants, a couple like cheetahs. And size. We finally got some. We got six boys with builds like a female gray seal's. Course, they're still young, some of them are wild as herons—that's O.K., they got the old desire. Every one of them is a snapping turtle or a raccoon. And I'll tell you something,' the sly, skunky veteran added, lowering his squeaky voice. 'We'll chew 'em up and lay 'em out this season.' A shrewish grin spread across the battered old face."

Leaving you with that, I remain pretty as a peacock, sassy as a jaybird, happy as a clam.

FOR DISCUSSION AND REVIEW

1. A metaphor, according to a widely used handbook, is "an implied analogy which imaginatively identifies one object with another and ascribes to the first one or more of the qualities of the second or invests the first with emotional or imaginative qualities associated with the second." The same handbook defines a simile as "a figure of speech in which a similarity between two objects is directly expressed, as in Milton's "A dungeon horrible, on all sides round,/ As one great furnace flamed." Here the comparison between the dungeon (Hell) and the great furnace is directly expressed in the *as* which labels the comparison a *simile*. Most *similes* are introduced by *as* or *like*. Which of these figures of speech is used in the title of Gilbert's article? Which is used in the phrase "a body that a grizzly bear could be proud of"? Do you think that Gilbert's faulting of this last comparison is justified, or would it be effective for most readers?

2. Consider the alternative comparisons offered by Gilbert: "wild as a heron," for example, or "loose as a mink." Are these alternatives acceptable? Why or why not?

3. After reading Gilbert's article, what conclusions can you draw concerning the characteristics of effective metaphors and similes? Consider the effectiveness of the following literary metaphors and similes.

a. I wandered lonely as a cloud.
William Wordsworth

b. That time of year thou mayst in me behold
When yellow leaves, or none, or few, do hang
Upon those boughs which shake against the cold,
Bare ruined choirs where late the sweet birds sang.
William Shakespeare

c. I saw eternity the other night
Like a great ring of pure and endless light,
All calm as it was bright;
And round beneath it, time in hours, days, years,
Driv'n by the spheres,
Like a vast shadow moved, in which the world
And all her train were hurled. . . .
Henry Vaughan

d. Her feet beneath her petticoat,
Like little mice stole in and out,
As if they feared the light. . . .
Sir John Suckling

e. Life, like a dome of many-colored glass,
Stains the white radiance of Eternity.
Percy Bysshe Shelley

f. He clasps the crag with crooked hands;
Close to the sun in lonely lands,
Ringed with the azure world, he stands.

The wrinkled sea beneath him crawls;
He watches from his mountain walls,
And like a thunderbolt he falls.
Alfred, Lord Tennyson

DAVID BURNHAM 7
Police Have a Slanguage of Their Own

Traditionally, the argot of the criminal has been a favorite topic for students of slang. Only recently, however, has anyone investigated the slang of the police for what it might reveal about policemen and their jobs. This essay and the brief lexicon that accompanies it attempt to illustrate the major differences between police slang and the slang of other subcultures.

"Did you collar the skell?"
"How long have you been back in the bag?"
"I see you got gold tin. Who's your rabbi?"

EACH OF THESE QUESTIONS IS IN THE SECRET LANGUAGE OF NEW York policemen, a language virtually unknown to the average New Yorker.

Like men in most professions, policemen have evolved a language to meet special needs, including the need for a "shorthand" to get work done quickly and efficiently, as a counterman calls an order to a short-order cook; the need to keep communication understandable to only friendly ears, and the need of "belonging," of knowing the code of the lodge.

Thus, when one policeman says to another. "Did you collar the skell?", he is asking, "Did you arrest the drunken derelict?"

"How long have you been back in the bag?" means: "When were you demoted from detective to uniformed patrol?"

The translation of "I see you got the gold tin, who's your rabbi?" is "I see you have been promoted to detective. Who's your high-ranked sponsor?"

Policemen's slang varies from city to city. When policemen sleep on duty in New York, they "coop"; when they sleep in Washington, they "huddle."

This suggests that unlike members of other occupations, such as physicians, architects and teachers, policemen seldom move from one city to another. The President's Crime Commission has noted this relative lack of mobility among policemen, attributing it, in part, to civil service requirements that differ from place to place and restrict the movement of policemen.

Again, in contrast to the secret language of other occupations, police slang appears to be largely unknown to the public. One explanation may be that the nature of police work—the difficult round-the-clock working hours, the specialized skills and common interests—limits the policeman's social contacts.

Dr. Geoffrey Wagner, a professor of English at City College and the author of "On the Wisdom of Words," said in a recent interview that group unity is sometimes the product of such group isolation.

"Slang is sometimes an expression of the thought 'If you speak like us, you are one of us,' " he said.

Dr. Wagner also noted that an important purpose of slang, according to a widely held theory, is to disguise what is actually being said.

"During the Battle of Britain," he said, "R.A.F. pilots simply couldn't talk about dying so they developed a lot of different euphemisms. Inmates in prison are said to use slang so the guards won't know what they're up to. Perhaps the police use slang when talking about some questionable activity so the public can't understand."

The durability of most police slang—many of the words were coined well before World War II—is another indication of the unchanging nature of policemen and police work. Compared with radical shifts in the slang used by the young, for example, police slang seems archaic.

Because many of the terms used by the police are so old, their derivations are not known. The origins of a few of them, however, are self-evident.

Thus, the civilian or policeman assigned to sweep the precinct station here is called a "broom." And the patrolman in every precinct assigned to handle clerical work is called a "1-24 man," after the paragraph number of an old department regulation that created the position.

The sources of other slang words can only be the subjects of speculation. The term for planting false evidence is "flake," which is possibly a reference to dandruff. Similarly, "on the arm"—a free meal or any other free item—might be a play on the expression "the long arm of the law."

From conversations with a number of policemen and former policemen, here is a sampling of other slang words used by the police here:

Fixer A fixed post in front of a consulate, school or other institution where a constant guard is maintained.
Flop To be dismissed from a desirable job such as assignment as a detective or plainclothes man. "Have you been flopped back into the bag?"
Fly To be moved from the regular precinct for a special assignment. Also sometimes called "aviating." "They flew us in from Queens for the demonstration."
Good Adjective for a local merchant who provides free meals and discount merchandise.
Glass Post A patrolman's beat that has stores with large plate-glass windows.
Go, In, or Take a Fall To arrest. A policeman, talking to someone he knows has been arrested several times before, might say, "Come on, buddy, you've got to go" or "You're in" or "Come on, you've got to take a fall."
Hairbag A veteran patrolman, also a patrolman with backbone.
Hook A high Police Department official with power to help his lower-ranking friends.
Kid An expression of mild disdain, as used by Officer Obie in the film "Alice's Restaurant" for anyone who is younger, has a lower rank or who is not a detective.
K.G. Known gambler.
Lu Lieutenant. A patrolman, speaking to a lieutenant, "Hey, Lu, what's up?"
Pad A list of stores and institutions that make regular payoffs. Also used in the following ways: "Is he on the pad?" "Is there an office pad?" (The opposite of an "office pad" is "a private contract.")
Paper To write parking tickets. "I really papered that block."
Rip A complaint against a policeman.

Rubber Gun Squad Policemen, either drunks or those mentally unbalanced, who have had their guns taken away from them.
Seat One of two assignments in a radio patrol car, a much desired posting. "Do you have a full-time seat?"
Shoo fly Usually a captain from borough headquarters who is assigned to make sure policemen are not cooping.
Squeal A citizen's report that he has been the victim of a crime.
Standup Guy Someone who is tough enough to take pointed questions without informing on his friends. A standup guy may be the neighborhood bookmaker, a fellow patrolman or the precinct commander.
Straight Eight A tour of duty in which a patrolman puts in a full day's work.
Story The patrolman's description of an arrest.
Ten-Thirteen A radio code signal meaning a policeman is in trouble and needs immediate help.

FOR DISCUSSION AND REVIEW

1. How does slang help to communicate quickly and efficiently? Cite examples from your own slang vocabulary.

2. In addition to speed and efficiency, what are some other advantages of slang?

3. After comparing the slang you use now with that you used several years ago, determine the extent to which it has changed. How do you account for the dynamic quality of your language in contrast to the stability of police slanguage?

5. Do you use any of the words included in the sample lexicon? If so, how do the meanings you assign the words differ from those assigned by the police? Explain the differences.

SAMUEL H. STEIN 8

The Semantics of Patient-Dentist Relations

Modern dentistry is becoming less painful all the time. What is still frightening for us as patients, however, is our general ignorance, even after explanations have been offered, of what is being done to us. Samuel Stein isolates and discusses a number of semantic problems of which dentists as well as patients should be more aware.

DENTAL PATIENTS, LIKE EVERYONE ELSE, LIVE IN A SEMANTIC ENvironment. They not only use words in their daily communication, but are bombarded by words over the radio and television to buy the toothpaste with GL-70; get "living lipstick"; buy the car with the "jet-away look," etc. An understanding of the impact of language on a person's behavior can help dentists establish better patient-dentist relations.

Patients aren't just good or bad—they show an infinite variety. Their backgrounds, experiences, and complexities of attitude influence their behavior in a dental office as everywhere else.

For instance, my secretary's husband came into my office with six remaining upper front teeth that swayed as he spoke. He did not want to have them extracted. "I can't stand false teeth," he said. "The thought of false teeth makes me sick to my stomach. My father had them and they were loose in his mouth. He kept them in a glass and they upset me every time I saw them." When he was reminded that his wife had had dentures (not "false teeth") for many years (which he had never seen out of her mouth), he remained for treatment—and he is now an enthusiastic denture-wearer, telling everyone else that they are foolish to postpone wearing "replacements."

A simple semantic premise would have spared this man years of discomfort and embarrassment: dentist_1 is not dentist_2; dentistry_{1925} is not dentistry_{1960}.

Both patients and dentists abstract. Patients leave out pertinent details about their past experiences in giving a history. A dentist's diagnosis is often influenced by conventional methods of procedure. Identifying different levels of abstraction—word, feeling, and thing—is pathological. Feelings are projected on to the outside world and the individual behaves as if "qualities" were in the object rather than inside himself. Awareness of the process of abstracting and projecting should develop an attitude of "to-me-ness." "We see things not as they are, but as we are." That goes for food, color, dentistry, or anything else. Without this awareness, we follow the misleading implication that we are talking only about the object, whereas in reality we are talking about our own feelings.

The "maps" made by patients are consequently often inadequate. A patient's statement: "This tooth is killing me" or "My whole head hurts," are maps of his feelings, not of any territory. "Does this tooth hurt when I spray it with warm water?"; "Does this tooth hurt when I tap it?" enables the dentist to make more accurate maps of the dental territory. The case histories that many patients give are also inaccurate, misleading maps: "Novocaine gives me the jitters," "I can't take gas." These patients use one experience to make a map of all future relations with different dentists.

. . .

That dentists can also make pretty poor maps is illustrated by the patient who had recurrent decay under an abutment tooth. "But," she insisted, "I was told this was a permanent bridge when the dentist inserted it two years ago." If a dentist tells a patient that he is making a permanent denture or a permanent bridge, he is making a misleading map—for all dental work is of necessity temporary, since people change, health changes, and mouths change.

. . .

One dentist assumed that everyone else made the same kind of shell-crowns that he did. When a patient presented him with an abscessed tooth, acting as an abutment for an interrupted bridge, he didn't observe that the crowns were cast (and fitted beautifully). He cut the bridge at the abscessed tooth, put his forceps on the tooth to be extracted, without cutting the crown on the second molar. The abscessed tooth came out easily, and so did the molar crown—with the patient's tooth attached to it. The patient then had to pay an additional fee for a partial denture, instead of a bridge, which was contracted for. An unhappy patient left that office—for good.

To the degree that a dentist makes adequate maps of a patient's teeth—to that degree will he render a better service to his patient.

General semantics should make dentists, as well as patients, aware that while language is man's greatest accomplishment and is useful in communication, it also has built into it many boobytraps, because we haven't learned to use language with full consciousness of abstracting—constantly checking words against reality and discarding them for better ones when necessary. Language freezes old concepts into words, which we pick up and use, unaware that they have outlived their usefulness (i.e., "race purity," "permanent teeth"). We must also be aware that words have no absolute meanings, but are akin to empty vessels into which we pour meanings. The "maps" that we make are but symbols for reality, and each person's reality is unique.

FOR DISCUSSION AND REVIEW

1. What does Stein mean by "dentist$_1$ is not dentist$_2$"?

2. Why did the patient feel comfortable wearing "dentures" or "replacements" while he refused to consider the possibility of "false teeth"? In a similar vein, which would you prefer to eat—a "first-class piece of dead cow" or "filet mignon"? Why? Why is it important for you to be conscious of your diction, or choice of words?

3. What does Stein mean by "maps" and "territories"? Why is it important to present accurate maps?

4. No word, according to S. I. Hayakawa, has exactly the same meaning twice. Discuss the examples in Stein's essay that illustrate this principle.

5. What boobytraps that Stein finds in the world of dentistry have you encountered in your relations with doctors, lawyers, dentists, and teachers?

STUART CHASE 9
Gobbledygook

Stuart Chase, well-known commentator on the dynamics of our language and author of The Power of Words *and* The Tyranny of Words, *takes us on a ramble through the world of obscure language, or gobbledygook, as it has come to be called. According to Chase, "gobbledygook not only flourishes in government bureaus but grows wild and lush in the law, the universities, and sometimes among the literati."*

SAID FRANKLIN ROOSEVELT, IN ONE OF HIS EARLY PRESIDENTIAL speeches: "I see one-third of a nation ill-housed, ill-clad, ill-nourished." Translated into standard bureaucratic prose his statement would read:

> It is evident that a substantial number of persons within the Continental boundaries of the United States have inadequate financial resources with which to purchase the products of agricultural communities and industrial establishments. It would appear that for a considerable segment of the population, possibly as much as 33.3333* of the total, there are inadequate housing facilities, and an equally sig-

* Not carried beyond four places.

nificant proportion is deprived of the proper types of clothing and nutriment.

This rousing satire on gobbledygook—or talk among the bureaucrats—is adapted from a report[1] prepared by the Federal Security Agency in an attempt to break out of the verbal squirrel cage. "Gobbledygook" was coined by an exasperated Congressman, Maury Maverick of Texas, and means using two, or three, or ten words in the place of one, or using a five-syllable word where a single syllable would suffice. Maverick was censuring the forbidding prose of executive departments in Washington, but the term has now spread to windy and pretentious language in general.

"Gobbledygook" itself is a good example of the way a language grows. There was no word for the event before Maverick's invention; one had to say: "You know, that terrible, involved, polysyllabic language those government people use down in Washington." Now one word takes the place of a dozen.

A British member of Parliament, A. P. Herbert, also exasperated with bureaucratic jargon, translated Nelson's immortal phrase, "England expects every man to do his duty":

> England anticipates that, as regards the current emergency, personnel will face up to the issues, and exercise appropriately the functions allocated to their respective occupational groups.

A New Zealand official made the following report after surveying a plot of ground for an athletic field:[2]

> It is obvious from the difference in elevation with relation to the short depth of the property that the contour is such as to preclude any reasonable developmental potential for active recreation.

Seems the plot was too steep.

An office manager sent this memo to his chief:

> Verbal contact with Mr. Blank regarding the attached notification of promotion has elicited the attached representation intimating that he prefers to decline the assigment.

Seems Mr. Blank didn't want the job.

> A doctor testified at an English trial that one of the parties was suffering from "circumorbital haematoma."

[1] This and succeeding quotations from F.S.A. report by special permission of the author, Milton Hall.

[2] This item and the next two are from the piece on gobbledygook by W. E. Farbstein, *New York Times,* March 29, 1953.

Seems the party had a black eye.

> In August 1952 the U.S. Department of Agriculture put out a pamphlet entitled: "Cultural and Pathogenic Variability in Single-Condial and Hyphaltip Isolates of Hemlin-Thosporium Turcicum Pass."

Seems it was about corn leaf disease.

On reaching the top of the Finsteraarhorn in 1845, M. Dollfus-Ausset, when he got his breath, exclaimed:

> The soul communes in the infinite with those icy peaks which seem to have their roots in the bowels of eternity.

Seems he enjoyed the view.

A governmental department announced:

> Voucherable expenditures necessary to provide adequate dental treatment required as adjunct to medical treatment being rendered a pay patient in in-patient status may be incurred as required at the expense of the Public Health Service.

Seems you can charge your dentist bill to the Public Health Service. Or can you?

Legal Talk

Gobbledygook not only flourishes in government bureaus but grows wild and lush in the law, the universities, and sometimes among the literati. Mr. Micawber was a master of gobbledygook, which he hoped would improve his fortunes. It is almost always found in offices too big for face-to-face talk. Gobbledygook can be defined as squandering words, packing a message with excess baggage and so introducing semantic "noise." Or it can be scrambling words in a message so that meaning does not come through. The directions on cans, bottles, and packages for putting the contents to use are often a good illustration. Gobbledygook must not be confused with double talk, however, for the intentions of the sender are usually honest.

I offer you a round fruit and say, "Have an orange." Not so an expert in legal phraseology, as parodied by editors of *Labor:*

> I hereby give and convey to you, all and singular, my estate and interests, right, title, claim and advantages of and in said orange, together with all rind, juice, pulp, and pits, and all rights and advantages therein . . . anything hereinbefore or hereinafter or in any other deed or

deeds, instrument or instruments of whatever nature or kind whatsoever, to the contrary, in any wise, notwithstanding.

The state of Ohio, after five years of work, has redrafted its legal code in modern English, eliminating 4,500 sections and doubtless a blizzard of "whereases" and "hereinafters." Legal terms of necessity must be closely tied to their referents, but the early solons tried to do this the hard way, by adding synonyms. They hoped to trap the physical event in a net of words, but instead they created a mumbo-jumbo beyond the power of the layman, and even many a lawyer, to translate. Legal talk is studded with tautologies, such as "cease and desist," "give and convey," "irrelevant, incompetent, and immaterial." Furthermore, legal jargon is a dead language; it is not spoken and it is not growing. An official of one of the big insurance companies calls their branch of it "bafflegab." Here is a sample from his collection:[3]

> One-half to his mother, if living, if not to his father, and one-half to his mother-in-law, if living, if not to his mother, if living, if not to his father. Thereafter payment is to be made in a single sum to his brothers. On the one-half payable to his mother, if living, if not to his father, he does not bring in his mother-in-law as the next payee to receive, although on the one-half to his mother-in-law, he does bring in the mother or father.

You apply for an insurance policy, pass the tests, and instead of a straightforward "here is your policy," you receive something like this:

> This policy is issued in consideration of the application therefor, copy of which application is attached hereto and made part hereof, and of the payment for said insurance on the life of the above-named insured.

Academic Talk

The pedagogues may be less repetitious than the lawyers, but many use even longer words. It is a symbol of their calling to prefer Greek and Latin derivatives to Anglo-Saxon. Thus instead of saying: "I like short clear words," many a professor would think it more seemly to say: "I prefer an abbreviated phraseology, distinguished for its lucidity." Your professor is sometimes right, the longer word may carry the meaning better—but not because it is long. Allen Upward in his book *The New Word* warmly advocates Anglo-Saxon English

[3] Interview with Clifford B. Reeves by Sylvia F. Porter, *New York Evening Post,* March, 14, 1952.

as against what he calls "Mediterranean" English, with its polysyllables built up like a skyscraper.

Professional pedagogy, still alternating between the Middle Ages and modern science, can produce what Henshaw Ward once called the most repellent prose known to man. It takes an iron will to read as much as a page of it. Here is a sample of what is known in some quarters as "pedageese":

> Realization has grown that the curriculum or the experiences of learners change and improve only as those who are most directly involved examine their goals, improve their understandings and increase their skill in performing the tasks necessary to reach newly defined goals. This places the focus upon teacher, lay citizen and learner as partners in curricular improvement and as the individuals who must change, if there is to be curriculum change.

I think there is an idea concealed here somewhere. I think it means: "If we are going to change the curriculum, teacher, parent, and student must all help." The reader is invited to get out his semantic decoder and check on my translation. Observe there is no technical language in this gem of pedageese, beyond possibly the word "curriculum." It is just a simple idea heavily oververbalized.

In another kind of academic talk the author may display his learning to conceal a lack of ideas. A bright instructor, for instance, in need of prestige may select a common sense proposition for the subject of a learned monograph—say, "Modern cities are hard to live in" and adorn it with imposing polysyllables: "Urban existence in the perpendicular declivities of megalopolis . . ." et cetera. He coins some new terms to transfix the reader—"mega-decibel" or "stratocosmopolis"—and works them vigorously. He is careful to add a page or two of differential equations to show the "scatter." And then he publishes, with 147 footnotes and a bibliography to knock your eye out. If the authorities are dozing, it can be worth an associate professorship.

While we are on the campus, however, we must not forget that the technical language of the natural sciences and some terms in the social sciences, forbidding as they may sound to the layman, are quite necessary. Without them, specialists could not communicate what they find. Trouble arises when experts expect the uninitiated to understand the words; when they tell the jury, for instance, that the defendant is suffering from "circumorbital haematoma."

Here are two authentic quotations. Which was written by a distinguished modern author, and which by a patient in a mental hospital? You will find the answer at the end of this essay.

1. Have just been to supper. Did not knowing what the woodchuck sent me here. How when the blue blue blue on the said anyone can do it that tries. Such is the presidential candidate.

2. No history of a family to close with those and close. Never shall he be alone to be alone to be alone to be alone to be alone to lend a hand and leave it left and wasted.

Reducing the Gobble

As government and business offices grow larger, the need for doing something about gobbledygook increases. Fortunately the biggest office in the world is working hard to reduce it. The Federal Security Agency in Washington,[4] with nearly 100 million clients on its books, began analyzing its communication lines some years ago, with gratifying results. Surveys find trouble in three main areas: correspondence with clients about their social security problems, office memos, official reports.

Clarity and brevity, as well as common humanity, are urgently needed in this vast establishment which deals with disability, old age, and unemployment. The surveys found instead many cases of long-windedness, foggy meanings, clichés, and singsong phrases, and gross neglect of the reader's point of view. Rather than talking to a real person, the writer was talking to himself. "We often write like a man walking on stilts."

Here is a typical case of long-windedness:

Gobbledygook as found: "We are wondering if sufficient time has passed so that you are in a position to indicate whether favorable action may now be taken on our recommendation for the reclassification of Mrs. Blank, junior clerk-stenographer, CAF 2, to assistant clerk-stenographer, CAF 3?"

Suggested improvement: "Have you yet been able to act on our recommendation to reclassify Mrs. Blank?"

Another case:

Although the Central Efficiency Rating Committee recognizes that there are many desirable changes that could be made in the present efficiency rating system in order to make it more realistic and more workable than it now is, this committee is of the opinion that no further change should be made in the present system during the current year. Because of conditions prevailing throughout the country and the resultant turnover in personnel, and difficulty in administering the

[4] Now the Department of Health, Education, and Welfare.

> Federal programs, further mechanical improvement in the present rating system would require staff retraining and other administrative expense which would seem best withheld until the official termination of hostilities, and until restoration of regular operations.

The F.S.A. invites us to squeeze the gobbledygook out of this statement. Here is my attempt:

> The Central Efficiency Rating Committee recognizes that desirable changes could be made in the present system. We believe, however, that no change should be attempted until the war is over.

This cuts the statement from 111 to 30 words, about one-quarter of the original, but perhaps the reader can do still better. What of importance have I left out?

Sometimes in a book which I am reading for information—not for literary pleasure—I run a pencil through the surplus words. Often I can cut a section to half its length with an improvement in clarity. Magazines like *The Reader's Digest* have reduced this process to an art. Are long-windedness and obscurity a cultural lag from the days when writing was reserved for priests and cloistered scholars? The more words and the deeper the mystery, the greater their prestige and the firmer the hold on their jobs. And the better the candidate's chance today to have his doctoral thesis accepted.

The F.S.A. surveys found that a great deal of writing was obscure although not necessarily prolix. Here is a letter sent to more than 100,000 inquirers, a classic example of murky prose. To clarify it, one needs to *add* words, not cut them:

> In order to be fully insured, an individual must have earned $50 or more in covered employment for as many quarters of coverage as half the calendar quarters elapsing between 1936 and the quarter in which he reaches age 65 or dies, whichever first occurs.

Probably no one without the technical jargon of the office could translate this: nevertheless, it was sent out to drive clients mad for seven years. One poor fellow wrote back: "I am no longer in covered employment. I have an outside job now."

Many words and phrases in officialese seem to come out automatically, as if from lower centers of the brain. In this standardized prose people never *get jobs,* they "secure employment"; *before* and *after* become "prior to" and "subsequent to"; one does not *do,* one "performs"; nobody *knows* a thing, he is "fully cognizant"; one never *says,* he "indicates." A great favorite at present is "implement."

Some charming boners occur in this talking-in-one's-sleep. For instance:

The problem of extending coverage to all employees, regardless of size, is not as simple as surface appearances indicate.

Though the proportions of all males and females in ages 16–45 are essentially the same . . .

Dairy cattle, usually and commonly embraced in dairying . . .

In its manual to employees, the F.S.A. suggests the following:

Instead of	*Use*
give consideration to	consider
make inquiry regarding	inquire
is of the opinion	believes
comes into conflict with	conflicts
information which is of a confidential nature	confidential information

Professional or office gobbledygook often arises from using the passive rather than the active voice. Instead of looking you in the eye, as it were, and writing "This act requires . . ." the office worker looks out of the window and writes: "It is required by this statute that . . ." When the bureau chief says, "We expect Congress to cut your budget," the message is only too clear; but usually he says, "It is expected that the departmental budget estimates will be reduced by Congress."

Gobbled: "All letters prepared for the signature of the Administrator will be single spaced."

Ungobbled: "Single space all letters for the Administrator." (Thus cutting 13 words to 7.)

Only People Can Read

The F.S.A. surveys pick up the point that human communication involves a listener as well as a speaker. Only people can read, though a lot of writing seems to be addressed to beings in outer space. To whom are you talking? The sender of the officialese message often forgets the chap on the other end of the line.

A woman with two small children wrote the F.S.A. asking what she should do about payments, as her husband had lost his memory. "If he never gets able to work," she said, "and stays in an institution would I be able to draw any benefits? . . . I don't know how I am going to live and raise my children since he is disable to work. Please give me some information. . . ."

To this human appeal, she received a shattering blast of gobbledygook, beginning, "State unemployment compensation laws do not provide any benefits for sick or disabled individuals . . . in order to qualify an individual must have a certain number of quarters of coverage . . ." et cetera, et cetera. Certainly if the writer had been thinking about the poor woman he would not have dragged in unessential material about old-age insurance. If he had pictured a mother without means to care for her children, he would have told her where she might get help—from the local office which handles aid to dependent children, for instance.

Gobbledygook of this kind would largely evaporate if we thought of our messages as two way—in the above case, if we pictured ourselves talking on the doorstep of a shabby house to a woman with two children tugging at her skirts, who in her distress does not know which way to turn.

Results of the Survey

The F.S.A. survey showed that office documents could be cut 20 to 50 per cent, with an improvement in clarity and a great saving to taxpayers in paper and payrolls.

A handbook was prepared and distributed to key officials.[5] They read it, thought about it, and presently began calling section meetings to discuss gobbledygook. More booklets were ordered, and the local output of documents began to improve. A Correspondence Review Section was established as a kind of laboratory to test murky messages. A supervisor could send up samples for analysis and suggestions. The handbook is now used for training new members; and many employees keep it on their desks along with the dictionary. Outside the Bureau some 25,000 copies have been sold (at 20 cents each) to individuals, governments, business firms, all over the world. It is now used officially in the Veterans Administration and in the Department of Agriculture.

The handbook makes clear the enormous amount of gobbledygook which automatically spreads in any large office, together with ways and means to keep it under control. I would guess that at least half of all the words circulating around the bureaus of the world are "irrelevant, incompetent, and immaterial"—to use a favorite legalism; or are just plain "unnecessary"—to ungobble it.

My favorite story of removing the gobble from gobbledygook concerns the Bureau of Standards at Washington. I have told it before but perhaps the reader will forgive the repetition. A New York

[5] By Milton Hall.

plumber wrote the Bureau that he had found hydrochloric acid fine for cleaning drains, and was it harmless? Washington replied: "The efficacy of hydrochloric acid is indisputable, but the chlorine residue is incompatible with metallic permanence."

The plumber wrote back that he was mighty glad the Bureau agreed with him. The Bureau replied with a note of alarm: "We cannot assume responsibility for the production of toxic and noxious residues with hydrochloric acid, and suggest that you use an alternate procedure." The plumber was happy to learn that the Bureau still agreed with him.

Whereupon Washington exploded: "Don't use hydrochloric acid; it eats hell out of the pipes!"

Note: The second quotation on p. 94 comes from Gertrude Stein's *Lucy Church Amiably*.

FOR DISCUSSION AND REVIEW

1. What is gobbledygook? Illustrate. How is it related to *Time*'s "nice-Nellyism" (pp. 16–20) and Mencken's occupational euphemisms (pp. 49–55)?

2. Why do bureaucrats, lawyers, and professors, among others, use gobbledygook? Is it ever justified?

3. Do you agree with Chase's paraphrases or translations of bureaucratic jargon on pages 90 and 91? Rewrite these passages differently from the way Chase has.

4. Look back to Orwell's list of questions to ask yourself before you begin to write (p. 29) and his list of rules for writing (p. 33). Having read Chase's essay, can you add to these lists?

WRITING

1. Edward Sapir and Benjamin Lee Whorf have put forth the theory that language shapes reality. Look at this example of an attempt to shape reality: ". . . a magnificently seared thickness of sizzling goodness that has been reduced by grinders of rarest Toledo steel to mouth-watering palate-tantalizers of Kansas City beef beaded with rich ruby globules served on a farm-fresh roll and laced lavishly with great oozing lashings of rarest mustards and onions from faraway Spain" (Russell Baker, "At Lunch"). Perhaps you recognize

this as a hamburger. Most menus are not this elaborate in their attempts at shaping reality; they do, however, lead the diner to believe that he is having an unusual eating experience, and phrases like the following are common: skillfully seasoned and basted with butter, festive red cranberry sauce, selected shrimp bathed in our own mouth-watering sauce, a bed of shredded lettuce, coffee by candlelight. Make an attempt to shape reality by using the following foods as the basis for composing two different menus, one for a "greasy spoon" diner and the other for an expensive gourmet restaurant: soup, fruit juice, ground beef, veal cutlet, fish, potatoes, corn, peas, tossed salad, bread, desserts, beverages.

2. Describe a person or an object in a short paragraph (no more than 100 words or so) using at least five similes and metaphors.

3. Repetition can be an effective writing device; but unless it is handled carefully, it will result in a tedious piece of writing. Rewrite the following paragraph, either eliminating repetition or reworking the repetitions to make a stronger effect.

> Day care centers should be available to all women who work and have no one to care for their children. Day care centers should not be available only to women who are raising their children alone or to families whose income is below the poverty level. All women who work should have available to them care for their children that is reliable, responsible, convenient, and that does not cost an exorbitant amount. Women who work need and must demand more day care centers. No woman should be prevented from working because of the lack of convenient and reliable facilities for child care.

4. In his essay "The Marks of an Educated Man" (*Context,* Spring, 1961), Alan Simpson presents the following example of gobbledygook, or, as he aptly dubs it, "verbal smog."

> It is inherent to motivational phenomena that there is a drive for more gratification than is realistically possible, on any level or in any type of personality organization. Likewise it is inherent to the world of objects that not all potentially desirable opportunities can be realized within a human life span. Therefore, any personality must involve an organization that allocates opportunities for gratifications, that systematizes precedence relative to the limited possibilities. The possibilities of gratification, simultaneously or sequentially, of all need-dispositions are severely limited by the structure of the object system and by the intra-systemic incompatibility of the consequences of gratifying them all.

What is the author trying to say? Rewrite the paragraph eliminating unnecessary verbiage.

5. Select one of the following situations and write a dialogue that accurately reflects the language of the people involved.

(a) Conference between a student and a teacher about the first paper of the semester
(b) Discussion between an executive and an auto mechanic about repairs to the former's Cadillac
(c) Conversation between a 10-year-old child and his/her mother about the condition of the child's room
(d) Interview by a newspaper reporter of a small town chief of police concerning a recent crime

6. In "The Semantics of Patient-Dentist Relations," Samuel Stein uses a metaphor common to semantics to explain the way in which language portrays reality. For many semanticists, "maps" are the words used to describe a "territory" or a particular reality. Just as a word is a symbol and may be confused with what it symbolizes, a map—"This tooth is killing me!" for example—may erroneously be meant as a description of a toothache. Such a statement says more about a person's feelings than about a toothache. The map-territory confusion is usually made up of a number of symbol-referent confusions but is a much more complex and significant phenomenon. Write an essay in which you explore either an example of map-territory confusion or an area in which false maps exist. The following questions may give you a start: Do you believe in superstitions? Is history a map? In what ways has your thinking about a certain subject changed since you were a child?

7. Elsewhere in his book *The Language of the Law,* David Mellinkoff states that "party line emergency statutes—bad enough in a lawyer's library—also invade the sanctity of the home. They require a notice in telephone books explaining the law to laymen." Mellinkoff quotes the following portions of the notices appearing in the California and New York directories, notices that were drafted from almost the same statutes:

California	*New York*
Penal Code section 384 makes it a misdemeanor	State law requires
for any person who shall willfully refuse to immediately relinquish a telephone party line	you to hang up the receiver of a party line telephone immediately
when informed that such line is needed for an emergency call . . .	when told the line is needed for an emergency call . . .
Also, any person who shall secure the use of a telephone party line	It is unlawful to take over a party line

by falsely stating that such line is needed for an emergency call shall be guilty of a misdemeanor.	by stating falsely that the line is needed for an emergency.

The California draftsman has taken the easy way—following the language of the statute, thus passing on to laymen technicality they don't need and words they don't understand. The New Yorker gives as much as the layman needs. He has avoided repetitions and chosen the ordinary, the direct, rather than the strange and roundabout. . . .

There is a small terroristic value in California's brandishing of the words *Penal Code, section 384, guilty, misdemeanor*. But for most citizens it is enough to learn from a telephone directory that conduct is against the law. Beyond the level of the parking ticket, when a layman needs to weigh the specific consequences of law-breaking, he is on his way to a lawyer or to prison. The New York draft is both shorter and more intelligible, with nothing essential lost.

Examine the party line emergency notice as it appears in your phone directory and write a brief essay in which you analyze the language used. Has the draftsman taken his audience into account, eliminated unnecessary legalese, and made the law intelligible to the layman? Highlight your analysis by comparing and contrasting your notice with those of California and New York.

8. One of the fascinating aspects of American English is its diversity, and one of the causes of this diversity is the specialized vocabularies of different occupations in America. Russell Baker's report of a fictitious symposium dealing with Little Miss Muffet, taken from *Poor Russell's Almanac,* illustrates several varieties of occupational Americanese:

Little Miss Muffet, as everyone knows, sat on a tuffet eating her curds and whey when along came a spider who sat down beside her and frightened Miss Muffet away. While everyone knows this, the significance of the event had never been analyzed until a conference of thinkers recently brought their special insights to bear upon it. Following are excerpts from the transcript of their discussion:

Sociologist: We are clearly dealing here with a prototypical illustration of a highly tensile social structure's tendency to dis- or perhaps even de-structure itself under the pressures created when optimum minimums do not obtain among the disadvantaged. Miss Muffet is nutritionally underprivileged, as evidenced by the subminimal diet of curds and whey upon which she forced to subsist, while the spider's cultural disadvantage is evidenced by such phenomena as legs exceeding standard norms, odd mating habits, and so forth.

In this instance, spider expectations lead the culturally disadvantaged to assert demands to share the tuffet with the nutritionally underprivileged. Due to a communications failure, Miss Muffet assumes without evidence that the spider will not be satisfied to share her tuffet, but will also insist on eating her curds and perhaps even her whey. Thus, the failure to preestablish selectively optimum norm structures diverts potentially optimal minimums from the expectation levels assumed to . . .

Militarist: Second-strike capability, sir! That's what was lacking. If Miss Muffet had developed a second-strike capability instead of squandering her resources on curds and whey, no spider on earth would have dared launch a first strike capable of carrying him right to the heart of her tuffet. I am confident that Miss Muffet had adequate notice from experts that she could not afford both curds and whey and, at the same time, support an early-spider-warning system. Yet curds alone were not good enough for Miss Muffet. She had to have whey, too. Tuffet security must be the first responsibility of every diner . . .

Book Reviewer: Written on several levels, this searing and sensitive exploration of the arachnid heart illuminates the agony and splendor of Jewish family life with a candor that is at once breathtaking in its simplicity and soul-shattering in its implied ambiguity. Some will doubtless be shocked to see such subjects as tuffets and whey discussed without flinching, but hereafter writers too timid to call a curd a curd will no longer . . .

Editorial Writer: Why has the Government not seen fit to tell the public all it knows about the so-called curds-and-whey affair? It is not enough to suggest that this was merely a random incident involving a lonely spider and a young diner. In today's world, poised as it is on the knife edge of . . .

Psychiatrist: Little Miss Muffet is, course, neither little nor a miss. These are obviously the self she has created in her own fantasies to escape the reality that she is a gross divorcee whose superego makes it impossible for her to sustain a normal relationship with any man, symbolized by the spider, who, of course, has no existence outside her fantasies. Little Miss Muffet may, in fact, be a man with deeply repressed Oedipal impulses, who sees in the spider the father he would like to kill, and very well may some day unless he admits that what he believes to be a tuffet is, in fact, probably the dining room chandelier, and that the whey he thinks he is eating is, in fact, probably . . .

Flower Child: Like this beautiful kid is on a bad trip, dig? Like . . .

Student Demonstrator: Little Miss Muffet, tuffets, curds, whey and spiders are what's wrong with education today. They're all irrelevant. Tuffets are irrelevant. Curds are irrelevant. Whey is irrelevant. Meaningful experience! How can you have relevance without meaningful experience? And how can there ever be meaningful experience without understanding? With understanding and meaningfulness and relevance, there can be love and good and deep seriousness and education today will be freed of slavery and Little Miss Muffet, and life will become meaningful and . . .

Child: This is about a little girl who gets scared by a spider.

(The child was sent home when the conference broke for lunch. It was agreed that he was too immature to subtract anything from the sum of human understanding.)

Try your hand at retelling the story of George Washington and the cherry tree or another familiar tale in some variety of Americanese.

9. Watch episodes from three different television shows in any one of the following categories: detectives, doctors, westerns, lawyers. Write an analysis of the professional language used in these shows and comment on the general accuracy of the language and the similarities among the shows.

NOTABLE QUOTATIONS

"The American, probably more than any other man, is prone to be apologetic about the trade he follows." *Mencken*

"Planned criticism takes two major forms: (1) saying-nothing and making it look like something, and (2) saying-something and making it look like nothing, or like something else." *Mellinkoff*

"American speech is conceded to be energetic and picturesque, possibly as an expression or reflection of national activity and variety." *Schultz*

"Among animals, only men seem susceptible to narcissism." *Gilbert*

"Like men in most professions, policemen have evolved a language to meet special needs, including the need for a "short hand" to get work done quickly and efficiently, as a counterman calls an order to a short-order cook; the need to keep communication understandable to only friendly ears, and the need of 'belonging,' of knowing the code of the lodge." *Burnham*

"Language freezes old concepts into words, which we pick up and use, unaware that they have outlived their usefulness." *Stein*

"We must also be aware that words have no absolute meanings, but are akin to empty vessels into which we pour meanings." *Stein*

"The 'maps' that we make are but symbols for reality, and each person's reality is unique." *Stein*

". . . we haven't learned to use language with full consciousness of abstracting—constantly checking words against reality and discarding them for better ones when necessary." *Stein*

"Many words and phrases in official use seem to come out automatically, as if from lower centers of the brain." *Chase*

"Professional or office gobbledygook often arises from using the passive rather than the active voice." *Chase*

PRISONERS OF LANGUAGE III

A language is not merely a means of communication; it is also an expression of shared assumptions. Language thus transmits implicit values and behavioral models to all those people who use it.

Elizabeth Burr, Susan Dunn, and Norma Farquhar

But if our language is perhaps an insidious cause for the perpetuation of racism, can it not also become the vehicle which propels us out of the mire of prejudice and hatred?

John A. Black

GORDON ALLPORT 1

Linguistic Factors in Prejudice

The concept of prejudice is the central concern of the readings in this section. In this selection from The Nature of Prejudice, *Gordon Allport examines the interaction between language and prejudice. Language plays a major role in the development and continuation of prejudice because human thinking is inextricably linked to language. Allport identifies and discusses some of the specific ways in which language, often very subtly, induces and shapes prejudice.*

WITHOUT WORDS WE SHOULD SCARCELY BE ABLE TO FORM CATEgories at all. A dog perhaps forms rudimentary generalizations, such as small-boys-are-to-be-avoided—but this concept runs its course on the conditioned reflex level, and does not become the object of thought as such. In order to hold a generalization in mind for reflection and recall, for identification and for action, we need to fix it in words. Without words our world would be, as William James said, an "empirical sand-heap."

Nouns That Cut Slices

In the empirical world of human beings there are some two and a half billion grains of sand corresponding to our category "the human race." We cannot possibly deal with so many separate entities in our thought, nor can we individualize even among the hundreds whom we encounter in our daily round. We must group them, form clusters. We welcome, therefore, the names that help us to perform the clustering.

The most important property of a noun is that it brings many grains of sand into a single pail, disregarding the fact that the same grains might have fitted just as appropriately into another pail. To state the matter technically, a noun *abstracts* from a concrete reality some one feature and assembles different concrete realities only with respect to this one feature. The very act of classifying forces us to overlook all other features, many of which might offer a sounder basis than the rubric we select. Irving Lee gives the following example:

> I knew a man who had lost the use of both eyes. He was called a "blind man." He could also be called an expert typist, a conscientious worker, a good student, a careful listener, a man who wanted a job. But he couldn't get a job in the department store order room where employees sat and typed orders which came over the telephone. The personnel man was impatient to get the interview over. "But you're a blind man," he kept saying, and one could almost feel his silent assumption that somehow the incapacity in one aspect made the man incapable in every other. So blinded by the label was the interviewer that he could not be persuaded to look beyond it.

Some labels, such as "blind man," are exceedingly salient and powerful. They tend to prevent alternative classification, or even cross-classification. Ethnic labels are often of this type, particularly if they refer to some highly visible feature, e.g., Negro, Oriental. They resemble the labels that point to some outstanding incapacity—*feeble-minded, cripple, blind man.* Let us call such symbols "labels of primary potency." These symbols act like shrieking sirens, deafening us to all finer discriminations that we might otherwise perceive. Even though the blindness of one man and the darkness of pigmentation of another may be defining attributes for some purposes, they are irrelevant and "noisy" for others.

Most people are unaware of this basic law of language—that every label applied to a given person refers properly only to one aspect of his nature. You may correctly say that a certain man is *human, a philanthropist, a Chinese, a physician, an athlete.* A given person may be all of these; but the chances are that *Chinese* stands out in your mind as the symbol of primary potency. Yet neither this nor any other classificatory label can refer to the whole of a man's nature. (Only his proper name can do so.)

Thus each label we use, especially those of primary potency, distracts our attention from concrete reality. The living, breathing, complex individual—the ultimate unit of human nature—is lost to sight. As in Fig. 1, the label magnifies one attribute out of all proportion

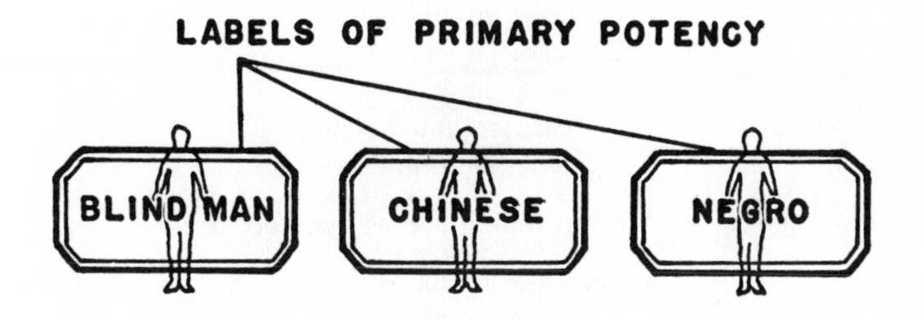

to its true significance, and masks other important attributes of the individual. . . .

A category, once formed with the aid of a symbol of primary potency, tends to attract more attributes than it should. The category labeled *Chinese* comes to signify not only ethnic membership but also reticence, impassivity, poverty, treachery. To be sure, . . . there may be genuine ethnic-linked traits, making for a certain *probability* that the member of an ethnic stock may have these attributes. But our cognitive process is not cautious. The labeled category, as we have seen, includes indiscriminately the defining attribute, probable attributes, and wholly fanciful, nonexistent attributes.

Even proper names—which ought to invite us to look at the individual person—may act like symbols of primary potency, especially if they arouse ethnic associations. Mr. Greenberg is a person, but since his name is Jewish, it activates in the hearer his entire category of Jews-as-a-whole. An ingenious experiment performed by Razran shows this point clearly, and at the same time demonstrates how a proper name, acting like an ethnic symbol, may bring with it an avalanche of stereotypes.

> Thirty photographs of college girls were shown on a screen to 150 students. The subjects rated the girls on a scale from one to five for *beauty, intelligence, character, ambition, general likability*. Two months later the same subjects were asked to rate the same photographs (and fifteen additional ones introduced to complicate the memory factor). This time five of the original photographs were

given Jewish surnames (Cohen, Kantor, etc.), five Italian (Valenti, etc.), and five Irish (O'Brien, etc.); and the remaining girls were given names chosen from the signers of the Declaration of Independence and from the Social Register (Davis, Adams, Clark, etc.).

When Jewish names were attached to photographs there occurred the following changes in ratings:

decrease in liking
decrease in character
decrease in beauty
increase in intelligence
increase in ambition

For those photographs given Italian names there occurred:

decrease in liking
decrease in character
decrease in beauty
decrease in intelligence

Thus a mere proper name leads to prejudgments of personal attributes. The individual is fitted to the prejudice ethnic category, and not judged in his own right.

While the Irish names also brought about depreciated judgment, the depreciation was not as great as in the case of the Jews and Italians. The falling of likability of the "Jewish girls" was twice as great as for "Italians" and five times as great as for "Irish." We note, however, that the "Jewish" photographs caused higher ratings in *intelligence* and in *ambition*. Not all stereotypes of out-groups are unfavorable.

The anthropologist, Margaret Mead, has suggested that labels of primary potency lose some of their force when they are changed from nouns into adjectives. To speak of a Negro soldier, a Catholic teacher, or a Jewish artist calls attention to the fact that some other group classifications are just as legitimate as the racial or religious. If George Johnson is spoken of not only as a Negro but also as a *soldier,* we have at least two attributes to know him by, and two are more accurate than one. To depict him truly as an individual, of course, we should have to name many more attributes. It is a useful suggestion that we designate ethnic and religious membership where possible with *adjectives* rather than with *nouns.*

Emotionally Toned Labels

Many categories have two kinds of labels—one less emotional and one more emotional. Ask yourself how you feel, and what thoughts you have, when you read the words *school teacher,* and then *school marm*. Certainly the second phrase calls up something more strict, more ridiculous, more disagreeable than the former. Here are four innocent letters: m-a-r-m. But they make us shudder a bit, laugh a bit, and scorn a bit. They call up an image of a spare, humorless, irritable old maid. They do not tell us that she is an individual human being with sorrows and troubles of her own. They force her instantly into a rejective category.

In the ethnic sphere even plain labels such as Negro, Italian, Jew, Catholic, Irish-American, French-Canadian may have emotional tone for a reason that we shall soon explain. But they all have their higher key equivalents: nigger, wop, kike, papist, harp, canuck. When these labels are employed we can be almost certain that the speaker *intends* not only to characterize the person's membership, but also to disparage and reject him.

Quite apart from the insulting intent that lies behind the use of certain labels, there is also an inherent ("physiognomic") handicap in many terms designating ethnic membership. For example, the proper names characteristic of certain ethnic memberships strike us as absurd. (We compare them, of course, with what is familiar and therefore "right.") Chinese names are short and silly; Polish names intrinsically difficult and outlandish. Unfamiliar dialects strike us as ludicrous. Foreign dress (which, of course, is a visual ethnic symbol) seems unnecessarily queer.

But of all these "physiognomic" handicaps the reference to color, clearly implied in certain symbols, is the greatest. The word Negro comes from the Latin *niger,* meaning black. In point of fact, no Negro has a black complexion, but by comparison with other blonder stocks, he has come to be known as a "black man." Unfortunately *black* in the English language is a word having a preponderance of sinister connotations: the outlook is black, blackball, blackguard, blackhearted, black death, blacklist, blackmail, Black Hand. In his novel *Moby Dick,* Herman Melville considers at length the remarkably morbid connotations of black and the remarkably virtuous connotations of white.

Nor is the ominous flavor of black confined to the English language. A cross-cultural study reveals that the semantic significance of black is more or less universally the same. Among certain Siberian tribes, members of a privileged clan call themselves "white bones," and refer to all others as "black bones." Even among Uganda Negroes there is some evidence for a white god at the apex of the theocratic hierarchy; certain it is that a white cloth, signifying purity, is used to ward off evil spirits and disease.

There is thus an implied value-judgment in the very concept of *white race* and *black race*. One might also study the numerous unpleasant connotations of *yellow,* and their possible bearing on our conception of the people of the Orient.

Such reasoning should not be carried too far, since there are undoubtedly, in various contexts, pleasant associations with both black and yellow. Black velvet is agreeable, so too are chocolate and coffee. Yellow tulips are well liked; the sun and moon are radiantly yellow. Yet it is true that "color" words are used with chauvinistic overtones more than most people realize. There is certainly condescension indicated in many familiar phrases: dark as a nigger's pocket, darktown strutters, white hope (a term originated when a white contender was sought against the Negro heavyweight champion, Jack Johnson), the white man's burden, the yellow peril, black boy. Scores of everyday phrases are stamped with the flavor of prejudice, whether the user knows it or not.

We spoke of the fact that even the most proper and sedate labels for minority groups sometimes seem to exude a negative flavor. In many contexts and situations the very terms *French-Canadian, Mexican,* or *Jew,* correct and nonmalicious though they are, sound a bit opprobrious. The reason is that they are labels of social deviants. Especially in a culture where uniformity is prized, the name of *any* deviant carries with it *ipso facto* a negative value-judgment. Words like *insane, alcoholic, pervert* are presumably neutral designations of a human condition, but they are more: they are finger-pointings at deviance. Minority groups are deviants, and for this reason, from the very outset, the most innocent labels in many situations imply a shading of disrepute. When we wish to highlight the deviance and denigrate it still further we use words of a higher emotional key: crackpot, soak, pansy, greaser, Okie, nigger, harp, kike.

Members of minority groups are often understandably sensitive to names given them. Not only do they object to deliberately insulting epithets, but sometimes see evil intent where none exists. Often the word Negro is spelled with a small *n,* occasionally as a studied insult, more often from ignorance. (The term is not cognate with white, which is not capitalized, but rather with Caucasian, which is.) Terms like "mulatto," or "octoroon" cause hard feeling because of the condescension with which they have often been used in the past. Sex differentiations are objectionable, since they seem doubly to emphasize ethnic difference: why speak of Jewess and not of Protestantess, or of Negress and not of whitess? Similar overemphasis is implied in the terms like Chinamen or Scotchman; why not American man? Grounds for misunderstanding lie in the fact that minority group members are sensitive to such shadings, while majority members may employ them unthinkingly.

The Communist Label

Until we label an out-group it does not clearly exist in our minds. Take the curiously vague situation that we often meet when a person wishes to locate responsibility on the shoulders of some out-group whose nature he cannot specify. In such a case he usually employs the pronoun "they" without an antecedent. "Why don't they make these sidewalks wider?" "I hear they are going to build a factory in this town and hire a lot of foreigners." "I won't pay this tax bill; they can just whistle for their money." If asked "who?" the speaker is likely to grow confused and embarrassed. The common use of the orphaned pronoun *they* teaches us that people often want and need to designate out-groups (usually for the purpose of venting hostility) even when they have no clear conception of the out-group in question. And so long as the target of wrath remains vague and ill-defined specific prejudice cannot crystallize around it. To have enemies we need labels.

Until relatively recently—strange as it may seem—there was no agreed-upon symbol for *communist*. The word, of course, existed but it had no special emotional connotation, and did not designate a public enemy. Even when, after World War I, there was a growing feeling of economic and social menace in this country, there was no agreement as to the actual source of the menace.

> A content analysis of the *Boston Herald* for the year 1920 turned up the following list of labels. Each was used in a context implying some threat. Hysteria had overspread the country, as it did after World War II. Someone must be responsible for the postwar malaise, rising prices, uncertainty. There must be a villain. But in 1920 the villain was impartially designated by reporters and editorial writers with the following symbols:
>
>> alien, agitator, anarchist, apostle of bomb and torch, Bolshevik, communist, communist laborite, conspirator, emissary of false promise, extremist, foreigner, hyphenated-American, incendiary, IWW, parlor anarchist, parlor pink, parlor socialist, plotter, radical, red, revolutionary, Russian agitator, socialist, Soviet, syndicalist, traitor, undesirable.

From this excited array we note that the *need* for an enemy (someone to serve as a focus for discontent and jitters) was considerably more apparent than the precise *identity* of the enemy. At any rate, there was no clearly agreed upon label. Perhaps partly for this reason the hysteria abated. Since no clear category of "communism" existed there was no true focus for the hostility.

But following World War II this collection of vaguely interchangeable labels became fewer in number and more commonly agreed upon. The out-group menace came to be designated almost always as *communist* or *red*. In 1920 the threat, lacking a clear label, was vague; after 1945 both symbol and thing became more definite. Not that people knew precisely what they meant when they said "communist," but with the aid of the term they were at least able to point consistently to *something* that inspired fear. The term developed the power of signifying menace and led to various repressive measures against anyone to whom the label was rightly or wrongly attached.

Logically, the label should apply to specifiable defining attributes, such as members of the Communist Party, or people whose allegiance is with the Russian system, or followers, historically, of Karl Marx. But the label came in for far more extensive use.

What seems to have happened is approximately as follows. Having suffered through a period of war and being acutely aware of devastating revolutions abroad, it is natural that most people should be upset, dreading to lose their possessions, annoyed by high taxes, seeing customary moral and religious values threatened, and dreading worse disasters to come. Seeking an explanation for this unrest, a single identifiable enemy is wanted. It is not enough to designate "Russia" or some other distant land. Nor is it satisfactory to fix blame on "changing social conditions." What is needed is a human agent near at hand: someone in Washington, someone in our schools, in our factories, in our neighborhood. If we *feel* an immediate threat, we reason, there must be a near-lying danger. It is, we conclude, communism, not only in Russia but also in America, at our doorstep, in our government, in our churches, in our colleges, in our neighborhood.

Are we saying that hostility toward communism is prejudice? Not necessarily. There are certainly phases of the dispute wherein realistic social conflict is involved. American values (e.g., respect for the person) and totalitarian values as represented in Soviet practice are intrinsically at odds. A realistic opposition in some form will occur. Prejudice enters only when the defining attributes of "communist" grow imprecise, when anyone who favors any form of social change is called a communist. People who fear social change are the ones most likely to affix the label to any persons or practices that seem to them threatening.

For them the category is undifferentiated. It includes books, movies, preachers, teachers who utter what for them are uncongenial thoughts. If evil befalls—perhaps forest fires or a factory explosion—it is due to communist saboteurs. The category becomes monopolistic, covering almost anything that is uncongenial. On the floor of the House of Representatives in 1946, Representative Rankin called

James Roosevelt a communist. Congressman Outland replied with psychological acumen, "Apparently everyone who disagrees with Mr. Rankin is a communist."

When differentiated thinking is at a low ebb—as it is in times of social crises—there is a magnification of two-valued logic. Things are perceived as either inside or outside a moral order. What is outside is likely to be called "communist." Correspondingly—and here is where damage is done—whatever is called communist (however erroneously) is immediately cast outside the moral order.

This associative mechanism places enormous power in the hands of a demagogue. For several years Senator McCarthy managed to discredit many citizens who thought differently from himself by the simple device of calling them communist. Few people were able to see through this trick and many reputations were ruined. But the famous senator has no monopoly on the device. As reported in the *Boston Herald* on November 1, 1946, Representative Joseph Martin, Republican leader in the House, ended his election campaign against his Democratic opponent by saying, "The people will vote tomorrow between chaos, confusion, bankruptcy, state socialism or communism, and the preservation of our Americal life, with all its freedom and its opportunities." Such an array of emotional labels placed his opponent outside the accepted moral order. Martin was re-elected. . . .

Not everyone, of course, is taken in. Demagogy, when it goes too far, meets with ridicule. Elizabeth Dilling's book, *The Red Network,* was so exaggerated in its two-valued logic that it was shrugged off by many people with a smile. One reader remarked, "Apparently if you step off the sidewalk with your left foot you're a communist." But it is not easy in times of social strain and hysteria to keep one's balance, and to resist the tendency of a verbal symbol to manufacture large and fanciful categories of prejudiced thinking.

Verbal Realism and Symbol Phobia

Most individuals rebel at being labeled, especially if the label is uncomplimentary. Very few are willing to be called *fascistic, socialistic,* or *anti-Semitic*. Unsavory labels may apply to others; but not to us.

An illustration of the craving that people have to attach favorable symbols to themselves is seen in the community where white people banded together to force out a Negro family that had moved in. They called themselves "Neighborly Endeavor" and chose as their motto the Golden Rule. One of the first acts of this symbol-sanctified band was to sue the man who sold property to Negroes. They then flooded the house which another Negro couple planned to occupy. Such were the acts performed under the banner of the Golden Rule.

Studies made by Stagner and by Hartmann show that a person's political attitudes may in fact entitle him to be called a fascist or a socialist, and yet he will emphatically repudiate the unsavory label, and fail to endorse any movement or candidate that overtly accepts them. In short, there is a *symbol phobia* that corresponds to *symbol realism.* We are more inclined to the former when we ourselves are concerned, though we are much less critical when epithets of "fascist," "communist," "blind man," "school marm" are applied to others.

When symbols provoke strong emotions they are sometimes regarded no longer as symbols, but as actual things. The expressions "son of a bitch" and "liar" are in our culture frequently regarded as "fighting words." Softer and more subtle expressions of contempt may be accepted. But in these particular cases, the epithet itself must be "taken back." We certainly do not change our opponent's attitude by making him take back a word, but it seems somehow important that the word itself be eradicated.

Such verbal realism may reach extreme length.

> The City Council of Cambridge, Massachusetts, unanimously passed a resolution (December, 1939) making it illegal "to possess, harbor, sequester, introduce or transport, within the city limits, any book, map, magazine, newspaper, pamphlet, handbill or circular containing the words Lenin or Leningrad."

Such naiveté in confusing language with reality is hard to comprehend unless we recall that word-magic plays an appreciable part in human thinking. The following examples, like the one preceding, are taken from Hayakawa.

> The Malagasy soldier must eschew kidneys, because in the Malagasy language the word for kidney is the same as that for "shot"; so shot he would certainly be if he ate a kidney.

> In May, 1937, a state senator of New York bitterly opposed a bill for the control of syphilis because "the innocence of children might be corrupted by a widespread use of the term. . . . This particular word creates a shudder in every decent woman and decent man."

This tendency to reify words underscores the close cohesion that exists between category and symbol. Just the mention of "communist," "Negro," "Jew," "England," "Democrats," will send some people into a panic of fear or a frenzy of anger. Who can say whether it is the word or the thing that annoys them? The label is an intrinsic part of any monopolistic category. Hence to liberate a person from ethnic or political prejudice it is necessary at the same time to liberate him from word fetishism. This fact is well known to students of general semantics who tell us that prejudice is due in large part to verbal realism and to symbol phobia. Therefore any program for the reduction of prejudice must include a large measure of semantic therapy.

FOR DISCUSSION AND REVIEW

1. Allport quotes William James's statement that without words our lives would be an "empirical sand-heap." What did James mean by the phrase? What are the implications of a world in which we could not determine categories?

2. Nouns or names provide an essential service in making categorization possible. Yet, according to Allport, nouns are also words that "cut slices." What is inherently unfair about nouns?

3. Why is the "orphaned pronoun *they*" used so often?

4. Allport seems to use the terms "noun," "label," and "symbol" interchangeably. Can you distinguish among these terms?

5. What are "labels of primary potency"? Why are they so important? Can and should we avoid the use of such labels?

6. Personal names are powerful "labels of primary potency." Consult an almanac for the real names of the celebrities listed below and then discuss the significance of the changes:

Tony Curtis
Mick Jagger
Simone Signoret
Roy Rogers
Raquel Welch
James Garner
Bob Dylan
Doris Day
John Wayne
Cyd Charisse
Anne Bancroft
Michael Caine
Jack Benny
Connie Francis
Ringo Starr
Hugh O'Brian

7. What do the terms "reification," "verbal realism," "symbol phobia," and "symbol realism" mean? How could you apply these terms to the whole range of "four-letter" or "taboo" words to make linguistic sense of the concept of pornography?

R. D. LAING 2
from **Knots**

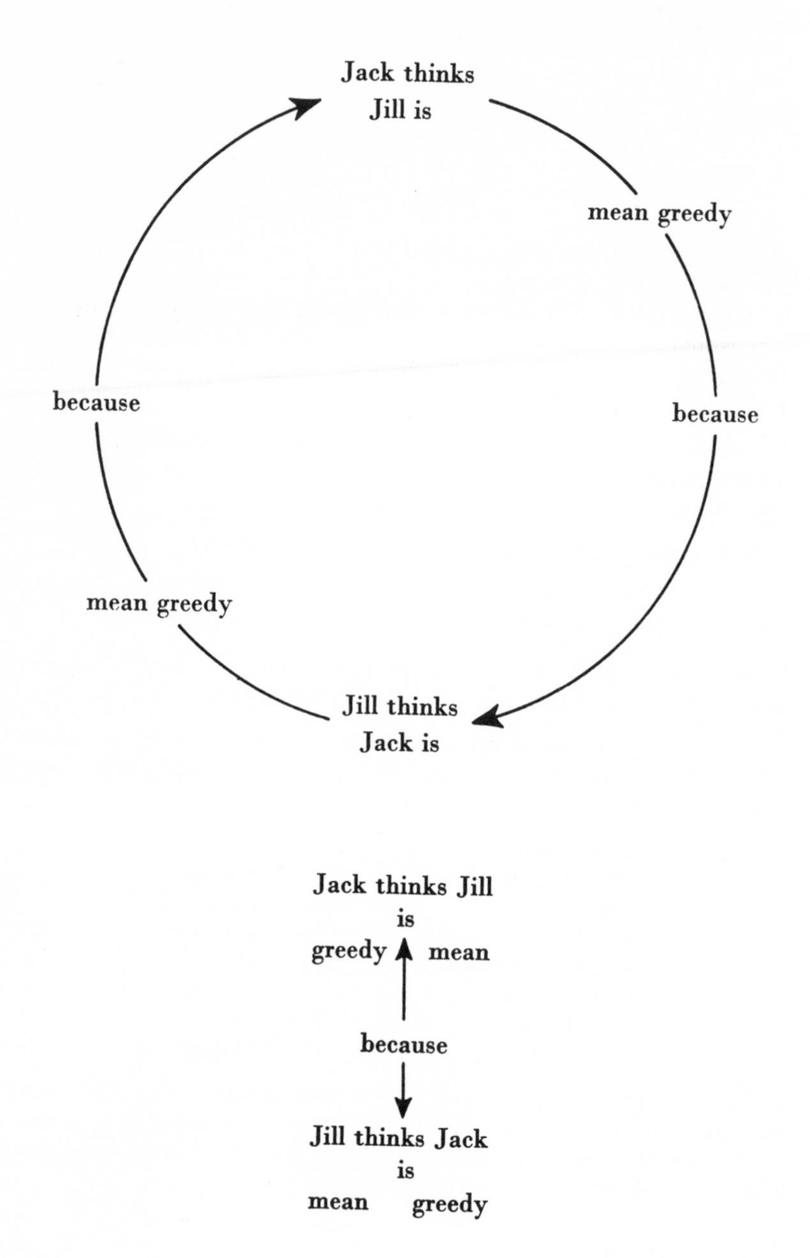

FOR DISCUSSION AND REVIEW

1. This poem comes from Laing's book *Knots,* in which the individual poems are untitled. Does "Knots" seem to you an appropriate title for this poem? Why or why not?

2. How does the physical format of Laing's poem contribute to its effect on the reader?

3. Attempt to construct a "knot" of your own.

OSSIE DAVIS 3
The English Language Is My Enemy!

A number of subgroups within American culture—most notably blacks and women—have called attention in recent years to the prejudicial nature of English. In this short article, author, playwright, and actor Ossie Davis, drawing his evidence from entries in Roget's Thesaurus, *argues that the English language makes "racial prejudgment" inevitable on the part of its speakers. For that reason, he believes, the English language is the black American's enemy.*

A SUPERFICIAL EXAMINATION OF ROGET'S THESAURUS OF THE ENglish Language reveals the following facts: the word WHITENESS has 134 synonyms; 44 of which are favorable and pleasing to contemplate, i.e. purity, cleanness, immaculateness, bright, shining, ivory, fair, blonde, stainless, clean, clear, chaste, unblemished, unsullied, innocent, honorable, upright, just, straight-forward, fair, genuine, trustworthy (a white man's colloquialism). Only ten synonyms for WHITENESS appear to me to have negative implications—and these only in the mildest sense: gloss over, whitewash, gray, wan, pale, ashen, etc.

The word BLACKNESS has 120 synonyms, 60 of which are distinctly unfavorable, and none of them even mildly positive. Among the offending 60 were such words as: blot, blotch, smut, smudge, sully, begrime, soot, becloud, obscure, dingy, murky, low-toned, threatening, frowning, foreboding, forbidden, sinister, baneful, dismal, thundery, evil, wicked, malignant, deadly, unclean, dirty, unwashed, foul, etc. . . . not to mention 20 synonyms directly related to race, such as: Negro, Negress, nigger, darky, blackamoor, etc.

When you consider the fact that *thinking* itself is sub-vocal speech —in other words, one must use *words* in order to think at all—you will appreciate the enormous heritage of racial prejudgment that lies in wait for any child born into the English Language. Any teacher good or bad, white or black, Jew or Gentile, who uses the English Language as a medium of communication is forced, willy-nilly, to teach the Negro child 60 ways to despise himself, and the white child 60 ways to aid and abet him in the crime.

Who speaks to me in my Mother Tongue damns me indeed! . . . the English Language—in which I cannot conceive my self as a black man without, at the same time, debasing myself . . . my enemy, with which to survive at all I must continually be at war.

FOR DISCUSSION AND REVIEW

1. If, as Davis observes, most of the definitions of "Blackness" are unfavorable, how does this contribute to prejudice against blacks?

2. Black Americans have been labeled colored, Negro, Afro-American, and currently, black. Construct a reasonable linguistic explanation for these shifts.

3. Both Davis and Allport discuss the importance of words for colors. Allport suggests that yellow may have as many unpleasant connotative values as black does. Consult a thesaurus or dictionary and discuss the entries for yellow.

4. Many creative writers have consciously used colors to symbolize various moods and personal traits, though some such usages have become trite from overuse. The best use of such symbolism not only plays upon various color stereotypes but also expands upon connotations by using colors in stimulating and thought-provoking combinations or clusters. What colors might you associate with the following: greed, anger, envy, lust, sickness, old age, bliss? Explain. Which associations strike you as clichés and which as fresh and effective?

HAIG A. BOSMAJIAN 4

The Language of Sexism

Increasingly, women are becoming aware of the extent to which English stigmatizes them as an inferior group. In this article, Haig Bosmajian, of the Department of Speech, University of Washington, identifies some aspects of the language that have helped maintain inequalities and injustices and shows why women should work to correct them.

OUR IDENTITIES, WHO AND WHAT WE ARE OR THINK WE ARE, HOW others see and define us, are greatly affected by language. The power of language to affect identity is reflected in the fact that language has been used again and again to define and dehumanize individuals or groups of individuals into submission. The Nazis used language to redefine and dehumanize the Jews to the point that elimination of the "Jewish bacilli," the "Jewish plague," and "Jewish vermin" seemed "reasonable" to the Nazi audiences. The language of white racism has been used for decades to "keep the nigger in his place." It was not until the 1960s that people like Stokely Carmichael, Malcolm X, Martin Luther King, and Floyd McKissick pointed to the need for blacks to stop allowing whites to define who the blacks were and are. Carmichael summed it up when he said to an audience of students

In the church we have the "clergyman," the "altar boy," the Father, Son, and Holy Ghost. Males dominate in Christianity not only in language but also in terms of the decision-making powers, a domination that can be attributed partly to the language of sexism. This male domination exists despite the fact that "every survey that measures sex differences in religiosity shows that females attend church more frequently than males, pray more often, hold firmer beliefs, cooperate more in church programs. This is true at all age levels from childhood to senior-citizen, and of both single and married women, of women gainfully employed and home-makers." But what is woman to do when in Scripture she is told: "Wives, submit yourselves unto your own husbands, as unto the Lord"? This, in the same book, Ephesians, which tells children to obey their parents and servants to be obedient to their masters. Somehow women, along with children and servants, end up subjects in the master-subject relationship.

Another effect of the language of sexism is that it makes the male visible and the female "the invisible woman." In a world of "chairmen," "churchmen," "spokesmen," "businessmen," "congressmen,"
jurymen," et cetera, the woman is not only secondary, she is invisible.
he invisible woman remains invisible when in a classroom of women
d men the teacher says that "each student must see to it that his
ignment is turned in on time" or when the President of the United
tes says that "each citizen must do his duty to alleviate injustice
inequality in this land." Once we consistently begin talking about
gresswomen," "jurywomen," "spokeswomen," "businesswomen,"
tera, the woman becomes much more visible. She becomes more
e outside of the stereotyped duties of housewifery and childbear-
o many males, of course, this increased visibility is a threat,
ten requests that males use this language that will accomplish
reased visibility of the female are viewed as "troublesome,"
at, ridiculed or seen as really unnecessary.
nvisibility of women was clearly demonstrated in a one-page
ad that appeared in *The New York Times* of April 4, 1971.
as made up of a large half-page drawing of President Nixon
corks in his ears and over the drawing were the words:
JORITY IS NOT SILENT. THE ADMINISTRATION
About a dozen individuals are vigorously attempting to
s out of the President's ears, and it appears that getting
t to uncork and listen is a man's job. Nowhere in this
does there appear a woman who can claim to be part of
which is "not silent," part of that group which is at-
ncork Nixon's ears. Considering the important roles
nen and women's organizations in the anti-war move-

at Morgan State College on January 16, 1967: "It [definition] is very, very important because I believe people who can define are masters." Individuals or groups of individuals who allow others to define them as lazy, ignorant, inferior, inhuman, et cetera, have given the power of defining who and what they are to others, and this power carries with it the master-subject relationship.

It is the intent of this essay to demonstrate that the "liberation" of women, the eradication of the sexual subject-master relationship, will have to be accompanied with a conscious effort on the part of women to allow themselves to be defined by men no longer. Although the language of sexism has been with us for a very long time, recent experience has demonstrated that a "minority group" intent on defining itself and eradicating the language that has, in part, been used to maintain inequalities, injustices, and subjugation can effect changes in language behavior. The blacks who have no longer allowed themselves to be defined by the whites are a freer people. Women need to do the same. As George Orwell has pointed out in his famous essay, "Politics and the English Language," the decadence of some of our language is probably curable. "Silly words and expressions have often disappeared, not through any evolutionary process but owing to the conscious action of a minority." Conscious action by women and men can reduce the usage of, and perhaps eliminate, the language of sexism.

This conscious effort to reduce and eliminate the language of sexism was reflected in the action of *The Old Mole,* an underground newspaper in the Boston area, when it announced that it would no longer accept manuscripts or letters that used "male supremacist language." In its announcement, *The Old Mole* stated:

> Use of this language reflects values and patterns of thought that are oppressive to half the people in the world and harmful to all. To use the word "balls" to mean courage implies that (1) balls have something to do with courage and that (2) women, because they don't have balls, don't have courage. Similarly, the words "castration" and "emasculation" imply acceptance of the myth that man is superior to woman because of the strength that having a penis gives him.
>
> These words reflect a power structure (men having power over women) that we want to change. One way we can work to change this is to challenge the use, conscious or unconscious, of words and phrases that go along with this power structure. In other words, we will not print letters that call women "broads" just as we would not print letters that call blacks "niggers."

The necessity for actively ridding our language of sexist terminology was recognized by Wilma Scott Heide, President of the

National Organization for Women, when she stated in a speech delivered at the University of Nebraska: "In any social movement, when changes are effected, the language sooner or later reflects the change. Our approach is different. Instead of passively noting the change, we are changing language patterns to actively effect the changes, a significant part of which is the conceptual tool of thought, our language."

While the media can do its part to reduce the usage of the language of sexism, the individual (female and male) can make a great contribution by making a conscious effort to reduce the language of sexism in everyday language behavior.

Examples of male supremist language are numerous, and as Aileen Hernandez, past president of NOW, has stated, our sexist language makes it abundantly clear that "in all areas that really count, we discount women." She presents the following examples of sexist language:

> "Mankind" is the generic term for all people or all males, but there is no similar dual meaning for "womankind." The masculine pronoun is used to refer to both men and women in general discussions.
>
> The Constitution of the United States is replete with sexist language — Senators and Representatives are "he"; the President is obviously "he" and even the fugitive from justice is "he" in our Constitution . . .
>
> But just in case we as women manage to escape the brainwashing that assigns us to "our place" in the order of things, the language continues to get the message across.
>
> There is a "housewife" but no "househusband"; there's a "housemother" but no "housefather"; there's a "kitchenmaid" but no "kitchenman"; unmarried women cross the threshold from "bachelor girl" to "spinster" to "old maid," but unmarried men are "bachelors" forever.

Other examples of the language of sexism abound. Writing in *Women: A Journal of Liberation,* Emily Toth points out that "generally, women lack their own words for professional positions: a woman must be a 'female judge,' 'female representative,' 'madam chairman,' or—in a ghastly pun—a 'female mailman.' " She notes that "one textbook defines Standard English as that language spoken by 'educated professional people and their wives.' " We find in *Webster's New World Dictionary of the American Language* the word "honorarium" defined as "a payment to a professional man for services on which no fee is set or legally obtainable." It was not until November 1971 that it was announced that the standard directory of scientists, *American Men of Science,* would henceforth be known as *American Men and Women of Science.* It was not until January 1972 that it was publicly noted that the faculty washroom doors for women in Philosophy Hall at Columbia University were labelled "WOMEN" and the washroom doors for men were labelled "FOR OFFICERS OF INSTRUCTION." So ingrained is the language of sexism that it is with great effort that people will refer to a "jury-woman," a "churchwoman," a "journeywoman," or a "chairwoman." Instead, the females end up "countrymen," "middlemen," "business-men," and "jurymen" when these groups are referred to generally.

The pervasiveness of the problem is exemplified by the fact th
the very women who are attempting to bring about the women's lib
ation fall into the trap of using the sexist language. The maga
Aphra presented on its "Contributors" page the following inform
about one of its contributors: "Berenice Abbot is to have a or
show at the Museum of Modern Art this winter. . . ." On
casion I heard a female speaker discussing child-adoption re
she remarked to her audience that "the women at the adopti
acted as middlemen." Even the National Organization f
(NOW) places men in higher precedence in its 1966 S
Purpose. The first paragraph of that Statement begin
and women who hereby constitute ourselves as the Na
zation for Women, believe the time has come for a
toward true equality for all women in America, an
equal partnership of the sexes, as part of the wor
of human rights now taking place within and be
borders." The firstness of "men" in "We, men
reveals that the "liberated" women find it har
of the language of sexism. The Statement, co
should begin, "We women and men. . . ." T
two phrases are entirely different.

The blacks of the 1960s recognized tha
the white's definition which relegated bla
status. Why was it, the blacks asked, tha
ian-American," a "German-American,"
the blacks were always "American N
Indian" the Indians were relegated t
own land!) Just as the blacks begar
and bringing into question the firstr
women have to use language m
phrases that define them as the
casions when "women and men
curate than "men and women
women are a majority in th
speak of "the women and n
men and women of this nat

ment, it is odd that nowhere in this one-page anti-war ad are women represented as attempting to get the "deaf" President to listen to the not-so-silent majority.

Even in the everyday world of memoes, the woman remains invisible:

TO: Deans, Directors, Chairmen, and Advisers
RE: Minority Student Awards
Gentlemen:
Letters of nomination are now being prepared. . . .

In the larger world of international politics, "the battle for men's minds" goes on decade after decade with apparently little interest in the women's minds. Or does the "battle for men's minds" suggest that women have no minds?

While women, like the blacks, have been kept in "their place" by language and have remained invisible for so long, unlike the blacks the women have not yet been dubbed as a "problem" in the sense of whites speaking of "the Negro problem." While Gunnar Myrdal presented the similarities between the treatment of blacks and women in his now famous Appendix 5 of *The American Dilemma,* interestingly he spoke of the "Negro problem" but not of the "Woman problem." The book is subtitled "The Negro Problem and Modern Democracy" and Appendix 5 is titled "A Parallel to the Negro Problem," titles carrying with them the connotation that the Negro *is* the problem. The continual use by the Nazis of the phrase "the Jewish problem" implied that the Jews were a problem. There was no "Jewish problem" until the Nazis linguistically created and defined this fiction. Similarly, there is no "Negro problem" in this country; what exists is a "white problem"—the bigotry, ignorance, and inhumanity of so many whites. But Myrdal does not speak of the "Woman problem"; instead, he refers to "the women's problem." In the first paragraph of his Appendix 5, we find him saying: "In studying a special problem like the Negro problem, there is always a danger that one will develop a quite incorrect idea of its uniqueness. It will, therefore, give perspective to the Negro problem and prevent faulty interpretation to sketch some of the important similarities between the Negro problem and the women's problem." It may be that we will begin to hear more about the "Woman problem" as women begin to make vocal and persuasive their demands for a halt to the inequalities, injustices, and inhumanity based on sex.

The ritual of women adopting the name of their husbands upon marriage also has its male supremist implications, as does the ritual of giving the newborn child the male parent's surname. "What's In A Name?" asks Julie Coryell in *Women: A Journal of Liberation.*

She answers the question, in part, by saying: "Plenty. Why is it that women take their husband's name on marriage? Why don't we keep our names if we want to? In studying about patriarchy, I learned that women and children came to bear the husband's name and father's name because he owned them. I am no one's possession but my own self. Social usage clarifies the potential sexual availability of a woman in her name. We are Miss so and so—fair game—or Mrs. (man's name)—safe, hands off, men—or Mrs. (woman's name)—divorced? Available? Probably. Mr. does not reveal a man's marital status. After all, what does marital status have to do with one's work and attitudes? Why must women continue to be forced to declare it unless it is truly relevant?"

The institution of marriage forces the woman to undergo a change from "woman" to "wife" while the man remains a "man." The minister says, "Do you take this woman to be your wife?" and then turns to the woman and asks, "Do you take this man to be your husband?" After both have said "I do" they are informed that they are now "man and wife," not "husband and wife." The wife then adopts her man's surname, exchanging one male's surname for another male's surname; and in almost all facets of life she is required to use her man's name. In September 1971, for example, a three judge Federal Court in Montgomery, Alabama ruled that a married woman does not have a constitutional right to have her driver's license issued in her maiden name. Although Myrdal did not discuss this matter, another similarity between the status and treatment of blacks and women is that they both have been given the names of their "masters."

In his book *Women and the Law,* Leo Kanowitz devotes several paragraphs to this practice of the married woman taking her husband's name. Kanowitz asserts that "the probable effects of this unilateral name change upon the relations between the sexes, though subtle in character, are profound. In a very real sense, the loss of a woman's surname represents the destruction of an important part of her personality and its submersion in that of her husband." As far as the law is concerned, it is the male, father and husband, who has the last word on what names the women and children shall bear. Kanowitz cites several laws and court decisions that reflect this male power of defining through naming. Among the conclusions which he presents, based on his examination of the law, are ". . . under many of the statutes that prescribe formal procedures for changing one's name, the right to do so has been expressly or impliedly denied to married women. No comparable restriction has been imposed upon married men. Finally, the law, once more either expressly or by implication, generally requires that a change in the husband's surname produce a corresponding change in that of his wife, but never the reverse."

As Faith A. Seidenberg has observed, not only does the woman become lost in the anonymity of her husband's name, but "her domicile is his no matter where she lives, which means she cannot vote or run for office in her place of residence if her husband lives elsewhere. If she wants an annulment and is over eighteen, in certain cases she cannot get one, but her husband can until he is twenty-one. In practice, if not in theory, she cannot contract for any large amount, borrow money, or get a credit card in her own name. She is, in fact, a nonperson with no name." What has occurred over the decades and centuries is that linguistically the law has institutionalized the language of sexism, and when the law gave the male the power to name the female it served to perpetuate his status of master in the master-subject relationship.

The power that comes with the privilege of naming another person is directly related to the centuries-old belief in the magic of words. "From time immemorial," writes Margaret Schlauch, "men have thought that there is some mysterious essential connection between a thing and the spoken name for it." If a man can use the name of his enemy to exercise an evil control and influence over that enemy, how much more power has that man who can control the naming of others? If "not only people, but plants, animals, forces of nature, gods, demons, in fact all creatures could be affected for good or ill by solemn pronunciation of their names in the proper context," how much more power has the person who not only pronounces their names but also designates for them his choice of names.

It should come as no surprise at this stage in history that these female "non-persons" are beginning to seriously demand the right to designate their own identities. What is surprising is that it has taken so long for women seriously to attempt to define themselves and demand the eradication of social, political, and economic discrimination that has, in part, been perpetuated by the language of sexism. A conscious effort to diminish the use of the language of sexism may be an important step towards eradicating man's inhumanity to women.

FOR DISCUSSION AND REVIEW

1. Explain how language was used to make the murder of millions of Jews by the Nazis acceptable to the German population. Consider this effect of language in relation to the following statement from a

recent essay in *Time:* "The feminist attack on social crimes may be as legitimate as it was inevitable. But the attack on words is only another social crime—one against the means and the hope of communication."

2. Thomas Szasz says, "The struggle for definition is veritably the struggle for life itself" (p. 39). Explain the relationship between this statement and Bosmajian's belief that it is important that women consciously work toward the elimination of the language of sexism. What bad effects does Bosmajian attribute to the language of sexism?

3. Consider the examples of "male supremist language" cited in the article; do you agree that they exemplify the existence of a pervasive problem? How do you react to the following substitutions that have been proposed (some more seriously than others):

chairperson	for	chairman
genkind	for	mankind
otto-it	for	ottoman
herstory	for	history
himicanes	for	hurricanes

Do some of these suggestions represent attempts to make a joke of a serious problem?

4. Do you find any serious suggestions for language change in Bosmajian's article or other articles you've read that are in fact linguistically preposterous, however well intentioned? Explain.

5. Like any attempt to change the status quo, women's attempts to change language have aroused a great deal of opposition. To what is the opposition reacting? Does this opposition seem justified? What techniques does it employ?

SCOTT, FORESMAN AND CO. 5

Does Language Libel the Left-Handed?

Not all objections to prejudicial language are as serious as those made by blacks and women. Some are more lighthearted, though an undercurrent of seriousness runs through the amusing examples given here. We should remember that for many centuries "left" and "evil" have been linked and that left-handedness was even thought to be more common among criminals and the insane.

HAVE YOU EVER NOTICED HOW LANGUAGE SEEMS TO DISCRIMINATE against left-handed people? The left-handed sometimes complain that every device from doorknobs to kitchen sinks is designed for right-handed people. Left-handers might well object also to the implications of designating the socially inept as "gauche" ("left" in French), the evil as "sinister" ("left" in Latin), and barbed flattery as a "left-handed compliment."

On the other hand, the skillful worker is "adroit" (French *à droit,* "to the right") and "dexterous" (from Latin *dexter,* "right" or "right hand"). The boss depends on the worker who is his "right-hand man." Who ever heard of anyone's having a "left-hand man"? When Stonewall Jackson was severely wounded, didn't General Lee say, "He has lost his left arm. I have lost my right arm"?

If a young lady complains after a dance that her partner had "two left feet," she is immediately understood to mean that he was impossibly awkward. Still, she may try to stay on the "right side" of him, so she will not lack for partners another time. For popularity many a girl will dance with a "gawky" (original meaning, "left" or "left-handed") boy occasionally.

Many successful athletes have been both left-handed and extremely well coördinated. No one in his "right mind" would deny that Sandy Koufax was a great baseball player. Nor has the sports world a corner on famous left-handers. Other "lefties" were Alexander the Great, Charlemagne, Leonardo da Vinci, and Holbein.

Yet, undeterred by the facts, we go right on with our canards. When a person becomes very mixed up indeed, we may say that he is "way out in left field," in contrast to "right-minded" individuals, whom everyone recognizes as "right as rain."

These aspersions on the one out of twenty—the estimated number of left-handed people in the world—have been cast for too long for there to be much hope of stopping them. It's enough to make a maligned left-hander send the next unsuspecting right-hander he meets to the store for a "left-handed monkey wrench."

FOR DISCUSSION AND REVIEW

1. Speculate about the origins of the derogatory connotations associated with "left." You may wish to consult an unabridged or historical dictionary such as *Webster's Third New International Dictionary* or the *Oxford English Dictionary*.

2. Does language really discriminate against left-handed people? Are there any other groups that language seems to treat in a similar manner?

ANNA TERESA BAZIAK
AND ROBERT KNOX DENTAN 6

The Language of the Hospital and Its Effects on the Patient

Most people will eventually spend some time in the hospital as patients. Until they have done so, however, they may not realize how disturbing the experience can be. A major cause of a patient's unease is often the sense of loss of identity, his feeling that he has become a "case" and is no longer an individual. In this article, a nurse and an anthropologist examine the language of the hospital subculture and some of its effects on the sick.

THE WRITERS WOULD LIKE TO INTRODUCE THEIR TOPIC BY QUOTING from an unpublished paper by their colleague and friend, Ida J. Orlando:

> An elderly patient, just arrived in the general ward of a modern hospital, is crying softly. While her sister helps her to bed, a harassed nurse rushes in, places a specimen bottle and several chart sheets on the bedside stand and immediately begins to write.
>
> "Do you have any jewelry with you?" asks the nurse.
>
> The patient moans and swallows hard, while the nurse sighs and wiggles her pen. "No," say the patient. "Oh, my God, help me." She covers her face with her hand, and moans.
>
> "Do you have any false teeth?"

Still moaning, the patient shakes her head, then suddenly tries to grab a small bottle from her sister. "Give me my pills, please don't take them away."

The sister jumps back, saying, "You know you can't keep them."

"Yes, but when I have the pain, I have to wait too long. I know this place, I've been here eight times." The old woman is sobbing.

"Now, you know you can't keep them here," interjects the nurse.

"I told you so," the sister adds.

"But I can't stand the pain. Oh, why doesn't God help me?"

"Can you give me a urine sample?" asks the nurse.

From an anthropologist's point of view a hospital is a relatively isolated subculture. Doctors and nurses often live on the grounds; they go from place to place via underground tunnels; they eat, sleep and dance within the hospital; get their clothes washed at the hospital laundry; buy presents at the hospital gift shop; and often do not leave the hospital grounds for days at a time.

Within hospital "culture," roles are strictly defined. The doctor is the dominant figure. He diagnoses symptoms and prescribes for his forty-odd patients. In hospitals these prescriptions are called "orders" and are entered in an "order book." The nurse is to carry out the doctor's orders. She is not even supposed to give a patient a hot water bottle without a written "order." A doctor or a nurse tends to refer to himself or herself as "we," which seems to be shorthand for "we, the Hospital." Last, the patient is to "cooperate"—another frequently used hospital term—to make it possible for doctors and nurses to function with a minimum of disturbance. The patient does not call himself "we." Requests made by the patient to the doctors and nurses are often called "complaints."

The contentions of this paper are (1) that instead of paying attention to the patient's idiosyncratic problems, which may stem from the new environment, the unfamiliar disease and the patient's past, doctors and nurses tend to *perceive* only certain features of the patient's condition, features which to an outsider may seem less significant than the ones which are ignored; (2) that this situation is the result of cultural and linguistic preconditioning.

Doctors are frequently taught to think in terms of symptoms to be diagnosed. Doctors' language both reflects and constitutes part of this training. For many doctors, then, the patient is a symptom-vehicle, and such doctors perceive and respond to symptoms instead of patients.

For example, after an examination, a doctor calls to a passing medical student, "Come on in here, there's a finger you can do." The doctor begins to describe the symptoms in a voice inaudible to the patient, whom they both ignore.

"Hmmmm," says the student, with enthusiasm. "Where do you open it?"

The doctor answers, again inaudibly, and concludes "You get him all cleaned up. The only thing you need is a number eleven blade."

Then he goes away.

In this example the neglect of the patient as a human being is striking. Although both the doctor and the medical student make comments which probably upset the patient, neither speaks to him. This neglect is made even more striking by the doctor's reference to the patient as a "finger." Apparently, all that either responds to under these circumstances is this abstraction from the total patient.

Traditionally, the nurse is trained to be the doctor's "handmaiden." Furthermore, she tends to respond to the doctor's "orders" (which are actually prescriptions) as if they were commands; indeed, the doctor often expects her to respond this way. Thus the patient may become an object upon which "orders" are to be carried out. This depersonalization of the patient may be carried so far that he is called by room number or symptom. This linguistic habit, in turn, increases the anonymity of the patient. The diagram on the following page illustrates this semantic relationship.

In the example with which this paper opens, the nurse's apparently inappropriate responses result from her "orders" to "admit" the patient.

Outside the hospital the nurse would probably have been sympathetic with the old woman's distress. Within the hospital, however, she responds to the "order" given her by her superiors, instead of to the patient. The nurse, therefore, ignores, *i.e.,* doesn't "perceive" any responses of the patient which cannot be used on the admission-form. In another example, a nurse is reporting on a patient, characteristically called by room number. We quote again from the paper by Orlando:

> "She has one more dose of repeat methergen to go."
>
> The head nurse interrupts, "Did you give her her Seconal? It's no use, you know, because it takes such a long time to wake her up."
>
> "I really had to shake her, too," answers the nurse.

To show that these inappropriate responses are the result of linguistic as well as cultural conditioning, take the example of Miss Reynolds.

> Three nurses and an aide are sitting in a ward office. A light flashes on the signal board indicating that a patient is calling for attention.

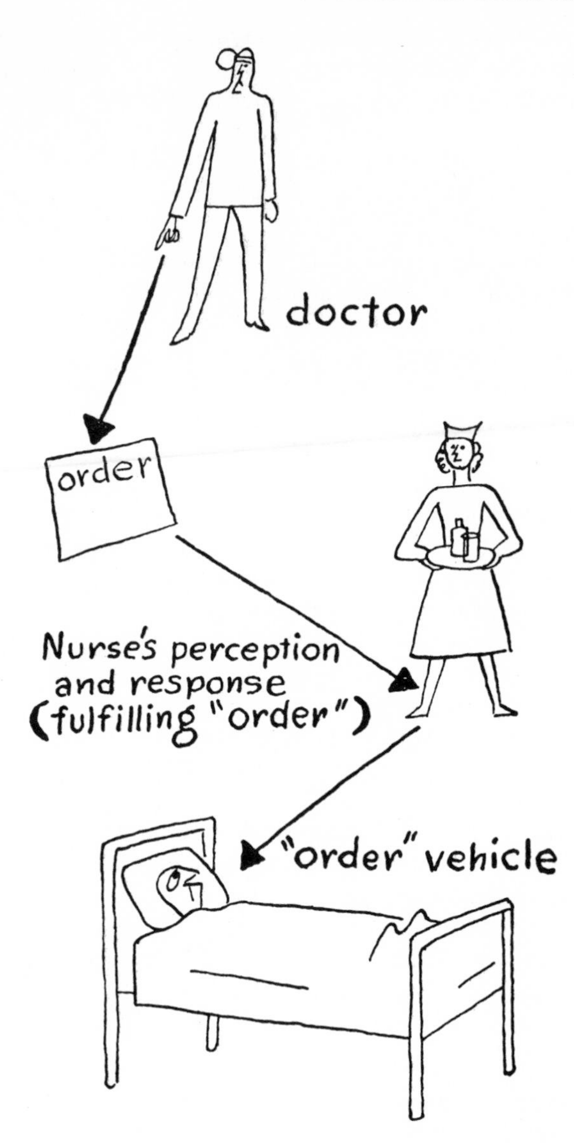

Nurse No. 1: Oh, brother, there's Miss Reynolds again.

Nurse No. 2: What does she want now? She's had her morning care.

Aide: I hate to go in. She'll keep me there an hour. She acts as if she can't lift a finger for herself.

Nurse No. 1 to Nurse No. 3: You're new here. Would you mind going in? We get enough of her when you're not here.

Nurse No. 3: All right.

(After having seen the patient, who was lonely, uncomfortable and in pain, Nurse No. 3 decided to try to change the attitude of the staff. She returned to the office.)

Nurse No. 3: Poor Miss Reynolds. She has such a hard time getting out of bed. She seemed so weak. I had to support her with my arm when she walked. What's wrong with her?

Nurse No. 1: Oh, she has metastatic carcinoma. She's been here for three weeks. I guess she does have some pain.

For three months, each time Nurse No. 3 came to the ward she asked if she might take care of Miss Reynolds. She followed this care by talking with the staff in this manner: "Miss Reynolds told me that she has no family. She said it makes being in the hospital especially lonely."

By the end of these three months, the behavior of the nurses toward Miss Reynolds had changed. They would fix her food in an attractive way, exercise more care in assisting her to move, bring her flowers from the rooms of discharged patients, and so forth.

What is striking here is that Miss Reynolds, the patient, has not changed at all, although the interpretant behavior of the staff has changed radically. This fact, it seems to us, indicates that the nurses were not responding to the flesh-and-blood Miss Reynolds, but to the word "Miss Reynolds" in a verbal context such as "Miss Reynolds is not *cooperative*." Since the phrase "Miss Reynolds" is phonemically unchanged, we are forced to the conclusion that it is the context of "*orders* which must be obeyed and with which Miss Reynolds does/does not interfere" that serves as the cue or sign for the nurses' interpretant behavior. Miss Reynolds is, phrase and person, irrelevant, except as a sign vehicle. But by manipulating the context in which the phrase "Miss Reynolds" occurred so that it no longer designated a situation in which obedience to "orders" was impeded but rather denoted a lonely, sick old woman, Nurse No. 3 was able to create a completely new interpretant behavior among the nurses.

Such a denotation would, outside hospital culture, be very likely to occur. The contention of this paper is not that the inappropriate behavior of nurses and doctors results from stupidity or inhumanity, but that it is conditioned by the subculture in which it occurs and by the language this subculture uses—a language in which prescriptions are "orders," patient's comments "complaints," and patients themselves numbers. Thus language is both the result and the cause of a situation in which sick people who come to an institution and take care of themselves are labeled "cooperative" and those who make demands on the personnel are labeled "uncooperative."

This sort of linguistic set-up seems to be an example of what

Charles Morris calls "semiosis." The doctors and nurses take account of the patient mediately, *i.e.,* by means of something else. Symptoms and "orders" are examples of what Morris calls "signs," insofar as doctors and nurses take account of the patient because of the presence of symptoms or orders. The patient is a "sign vehicle" and the behavior of the doctors and nurses is "interpretant."

The hospital is a very complex community. We have looked only at one aspect of this community and at how this aspect seems to inhibit the avowed functions of the hospital—namely, the meeting of a sick person's physical and emotional needs.

FOR DISCUSSION AND REVIEW

1. Baziak and Dentan's article opens with a short scene involving an elderly patient, her sister, and a nurse. The authors argue that "the nurse's apparently inappropriate responses [in this scene] result from her 'orders' to 'admit' the patient." Explain this statement—that is, which of the nurse's responses are inappropriate? How are they inappropriate? How did her "orders" to "admit" the patient cause this inappropriate behavior?

2. How does the fact that "a hospital is a relatively isolated subculture" in which "roles are strictly defined" affect the character of the language used by hospital staff in talking to and about patients? What is the effect on the patient if he feels that he is considered a collection of symptoms rather than a human being?

3. The change in the nurses' behavior toward Miss Reynolds shows that their behavior was partially the result of linguistic conditioning. Explain.

The Language of Neglect: Other Cases 7

Although we are all prisoners of language—other people's and our own—some groups in America are more obviously trapped than others. The short excerpts that follow identify several of these groups: the poor; the poorly educated; minority ethnic groups; children; the aged; and the sick.

DORIS R. ENTWISLE

from Semantic Systems of Children: Some Assessments of Social Class and Ethnic Differences

WHEN LOWER-CLASS PERSONS INTERACT WITH PERSONS FROM HIGHER social strata under impersonal and public conditions, members of the lower class are identified primarily by dress and speech. Dress is fast fading as a source of social-class cues; the disparity between the type and quality of clothing worn by members of various social classes lessens each year. Speech, however, continues to furnish reliable cues, for persons retain, to a surprising degree, linguistic habits and inflections learned in childhood. Ten to fifteen seconds of speech are sufficient to make reliable judgments of social status. Pronunciation of a single word by an invisible speaker ("arrow" at the other end of a telephone line) is sufficient to establish the identity of the speaker as a Negro. Such an identification may have many consequences. If the caller is seeking a taxi, he might expect a longer wait than a Caucasian customer. If the caller seeks information from a branch of the city or state government he might find himself shunted from one extension to another or simply cut off.

Life chances may thus be directly shaped by linguistic habits that influence interpersonal relations, partly because speech instantaneously identifies members of a particular social group. Even more drastically, if cognition and language are as closely related as now supposed, life chances may be shaped more subtly by inadequate cognitive habits and skills. A lower-class person may fail to achieve upward mobility partly for motivational reasons—he is not socialized to strive for status or other goals the middle class prizes. But this may be also partly for cognitive reasons—he fails to perceive his environment in terms sufficiently differentiated so that he can recognize opportunities, or size up situations quickly and accurately, or even be aware in some cases that more than one alternative for action exists. In addition, if his speech identifies him as a member of an outgroup, when tagged as a member of that group he may be endowed with all the other modal attributes of that group—relatively low economic status, low educational status, values that emphasize immediate rather than delayed gratifications, relatively low power in the social hierarchy, or even having certain political leanings.

from The Invisible Minority: Report of the NEA-Tucson Survey of the Teaching of Spanish to the Spanish Speaking

The Spanish-Speaking Home

LET US SEE WHAT HAPPENS TO THE AVERAGE MEXICAN-AMERICAN child when he starts school. He comes to school speaking Spanish. He knows some English but has used it infrequently. The language of his home, the language of his childhood, his first years, is Spanish. His environment, his experiences, his very personality have been shaped by it.

To understand how totally Spanish the background of such a child may be, consider the results of a study made in 1965 in San Antonio, Texas, and reported to the El Paso conference of foreign language teachers. Six hundred Mexican-American adults were interviewed in San Antonio, and it was found that 71 percent of husbands and wives spoke only Spanish to each other. Among the grandparents, 94 percent spoke only Spanish to their children and 89 percent spoke only Spanish to their grandchildren.

Understandably, therefore, the child from this Spanish-saturated environment, once embarked on his school career, finds himself in a strange and even threatening situation. The language of instruction is English. Yet English, as John M. Sharp expressed it at the El Paso conference, may be "no less a foreign language to him that it would be to a child from Argentina or Colombia. He suddenly finds himself not only with the pressing need to master a (to him) alien tongue, but, also at the same time, to make immediate use of it in order to function as a pupil. His parents, to whom he has always looked for protection and aid, can be of no help at all to him in his perplexity. Moreover, as a result of cultural and economic differences between the English-speaking and Spanish-speaking segments of his community, many of the objects, social relationships and cultural attitudes presented to him in his lessons, though perfectly familiar to an Anglo youngster, lie without the Latin American's home experience. Accordingly, the problem of learning English is, for him, enormously increased by his unfamiliarity with what objects and situations the no less unfamiliar words and phrases stand for."

. . .

Fitting the Stereotype

Nor is it only a different language that the newly-arrived Mexican-American child encounters. He also encounters a strange and different set of cultural patterns, an accelerated tempo of living and, more often than not, teachers who, though sympathetic and sincere, have little understanding of the Spanish-speaking people, their customs, beliefs and sensitivities. He is given an intelligence test in which language and cultural and socio-economic background are depressing factors. He may have fully as much intellectual potential as his Anglo-

American classmates, but he shows up on the test as a "low achiever." He tends thus to become stereotyped in the eyes of the adults whose lives impinge on his. All of them—teachers, administrators, even parents—expect little of him, and he usually measures up (or down) to their expectations.

If he knows little or no English, he may be placed in a special class with other non-English-speaking children for a year and then "promoted" to the first grade the following year. But that means he must go through school a year behind other children of his age, and this embarrasses him.

Even if he speaks both English and Spanish, he may be only nominally bilingual—not truly so. He may have, as he often does, a low level of literacy in both languages. He watches television at home, as do his Anglo-American schoolmates. He listens to the radio. Soon he is speaking a language which is neither Spanish nor English but a mixture of the two—a kind of linguistic hybrid. He doesn't speak English correctly and he doesn't speak Spanish correctly.

There is something sadly paradoxical about the schools' well-meaning effort to make the Mexican-American child "talk American"—to eradicate his Spanish. For they are at the same time working strenuously to teach Spanish to the Anglo-American student, acclaiming the advantages of being able to communicate fluently in a language other than one's own. The National Defense Education Act is providing funds to schools to strengthen the teaching of modern foreign languages as well as mathematics, science, and other subjects. And so, while they strive to make the monolingual student bilingual, they are making—or trying to make the bilingual student monolingual.

. . .

The Damaged Self-Image

The harm done the Mexican-American child linguistically is paralleled—perhaps even exceeded—by the harm done to him as a person. In telling him that he must not speak his native language, we are saying to him by implication that Spanish and the culture which it represents are of no worth. Therefore (it follows) the people who speak Spanish are of no worth. Therefore (it follows again) this particular child is of no worth. It should come as no surprise to us, then, that he develops a negative self-concept—an inferiority complex. If he is no good, how can he succeed? And if he can't succeed, why try?

LYNN R. OSBORN

from Language, Poverty, and the North American Indian

THE CONDITIONS, SYMPTOMS, AND RESULTS OF POVERTY-LEVEL EXISTENCE in the United States during the last several decades have hardly anywhere been more appalling than among the nation's first citizens, the North American Indians. Although both the present picture and the future outlook are brighter today, their poverty problems are still the most serious faced by any group in this country during the latter half of the twentieth century.

Contrary to the widely held myth of the "vanishing Americans," the Indian population of the United States actually is increasing at a markedly faster rate than the general population. The 1960 census reported well over a half-million Indian citizens. It is estimated that this figure currently has risen to approximately six hundred thousand with two-thirds of this population living on or near government reservations in twenty-five states. Should the present rate maintain during the decade of the '70's, the number will have risen to over eight hundred thousand by 1980. This projected growth would reflect a population expansion of well over 300 percent in less than a century from the reported low of two hundred forty thousand in the 1890's. Thus the future concern is not only one of degree, but of numbers as well.

The circumstances of contemporary Indian poverty on the reservations have been well-summarized by Nash (in a press release dated in 1964):

1. Unemployment on the reservations runs between 40 and 50%—seven or eight times the national average.
2. Family income on the reservations averages between one-fourth and one-third the national average.
3. Nine out of ten Indian families live in housing that is far below minimum standards of comfort, safety, and decency.
4. Average schooling of young adults on the reservations is only eight years—two-thirds of the national average.
5. The average age at death on the reservation is 42 years, two-thirds the figure for the national population.

. . .

In examining factors thought to be responsible for the extremely high dropout rate among Indian freshmen enrolled at Northern Arizona University, Thompson found lack of proficiency in the English language to rank at the top of the list:

> English for these students had to be learned in the elementary and high-school grades as a second language, which means that these students have acquired their formal education in what to them is a foreign language. A few of them may have been fortunate enough to have had teachers well prepared in teaching English as a second language, but in all probability most did not. . . . Some Indian college students still find it difficult to think in English, and some are attempting to handle college subject matter with less than high-school reading tools. On the other hand, evidence points to the fact that most of these same college students if tested with instruments that eliminate English language factors score average or better with respect to potential ability. Nevertheless, struggling with the language problem has a damaging effect on their confidence in themselves. . . . The failing grade problem complicated by financial problems and sub-standard capability in the English language forms a web more frustrating than many students can take. . . . For many of them, walking away is the only solution they know.

. . .

As one attempts to examine relationships between the language capabilities of the Indian and his state of poverty, this examination must take into account an imposing array of disparate languages and dialects—some of which are disappearing and, in contrast, others in which the number of potential speakers is increasing. It also is apparent, to repeat the words of Thompson, that "a good command of the English language today, more than ever before, is the master key to Indians' successful transition to twentieth century living." The degree of acquisition and usage of this "master key" varies widely from those older Indians who speak little or no English at all to some of the younger generation who learned English as their first language and are totally unfamiliar with their native languages. The manner and form in which English as a second language has been taught have evolved from an earlier philosophy of total obliteration of the native language to the current belief of many that the Indian child should be educated for productive citizenship in both the Indian and non-Indian communities and, hence, must be literate in both languages.

Several of the better studies concerning Indian education have dealt with scholastic ability and achievement. The results of these have indicated that the Indian child has no inherited educational disadvantage when compared with his non-Indian peers. When measures not dependent upon knowledge of the English language have been utilized, the Indian child has been found to perform within the national norms. In some instances, indeed, the Indian pupil has exhibited certain performances superior to those of the non-Indian.

It has been shown that the Indian child seems to compensate for his language differences in the early elementary grades. However, from about the fourth grade, when English proficiency becomes a crucial factor in academic success, he frequently begins to fall behind his non-Indian classmates in scholastic performance.

Closely linked with this lag in academic achievement is a progressively higher incidence of dropouts among Indian school children. The rate steadily increases through the upper elementary, intermediate, and secondary grades until it ultimately is manifested in the extremely small number of Indian young people who graduate from college. Surveys of vocational success and satisfaction among employed Indians also have revealed close ties to employee proficiency in English. Similar links have been observed in the relatively few studies reported which deal with the urbanization of Indian populations.

S. I. HAYAKAWA

from On Communication with Children

[WHEN CHILDREN] START TO TALK THERE IS ALWAYS THE CONSTANT problem of interpretation. There is a sense in which small children are recent immigrants in our midst. They have trouble both in understanding and in using the language, and they often make errors. So many people (you can notice this in the supermarkets, especially with two- and three-year-old children) talk to their children and get angry at them because the children don't seem to mind, and anyone standing around can tell that the children just haven't understood what mother said. But mother feels, "Well, I said it, didn't I? What's wrong with the child that he doesn't understand? It's English, isn't it?" But, as I say, the child is a recent immigrant in our midst and there are things that the child doesn't understand.

There are curious instances. Once, when our little girl was three years old, she found the bath too hot and she said, "Make it warmer." It took me a moment to figure out that she meant, "Bring the water more nearly to the condition we call warm." It makes perfectly good sense if you look at it that way. Confronted with unusual formulations such as these which children constantly make, it seems to me that many of us react with incredible lack of imagination. Sometimes children are laughed at for making silly statements when it only requires looking at them—at their way of abstracting and their way of formulating their abstractions—to see that they are not silly at all.

IONA AND PETER OPIE

from The Lore and Language of Schoolchildren

CHILDREN ARE NOT SQUEAMISH ABOUT TELLING AN UNPOPULAR KID that he or she is not wanted, and juvenile language is well stocked (and apparently always has been) with expressions inviting a person's departure, for instance: "Away with you—no salt in our sugar!," bamboosh, bat off, beat it, beetle off, blot off, bugger off, bunk (or "Do a bunk!"), buzz off (and facetiously "What does the bee say?—Buzz!"), cleaff off (Lincoln), clear off (often used patronizingly "Clear off, son," "Clear out, you kids"), crab (Manchester), dig the dirt, disappear, do a mickey, dog off, drift, fizz, flit, float away, f— off, get scarce, get weaving, gerraway (often with a threat "—or else!"), git (short for "get going"), go and bale out, go and have a roll, go and jump in the cut (= canal, Liverpool), go and run up a tree (or "Run up a tree and branch off"), "Go home your ma's got cake," go on—blow, hit grit, hit the trail, hop it (often spelt as one word "oppit"), hook it, make yourself scarce, mooch (Liverpool), move along, move off, nash away (Kirkcaldy), on your way lad, pack your bags and go, push off, quit, remove your carcass, scarper, scat, scoosh (Kirkcaldy), scoot, scram, scramoosh, scrub off (Lydney), scudabunk (Scotland), shag off, shave off (Birmingham), shift off, shit off, shove off, skedaddle, skidoosh, skip it, sling your hook, split the breeze, take off, travel, turf or turf out of it, vamoose, vanish, waft away, catch a passing sputnik, and (one child) "Would you mind going please."

These terms supplied by twentieth-century children may be compared with those given 360 years ago by Richard Carew in his *Epistle on the Excellency of the English Tongue, c.* 1595: 'When wee would be rid of one, wee vse to saye *Bee going, trudge, pack, be faring, hence, awaye, shifte,* and, by circumlocution, *rather your roome then your companye, Letts see your backe, com againe when I bid you, when you are called, sent for, intreated, willed, desiered, inuited, spare vs your place, another in your steede, a shipp of salte for you, saue your credite, you are next the doore, the doore is open for you, theres noe bodye holdes you, no bodie teares your sleeue,* &c.'

The present-day directions are, of course, not infrequently accompanied by a personal description or family history of him whose absence is required. The following excommunication is commonly pronounced in Aberdeen:

Awa ye ham,
Yer mither's a bam,
Yer auld man's a darkie.

Bam is a local term in Aberdeen for a silly ass.

CATHERINE M. NORRIS

from Greetings from the Lonely Crowd

WE READ FEW SOCIAL SCIENCE STUDIES ABOUT HOSPITALS BEFORE we have some clues to our *real* versus *ideal* concept of patient role. In practice, the patient does not receive individualized, loving care since he is often cared for by as many as twenty-five to thirty people a day. These are comparatively short contacts and some people don't even take the time to introduce themselves. We expect, write the social scientists, the patient to learn to conform to a patient role. He must learn what prerogatives he loses when coming to the hospital and to accept this loss whether it is in terms of external symbols like clothes, papers and valuables or in terms of privacy and independence. He learns the rules under which he must function and the ways he must behave to get what he deems his fair share of attention. He learns what he may question and what he must never question. The onus of responsibility for getting along in the hospital is on the patient. If he does not learn the role, he may be labeled "uncooperative, attention getting, overdemanding," or "having no insight into his problems." He learns that to receive all the rewards that nursing and medicine have to offer, he must be compliant with doctors and nurses and be brave in such adversities as pain or a dreaded diagnosis.

TERRI SCHULTZ

from Who Needs the Aged Anyhow?

ONCE HER WHOLE LIFE HAD BEEN CHILDREN: LAUGHING, SPIRITED, roistering kids whose healthy clamor was her music, and the rhythm to her life. For Ms. Clara Wright had been a school teacher; in what she thinks of now as "my other life," she taught physical education.

I found her, not long ago, old beyond her 68 years and intimidated by her new environment. Even before she spoke, her sad brown eyes told me how this sensitive *senior American* was coping.

"One day here is like the next," she said of the Rosewood Manor Nursing Home on Chicago's North Side. "Pretty soon I'll be like Robinson Crusoe. I'll have to put six marks on the wall and cross it with a seventh to keep track of the weeks."

What she next told me, I had already guessed: "I never used to be lonely. I always had kids to laugh with and someone close by who knew my name and looked at me when they spoke."

"And someone who would listen?" I asked.

"Yes, someone who was *capable* of listening . . . and caring."

Clara Wright has been a nursing home patient seven months. She summed up her new life, with all its routines and constrictions, by saying: "It's a life of sleep."

"Isn't that wonderful," she added, "a life of sleep?"

SHARON R. CURTIN

from Nobody Ever Died of Old Age

I GAVE MISS LARSON A BATH IN HER ROOM THAT MORNING, OVER THE strenuous objections of the charge nurse, who felt I was encouraging separation and dependence. I felt guilty, and my hands were unnecessarily rough as I turned and bathed Miss Larson. It was as if I blamed her for placing me in a position where I had to be miserable, observe misery. How could she do it to me?

The resentment I felt so strongly that first morning seems endemic in places where the aged live. The custodians, whether medically trained or administrative, always seem to have some anger, some residual hatred or fear of their charges. Sometimes I felt it was fear of one's own aging process, or just anger at having to do a very difficult job. Sometimes I saw it as a sort of natural turning away from another's misery, the way one will ignore the open trousers of an old man on the subway. But even if it was a sense of delicacy, of not wanting to intrude on the last years these old people had on earth, it soon progressed to another level. Because the attendants had to physically care for, handle the aging bodies of these old people, they began to treat them as if they were infants, unhearing, uncaring, unable to speak or communicate in any way. The patients were uniformly called honey or dearie or sweetie—or sometimes naughty girl if they soiled their beds—just as one tends to call children by pet names. At that level, the attendants expected gratitude or at least silent acquiescence from the old people and their families. The bodies were kept clean, fed, powdered, combed, and clothed. They were as infants, without modesty or sex or privacy.

The next level involved treating the patients as inanimate objects rather than as any kind of human being, adult or infant. This attitude was most frequent in older staff members and is understandably defensive. "Ahhh, she's *just* an old lady," they would say. "She's *just* an old lady." And that seemed to justify all manner of things, including the way blind patients were fed or not fed, according to whim; or how soon an old man was cleaned and his linen changed after he soiled his bed.

FOR DISCUSSION AND REVIEW

1. Entwisle says that "speech instantaneously identifies members of a particular social group." Do you agree? Why are cues other than speech of less importance in America today?

2. How does the background of the average Mexican-American child interfere with his school career? Explain the statement: "The harm done the Mexican-American child linguistically is paralleled—perhaps even exceeded—by the harm done to him as a person."

3. Discuss the relationship between the living conditions on the reservations of American Indians and the Indians' experience with the English language.

4. The examples of children's "sending away" language cited by Opie and Opie are British. List as many American examples as you can.

5. Describe the relationship between language and the "patient role."

6. Clara Wright and Miss Larson share a condition common to the elderly: they are lonely and they have lost their sense of identity. This loss of identity comes partly from loss of job and partly from loss of name. Consider the implications of Curtin's statement: "The patients were uniformly called honey or dearie or sweetie—or sometimes naughty girl if they soiled their beds—just as one tends to call children by pet names."

WRITING

1. Our first impression of strangers is based on their physical appearance, the way they dress, how they talk, and their names. Sometimes our reaction to a person's name is personal. For example, perhaps our favorite aunt was named Gertrude, and we are favorably disposed to anyone we meet named Gertrude. Some reactions to names, however, are not personal but rather reflect expectations widely shared by Americans. Thus most people would find it difficult to think of Queen Lizzie instead of Queen Elizabeth. Test these statements by matching each occupation in the lefthand column with a name in the righthand column. Write a paragraph explaining two of your choices.

1. member of a teenage street gang	a. William L. Thompson
2. shortstop for the Boston Red Sox	b. W. Louis Thompson
3. novelist	c. Bill Thompson
4. financier	d. Lou Thompson
5. evangelist	e. Billy Lou Thompson
	f. Willie Thompson
	g. W. L. Thompson

2. Many prospective parents spend a lot of time thinking about names for their children. Using your own last name as a surname, list three masculine and three feminine first names that you find appealing and three that you find distasteful. Write a short essay in which you explain the reasons for your choices.

3. Businessmen are very conscious of the connotations of the names they give their products. Automobile manufacturers, for example, have drawn heavily on animal names—Impala, Pinto, Cougar, Mustang, Thunderbird, Jaguar, Cricket, Skylark, and Charger—to suggest the strength, size, and speed of the various models. If an automobile can be named Cobra, why not Rattler or Sidewinder? Make up a brand name with unappealing connotations and write an advertisement of a paragraph or two for the product—for instance, the Buick Buffalo, Antelope, or Ostrich.

4. As a writing project, analyze the names various manufacturers have given soap products, and categorize these names according to the sense impressions or images they suggest. Write an essay in which you evaluate these names and suggest alternative images and names you would give several of the products.

5. Members of a group often have different perceptions of the characteristics of that group from those held by outsiders. What is your own image of the racial, national, religious, and social groups to which you belong? How do nonmembers view these groups? Write an essay in which you compare the two images and attempt to account for the differences.

6. The following article appeared in the New York *Times* in 1968. Read it carefully and write a letter to the *Times* in which you either support or attack the UN report. Your analysis should take into account the presentation of the ideas as well as the purpose of the report.

> UN GROUP URGES DROPPING OF WORDS WITH RACIST TINGE
>
> In an effort to combat racial prejudice, a group of United Nations experts is urging sweeping revision of the terminology used by teachers, mass media and others dealing with race.
>
> Words such as Negro, primitive, savage, backward, colored, bushman and uncivilized would be banned as either "contemptuous, unjust or inadequate." They were described as aftereffects of colonialism.
>
> The report said that the terms were "so charged with emotive potential that their use, with or without conscious pejorative intent, to describe or characterize certain ethnic, social or religious groups, generally provoked an adverse reaction on the part of these groups."
>
> The report said further that even the term "race" should be used with particular care since its scientific validity was debatable and that it "often served to perpetuate prejudice." The experts suggested that the word "tribe" should be used as sparingly as possible, since most of the "population groups" referred to by this term have long since ceased to be tribes or are losing their tribal character. A "native" should be called "inhabitant," the group advised, and instead of "paganism" the words "animists," "Moslems," "Brahmans" and other precise words should be used. The word "savanna" is preferable to "jungle," and the new countries should be described as "developing" rather than "under-developed," the experts said.

7. Ludwig Wittgenstein's statement "The limits of my language are the limits of my world" is often quoted. Write an essay in which you illustrate the application of this idea to some group that you consider to be prisoners of language. Support your generalizations with carefully selected details.

8. Eugene Goodheart says that "language unwittingly reflects on the man who uses it rather than on the object of its use" (*The Nation,* April 6, 1970). While Goodheart is talking here about abusive language, his statement can be interpreted more generally. Find examples from your reading, in this book or elsewhere, to support this statement. In a paper, tell what is revealed about the writer (or writers).

NOTABLE QUOTATIONS

"Most people are unaware of this basic law of language—that every label applied to a given person refers properly only to one aspect of his nature." *Allport*

"Especially in a culture where uniformity is prized, the name of *any* deviant carries with it *ipso facto* a negative value-judgment." *Allport*

"Until we label an out-group it does not clearly exist in our minds." *Allport*

"When symbols provoke strong emotions they are sometimes regarded no longer as symbols but as actual things." *Allport*

"Our identities, who and what we are or think we are, how others see and define us, are greatly affected by language." *Bosmajian*

"A conscious effort to diminish the use of the language of sexism may be an important step towards eradicating man's inhumanity to women." *Bosmajian*

"For many doctors . . . the patient is a symptom-vehicle, and such doctors perceive and respond to symptoms instead of patients." *Baziak and Dentan*

"Dress is fast fading as a source of social-class cues. . . . Speech, however, continues to furnish reliable cues. . . ." *Entwisle*

INFLUENCING LANGUAGE IV

"When I use a word," Humpty Dumpty said in a rather scornful tone, "it means just what I choose it to mean—neither more nor less."

"The question is," said Alice, "whether you can make words mean so many different things."

"The question is," said Humpty Dumpty, "which is to be master—that's all."

Lewis Carroll, *Through the Looking Glass*

In order to be a great writer a person must have a built-in, shock-proof crap detector."

Ernest Hemingway

PAUL STEVENS 1

Weasel Words: God's Little Helpers

Commercials are a very real part of our daily lives. As a recent television critic reported in TV Guide, Jeopardy *"came on at 11* A.M. *and was interrupted as follows: at 11:03 for two 30-second spots, at 11:12 for four 30s, at 11:18 for a one-minute network promo, 11:26 for two 30s and at 11:28 for a close-out with nearly a minute more of network blurbs and two 30s and a 10-second spot." In his book* I Can Sell You Anything, *Paul Stevens, a writer of television commercials, reveals the secrets of successful advertising. Advertisers really don't have to substantiate their claims since they make you, the consumer, hear things that aren't being said. Stevens' guide to "commercialese" serves as a helpful handbook for the consumer.*

FIRST OF ALL, YOU KNOW WHAT A WEASEL IS, RIGHT? IT'S A SMALL, slimy animal that eats small birds and other animals, and is especially fond of devouring vermin. Now, consider for a moment the kind of winning personality he must have. I mean, what kind of a guy would get his jollies eating rats and mice? Would you invite him to a party? Take him home to meet your mother? This is one of the slyest and most cunning of all creatures; sneaky, slippery, and thoroughly obnoxious. And so it is with great and warm personal regard for these attributes that we humbly award this King of All Devious the honor of bestowing his name upon our golden sword: the weasel word.

A weasel word is "a word used in order to evade or retreat from a direct or forthright statement or position" (Webster). In other words, if we can't say it, we'll weasel it. And, in fact, a weasel word has become more than just an evasion or retreat. We've trained our weasels. They can do anything. They can make you hear things that aren't being said, accept as truths things that have only been implied, and believe things that have only been suggested. Come to think of it, not only do we have our weasels trained, but they, in turn, have got you trained. When *you* hear a weasel word, you automatically hear the implication. Not the real meaning, but the meaning *it* wants *you* to hear. So if you're ready for a little re-education, let's take a good look under a strong light at the two kinds of weasel words.

Words That Mean Things They Really Don't Mean

Help

That's it. "Help." It means "aid" or "assist." Nothing more. Yet, "help" is the one single word which, in all the annals of advertising, has done the most to say something that couldn't be said. Because "help" is the great qualifier; once you say it, you can say almost anything after it. In short, "help" has helped help us the most.

Helps keep you young
Helps prevent cavities
Helps keep your house germ-free

"Help" qualifies everything. You've never heard anyone say, "This product will keep you young," or "This toothpaste will positively prevent cavities for all time." Obviously, we can't say anything like that, because there aren't any products like that made. But by adding that one little word, "help," in front, we can use the strongest language possible afterward. And the most fascinating part of it is, you are immune to the word. You literally don't hear the word "help." You only hear what comes after it. And why not? That's strong language, and likely to be much more important to you than the silly little word at the front end.

I would guess that 75 percent of all advertising uses the word "help." Think, for a minute, about how many times each day you hear these phrases:

Helps stop . . .
Helps prevent . . .
Helps fight . . .
Helps overcome . . .
Helps you feel . . .
Helps you look . . .

I could go on and on, but so could you. Just as a simple exercise, call it homework if you wish, tonight when you plop down in front of the boob tube for your customary three and a half hours of violence and/or situation comedies, take a pad and pencil, and keep score. See if you can count how many times the word "help" comes up during the commercials. Instead of going to the bathroom during the pause before Marcus Welby operates, or raiding the refrigerator prior to witnessing the Mod Squad wipe out a nest of dope pushers, stick with it. Count the "helps," and discover just how dirty a four-letter word can be.

Like

Coming in second, but only losing by a nose, is the word "like," used in comparison. Watch:

It's like getting one bar free
Cleans like a white tornado
It's like taking a trip to Portugal

Okay. "Like" is a qualifier, and is used in much the same way as "help." But "like" is also a comparative element, with a very specific purpose; we use "like" to get you to stop thinking about the product per se, and to get you thinking about something that is bigger or better or different from the product we're selling. In other words, we can make you believe that the product is more than it is by likening it to something else.

Take a look at that first phrase, straight out of recent Ivory Soap advertising. On the surface of it, they tell you that four bars of Ivory cost about the same as three bars of most other soaps. So, if you're going to spend a certain amount of money on soap, you can buy four bars instead of three. Therefore, it's like getting one bar free. Now, the question you have to ask yourself is, "Why the weasel? Why do they say 'like'? Why don't they just come out and say, 'You get one bar free'?" The answer is, of course, that for one reason or another, you really don't. Here are two possible reasons. One: sure, you get four bars, but in terms of the actual amount of soap that you get, it may very well be the same as in three bars of another brand.

Remember, Ivory has a lot of air in it—that's what makes it float. And air takes up room. Room that could otherwise be occupied by more soap. So, in terms of pure product, the amount of actual soap in four bars of Ivory may be only as much as the actual amount of soap in three bars of most others. That's why we can't—or won't—come out with a straightforward declaration such as, "You get 25 percent more soap," or "Buy three bars, and get the fourth one free."

Reason number two: the actual cost and value of the product. Did it ever occur to you that Ivory may simply be a cheaper soap to make and, therefore, a cheaper soap to sell? After all, it doesn't have any perfume or hexachlorophene, or other additives that can raise the cost of manufacturing. It's plain, simple, cheap soap, and so it can be sold for less money while still maintaining a profit margin as great as more expensive soaps. By way of illustrating this, suppose you were trying to decide whether to buy a Mercedes-Benz or a Ford. Let's say the Mercedes cost $7,000, and the Ford $3,500. Now the Ford salesman comes up to you with this deal: as long as you're considering spending $7,000 on a car, buy my Ford for $7,000 and I'll give you a second Ford, free! Well, the same principle can apply to Ivory: as long as you're considering spending 35 cents on soap, buy my cheaper soap, and I'll give you more of it.

I'm sure there are other reasons why Ivory uses the weasel "like." Perhaps you've thought of one or two yourself. That's good. You're starting to think.

Now, what about that wonderful white tornado? Ajax pulled that one out of the hat some eight years ago, and you're still buying it. It's a classic example of the use of the word "like" in which we can force you to think, not about the product itself, but about something bigger, more exciting, certainly more powerful than a bottle of fancy ammonia. The word "like" is used here as a transfer word, which gets you away from the obvious—the odious job of getting down on your hands and knees and scrubbing your kitchen floor—and into the world of fantasy, where we can imply that this little bottle of miracles will supply all the elbow grease you need. Isn't that the name of the game? The whirlwind activity of the tornado replacing the whirlwind motion of your arm? Think about the swirling of the tornado, and all the work it will save you. Think about the power of that devastating windstorm; able to lift houses, overturn cars, and now, pick the dirt up off your floor. And we get the license to do it simply by using the word "like."

It's a copywriter's dream, because we don't have to substantiate anything. When we compare our product to "another leading brand," we'd better be able to prove what we say. But how can you compare ammonia to a windstorm? It's ludicrous. It can't be done. The whole statement is so ridiculous it couldn't be challenged by the government or the networks. So it went on the air, and it worked. Because the little word "like" let us take you out of the world of reality, and into your own fantasies.

Speaking of fantasies, how about that trip to Portugal? Mateus Rosé is actually trying to tell you that you will be transported clear across the Atlantic Ocean merely by sipping their wine. "Oh, come on," you say. "You don't expect me to believe that." Actually, we don't expect you to believe it. But we do expect you to get our meaning. This is called "romancing the product," and it is made possible by the dear little "like." In this case, we deliberately bring attention to the word, and we ask you to join us in setting reality aside for a moment. We take your hand and gently lead you down the path of moonlit nights, graceful dancers, and mysterious women. Are we saying that these things are all contained inside our wine? Of course not. But what we mean is, our wine is part of all this, and with a little help from "like," we'll get you to feel that way, too. So don't think of us as a bunch of peasants squashing a bunch of grapes. As a matter of fact, don't think of us at all. Feel with us.

"Like" is a virus that kills. You'd better get immune to it.

Other Weasels

"Help" and "like" are the two weasels so powerful that they can stand on their own. There are countless other words, not quite so potent, but equally effective when used in conjunction with our two basic weasels, or with each other. Let me show you a few.

VIRTUAL OR VIRTUALLY. How many times have you responded to an ad that said:

Virtually trouble-free . . .
Virtually foolproof . . .
Virtually never needs service . . .

Ever remember what "virtual" means? It means "in essence or effect, but not in fact." Important—"but not in fact." Yet today the word "virtually" is interpreted by you as meaning "almost or just about the same as. . . ." Well, gang, it just isn't true. "Not," in fact, means not, in fact. I was scanning, rather longingly I must confess, through the brochure Chevrolet publishes for its Corvette, and I came to this phrase: "The seats in the 1972 Corvette are virtually handmade." They had me, for a minute. I almost took the bait of that lovely little weasel. I almost decided that those seats were just about completely handmade. And then I remembered. Those seats were not, *in fact,* handmade. Remember, "virtually" means "not, in fact," or you will, in fact, get sold down the river.

ACTS OR WORKS. These two action words are rarely used alone, and are generally accompanied by "like." They need help to work, mostly because they are verbs, but their implied meaning is deadly, nonetheless. Here are the key phrases:

Acts like . . .
Acts against . .
Works like . . .
Works against . . .
Works to prevent (or help prevent) . . .

You see what happens? "Acts" or "works" brings an action to the product that might not otherwise be there. When we say that a certain cough syrup "acts on the cough control center," the implication is that the syrup goes to this mysterious organ and immediately makes it better. But the implication here far exceeds what the truthful promise should be. An act is simply a deed. So the claim "acts on" simply means it performs a deed on. What that deed is, we may never know.

The rule of thumb is this: if we can't say "cures" or "fixes" or use any other positive word, we'll nail you with "acts like" or "works against," and get you thinking about something else. Don't.

Miscellaneous Weasels

CAN BE. This is for comparison, and what we do is to find an announcer who can really make it sound positive. But keep your ears open. "Crest can be of significant value when used in . . . ," etc., is indicative of an ideal situation, and most of us don't live in ideal situations.

UP TO. Here's another way of expressing an ideal situation. Remember the cigarette that said it was aged, or "cured for up to eight long, lazy weeks"? Well, that could, and should, be interpreted as meaning that the tobaccos used were cured anywhere from one hour to eight weeks. We like to glamorize the ideal situation; it's up to you to bring it back to reality.

AS MUCH AS. More of the same. "As much as 20 percent greater mileage" with our gasoline again promises the ideal, but qualifies it.

REFRESHES, COMFORTS, TACKLES, FIGHTS, COMES ON. Just a handful of the same action weasels, in the same category as "acts" and "works," though not as frequently used. The way to complete the thought here is to ask the simple question, "How?" Usually, you won't get an answer. That's because, usually, the weasel will run and hide.

FEEL *or* THE FEEL OF. This is the first of our subjective weasels. When we deal with a subjective word, it is simply a matter of opinion. In our opinion, Naugehyde has the feel of real leather. So we can say it. And, indeed, if you were to touch leather, and then touch Naugehyde, you may very well agree with us. But that doesn't mean it is real leather, only that it feels the same. The best way to handle subjective weasels is to complete the thought yourself, by simply saying, "But it isn't." At least that way you can remain grounded in reality.

THE LOOK OF *or* LOOKS LIKE. "Look" is the same as "feel," our subjective opinion. Did you ever walk into a Woolworth's and see those $29.95 masterpieces hanging in their "Art Gallery"? "The look of a real oil painting," it will say. "But it isn't," you will now reply. And probably be $29.95 richer for it.

Words That Have No Specific Meaning

If you have kids, then you have all kinds of breakfast cereals in the house. When I was a kid, it was Rice Krispies, the breakfast cereal that went snap, crackle, and pop. (One hell of a claim for a product that is supposed to offer nutritional benefits.) Or Wheaties, the breakfast of champions, whatever that means. Nowadays, we're forced to a confrontation with Quisp, Quake, Lucky Stars, Cocoa-Puffs, Clunkers, Blooies, Snarkles and Razzmatazz. And they all have one thing in common: they're all "fortified." Some are simply "fortified with vitamins," while others are specifically "fortified with vitamin D," or some other letter. But what does it all mean?

"Fortified" means "added on to." But "fortified," like so many other weasel words of indefinite meaning, simply doesn't tell us enough. If, for instance, a cereal were to contain one unit of vitamin D, and the manufacturers added some chemical which would produce two units of vitamin D, they could then claim that the cereal was "fortified with twice as much vitamin D." So what? It would still be about as nutritional as sawdust.

The point is, weasel words with no specific meaning don't tell us enough, but we have come to accept them as factual statements closely associated with something good that has been done to the product. Here's another example.

Enriched

We use this one when we have a product that starts out with nothing. You mostly find it in bread, where the bleaching process combined with the chemicals used as preservatives renders the loaves totally void of anything but filler. So the manufacturer puts a couple of drops of vitamins into the batter, and presto! It's enriched. Sounds great when you say it. Looks great when you read it. But what you have to determine is, is it really great? Figure out what information is missing, and then try to supply that information. The odds are, you won't. Even the breakfast cereals that are playing it straight, like Kellogg's Special K, leave something to be desired. They tell you what vitamins you get, and how much of each in one serving. The catch is, what constitutes a serving? They say, one ounce. So now you have to whip out your baby scale and weigh one serving. Do you have any idea how much that is? Maybe you do. Maybe you don't care. Okay, so you polish off this mound of dried stuff, and now what? You have ostensibly received the minimum, repeat, minimum dosage of certain vitamins for the day. One day. And you still have to go find the vitamins you didn't get. Try looking it up on a box of frozen peas. Bet you won't find it. But do be alert to "fortified" and "enriched." Asking the right questions will prove beneficial.

Did you buy that last sentence? Too bad, because I weaseled you, with the word "beneficial." Think about it.

Flavor and taste

These are two totally subjective words that allow us to claim marvelous things about products that are edible. Every cigarette in the world has claimed the best taste. Every supermarket has advertised the most flavorful meat. And let's not forget "aroma," a subdivision of this category. Wouldn't you like to have a nickel for every time a room freshener (a weasel in itself) told you it would make your home "smell fresh as all outdoors"? Well, they can say it, because smell, like taste and flavor, is a subjective thing. And, incidentally, there are no less than three weasels in that phrase. "Smell" is the first. Then, there's "as" (a substitute for the ever-popular "like"), and, finally, "fresh," which, in context, is a subjective comparison, rather than the primary definition of "new."

Now we can use an unlimited number of combinations of these

weasels for added impact. "Fresher-smelling clothes." "Fresher-tasting tobacco." "Tastes like grandma used to make." Unfortunately, there's no sure way of bringing these weasels down to size, simply because you can't define them accurately. Trying to ascertain the meaning of "taste" in any context is like trying to push a rope up a hill. All you can do is be aware that these words are subjective, and represent only one opinion—usually that of the manufacturer.

Style and good looks

Anyone for buying a new car? Okay, which is the one with the good looks? The smart new styling? What's that you say? All of them? Well, you're right. Because this is another group of subjective opinions. And it is the subjective and collective opinion of both Detroit and Madison Avenue that the following cars have "bold new styling": Buick Riviera, Plymouth Satellite, Dodge Monaco, Mercury Brougham, and you can fill in the spaces for the rest. Subjectively, you have to decide on which bold new styling is, indeed, bold new styling. Then, you might spend a minute or two trying to determine what's going on under that styling. The rest I leave to Ralph Nader.

Different, special, and exclusive

To be different, you have to be not the same as. Here, you must rely on your own good judgment and common sense. Exclusive formulas and special combinations of ingredients are coming at you every day, in every way. You must constantly assure yourself that, basically, all products in any given category are the same. So when you hear "special," "exclusive," or "different," you have to establish two things: on what basis are they different, and is that difference an important one? Let me give you a hypothetical example.

All so-called "permanent" antifreeze is basically the same. It is made from a liquid known as ethylene glycol, which has two amazing properties: It has a lower freezing point than water, and a higher boiling point than water. It does not break down (lose its properties), nor will it boil away. And every permanent antifreeze starts with it as a base. Also, just about every antifreeze has now got antileak ingredients, as well as antirust and anticorrosion ingredients. Now, let's suppose that, in formulating the product, one of the companies comes up with a solution that is pink in color, as opposed to all the others, which are blue. Presto—an exclusivity claim. "Nothing else looks like it, nothing else performs like it." Or how about, "Look at ours, and look at anyone else's. You can see the difference our exclusive formula makes." Granted, I'm exaggerating. But did I prove a point?

A Few More Goodies

At Phillips 66, it's performance that counts
Wisk puts its strength where the dirt is
At Bird's Eye, we've got quality in our corner
Delicious and long-lasting, too

Very quickly now, let's deflate those four lines. First, what the hell does "performance" mean? It means that this product will do what any other product in its category will do. Kind of a back-handed reassurance that this gasoline will function properly in your car. That's it, and nothing more. To perform means to function at a standard consistent with the rest of the industry. All products in a category are basically the same.

Second line: What does "strength" or "strong" mean? Does it mean "not weak"? Or "superior in power"? No, it means consistent with the norms of the business. You can bet your first-born that if Wisk were superior in power to other detergents, they'd be saying it, loud and clear. So strength is merely a description of a property inherent in all similar products in its class. If you really want to poke a pin in a bubble, substitute the word "ingredients" for the word "strength." That'll do it every time.

Third line: The old "quality" claim, and you fell for it. "Quality" is not a comparison. In order to do that, we'd have to say, "We've got better quality in our corner than any other frozen food." Quality relates only to the subjective opinion that Bird's Eye has of its own products, and to which it is entitled. The word "quality" is what we call a "parity" statement; that is, it tells you that it is as good as any other. Want a substitute? Try "equals," meaning "the same as."

Fourth line: How delicious is delicious? About the same as good-tasting is good-tasting, or fresher-smelling is fresher-smelling. A subjective opinion regarding taste, which you can either accept or reject. More fun, though, is "long-lasting." You might want to consider writing a note to Mr. Wrigley, inquiring as to the standard length of time which a piece of gum is supposed to last. Surely there must be a guideline covering it. The longest lasting piece of gum I ever encountered lasted just over four hours, which is the amount of time it took me to get it off the sole of my shoe. Try expressing the line this way: "It has a definite taste, and you may chew it as long as you wish." Does that place it in perspective?

There are two other aspects of weasel words that I should mention here. The first one represents the pinnacle of the copywriter's craft, and I call it the "Weasel of Omission." Let me demonstrate:

Of America's best-tasting gums, Trident is sugar-free

Disregard, for a moment, the obvious subjective weasel "best-tasting." Look again at the line. Something has been left out. Omitted very deliberately. Do you know what that word is? The word that's missing is the word "only," which should come right before the name of the product. But it doesn't. It's gone. Left out. And the question is, why? The answer is, the government wouldn't let them. You see, they start out by making a subjective judgment, that their gum is among the best-tasting. That's fine, as far as it goes. That's their opinion. But it is also the opinion of every other maker of sugar-free gum that his product is also among the best-tasting. And, since both of their opinions must be regarded as having equal value, neither one is allowed the superiority claim, which is what the word "only" would do. So Trident left it out. But the sentence is so brilliantly constructed, the word "only" is so heavily implied, that most people hear it, even though it hasn't been said. That's the Weasel of Omission. Constructing a set of words that forces you to a conclusion that otherwise could not have been drawn. Be on the lookout for what isn't said, and try to fill the gaps realistically.

The other aspect of weasels is the use of all those great, groovy, swinging, wonderful, fantastic, exciting and fun-filled words known as adjectives. Your eyes, ears, mind, and soul have been bombarded by adjectives for so long that you are probably numb to most of them by now. If I were to give you a list of adjectives to look out for, it would require the next five hundred pages, and it wouldn't do you any good, anyway. More important is to bear in mind what adjectives do, and then to be able to sweep them aside and distinguish only the facts.

An adjective modifies a noun, and is generally used to denote the quality or a quality of the thing named. And that's our grammar lesson for today. Realistically, an adjective enhances or makes more of the product being discussed. It's the difference between "Come visit Copenhagen," and "Come visit beautiful Copenhagen." Adjectives are used so freely these days that we feel almost naked, robbed, if we don't get at least a couple. Try speaking without adjectives. Try describing something; you can't do it. The words are too stark, too bare-boned, too factual. And that's the key to judging advertising. There is a direct, inverse proportion between the number of adjectives and the number of facts. To put it succinctly, the more adjectives we use, the less we have to say.

You can almost make a scale, based on that simple mathematical premise. At one end you have cosmetics, soft drinks, cigarettes, products that have little or nothing of any value to say. So we get them all dressed up with lavish word and thought images, and present you with thirty or sixty seconds of adjectival puffery. The other end of the scale is much harder to find. Usually, it will be occupied by a new product that is truly new or different. . . . Our craving for adjectives has become so overriding that we simply cannot listen to what is known as "nuts and bolts" advertising. The rest falls somewhere in the middle; a combination of adjectives, weasels, and semi-truths. All I can tell you is, try to brush the description aside, and see what's really at the bottom.

. . .

The Fruit Basket

In this country today there are probably more products with the word "lemon" on the label than there are lemons. It started as a fad; somebody got the idea of putting lemons into a household product, and whammo! The thing took off. Now there are lemons in detergents, cleaning products, shampoos, even toilet paper, and there's no end in sight. It brings up two very interesting points to make about this fad/trend gone wild.

Point one: What is it about the poor little lemon that holds so much magic? How can someone say of their product, "The juice of one whole lemon, one whole lemon sets you free?" Imagine being set free by a lemon. Someone else explains it: "Lemons are nature's own grease-cutters." Oh, I see. In other words, when God created lemons, He did so because He knew that, one day, we would be troubled by caked-on grease in our ovens. Or excessively oily hair. Or built-up wax on our kitchen floors. Why is it that everyone is into lemons? Especially when modern science, with its technology, has already developed grease-cutters, bleaches, and cleaning compounds that far and away exceed, in power, even the wildest delusions of grandeur of the lemon.

Probably because of the general trend of going back to nature, back to things that are pure and natural. As a country, we are finally becoming aware of the condition of our water and air and land, and we are trying to sublimate our guilt feelings by making some small gesture away from the artificial, chemical environment we have all helped to create. The manufacturers and the advertisers have cashed in on this knowledge, by sticking a lemon onto everything that isn't moving. The lemon stands for freshness, naturalness. Its color is clean, its scent is fresh and pleasant, and its connotation is of going back to nature. So we make our small gesture, while the manufacturers and advertising agencies make their big profits, and we forget one or two salient facts: The laundry detergents with lemons all over them are still basically detergents, full of polluting phosphates, harmful chemicals, and potentially dangerous enzymes; the lemon shampoo is still basically a detergent; the lemon-printed, lemon-scented toilet paper is still full of dye, which will continue polluting the water. But we are satisfying our guilts, and we will continue to participate in the trend.

You know what's ironic about all this? The advertising industry played a key role in making Americans aware of the continued destruction of our land. Now we're playing a key role in continuing it.

Point two: What makes you so sure that all the products with lemons on them are really made of lemons? What about all those sly weasels like "lemony," "the smell of real lemons," and "lemon-active"? And best of all, "lemon-refreshed Mr. Clean"? What do you think the chances are that a real, genuine lemon has gotten within fifty yards of those factories? . . . Chances are that most of these lemon-fresh things have been created out of chemicals. They're artificial. We have taken a trend, based on a genuine desire, and turned it around to our own use. The buzz word for this year is "lemon," and the magic is in the amount of products the word will sell, regardless of how it's phrased. You have been caught up in a buzz word whose good intentions have long since been swept under the rug.

And the end of the fad/trend is still not in sight. "Lime" is beginning to make a run at it, and will do well as an alternative, once you get saturated with "lemon." Watch also for "citrus" to carve a place. Want it wilder? How about strawberry face cream? It's available, you know. Another truly wonderful one is Peach Thrill, a dishwashing liquid. I think that by the time this thing has run its course, we of the Avenue will have exploited it to its fullest, including such things as "Tangerine-powered Top Job," "Avocadoey Ivory Snow," and the biggest sure-fire hit of all, "Prune-Activated Sani-Flush."

One more word about fads in general. To be fair to yourself, you must be able to distinguish between a fad and a trend. To do so, you need to discount the fad advertising, which is always a direct reflection of the product, and examine the product on its own merits. If this is impossible, vis-à-vis a direct mail sale, then forget about it altogether. The wait-and-see policy is generally the best one to follow; if the product has merit as a new category, it will be available for some time to come, and others will follow it. If it turns out to be a fly-by-night thing, you're better off without it. True fad advertising, for higher-priced products, will be high-pressure and have a note of urgency. In lower-priced products, it will try to capitalize on a current phrase or contemporary word. It may not hurt you in the low-priced area, but expensive fads can burn you badly.

Fun Foods

This category is devoted to things made to be ingested, which either have no nutritional or health value, or are not sold as having these values. I include beer, wine, soft drinks, coffee, tea, candy, and most breakfast cereals. As a general point of view, all of these are sold basically on emotionalism, because by definition they have nothing else to offer. Within that framework, I find that they break down into seven approaches, as follows:

1. Good, better, best. A statement by the manufacturer asserting that his product is the best one around. This is not a comparison of any kind; it is simply a subjective opinion being expressed by a somewhat partial judge.
2. Taste/taste imagery. Either a claim of superior taste, or one which attempts to describe the taste in imaginative terms. The latter is particularly evident in candies and cereals.
3. Best-selling/boast. We've already been through this one.
4. You. Remember in the chapter on claims, we talked about "saying something about the user"? It's rampant here, particularly in drinks.
5. Description/recipe. Often fun food advertising will simply describe itself in the most delicious terms, very often taking the form of a recipe. This is rather innocuous stuff, if you are alert to the weasels used.
6. Exploitation. A variation of the "fad" advertising, usually found with products that have been around a long time, and are now getting on the bandwagon.
7. Catch phrases. Most often used with kids, to try to start a fad, or as a memory device.

I have divided the fun food categories into each of the seven approaches. We begin with:

GOOD, BETTER, BEST

You can pay more, but you can't buy a better beer than Brew 102
The first malt liquor good enough to be called Budweiser
Gallo. Great wine from the new country
Isabel . . . Queen of Portuguese Rosé

Gallo. A better breed of duck
Cora, the world's finest vermouth
Hot Nestles' cocoa is the very best

TASTE/TASTE IMAGERY

Schmidt's Beer: give your thirst a taste of life
Piper Champagne . . . turns an occasion into a celebration
Mogen David Concord Grape Wine. Part of the sweet life
Taste the difference Taylor makes
Alexis Lichine wines are full of flavor
Lancer's . . . because it tastes so special
Piper. The jubilant champagne, imported from France
Enjoy the traditional flavor of Spain, in Spanada
Zapple . . . that cinnamon apple flavor will sure make your tongue happy
Henry Marchant. I make the most delicious cold duck in the world [also could apply to "Good, Better, Best" group]
Boone's Farm Apple Wine. A startling new drink with the fresh, crisp taste of juicy red apples
Diet Pepsi. Tastes so great, you'll do a double-take
Shasta Root Beer. The foam that you feel
Folger's. You can almost taste the aroma
Nestles' Strawberry Quik. It'll tickle you pink
Quik really satisfies your chocolate thirst
You make my mouth so happy, Caravelle [see Zapple!]
Krackel. It's got a taste you can hear
Sara Lee Chocolates . . . taste even better than you can imagine
Chocolate never felt as good as Choco-Lite
Milky Way satisfies your candy hunger [see Quik!]
Chunky. Extra thick for extra flavor
Sanders Milk Chocolate . . . melt-in-your-mouth good
Bosco, the chocolate syrup that tastes like chocolate candy
Hershey's Instant makes milk taste like a Hershey Bar
Fruity Pebbles taste like a bowl of noisy fruit
Cocoa Pebbles are cocoa-mocoa good
Alpha Bits . . . ABC Delicious
Quangeroos. It looks orange and tastes orange
Maple Zoom . . . rich maple flavor is added [weasel, ho!]
Cocoa Krispies . . . tastes like a chocolate milk shake, only crunchy
Count Chocula . . . super sweeties for monsterous chocolate flavor
Franken Berry . . . strawberry sweeties, for monsterous strawberry flavor

BEST-SELLING/BOASTING

When you say Budweiser, you've said it all

Paul Masson Very Cold Duck. It's America's best-selling premium cold duck
Martini & Rossi . . . it's a world favorite
Noilly Prat is the best-selling French dry vermouth in America
Nestea. America's favorite instant
There's more for you, more for me, in Nabisco's brand of candy
Everybody likes Kraft Fudgies
Famous people love Fifth Avenue candy bar

YOU

Schaeffer is the one beer to have when you're having more than one
Schaeffer: for the more than one beer man
Mogen David Pink Catawba Wine. You really should try it
Be a name-dropper. Propose Mogen David Blackberry Wine
Lejon Wooden Cask Chablis. For people who know something about wine
Lejon Champagne. For people who know something about life
Show that you care. Give the best there is. Harvey's Bristol Cream Sherry
Lancer's . . . for the good life
Dubonnet. Whenever you and your little old lady get together
Dr. Pepper. You've got to try it to love it
Lipton. The tea you never get tired of
Sanka Coffee. If caffeine adds to your day
What do you want most from coffee? That's what you get most from Hills

DESCRIPTION/RECIPE

It's the water that makes it Olympia Beer
Hamm's: a beer brewed with the water best for brewing
Cold-brewed Ballantine Beer
Manischewitz Cream White Concord. Double-blended for extra smoothness
Sal Misark. It really crackles
Boone's Farm Apple Wine. It's the wine that grows on trees
RC Cola: easy on the syrup, easy on the gas
Canada Dry Club Soda, with a long-lasting bubble
Tender Leaf: the strong tea with the tender name
Swee-Touch-Nee Iced Tea. The cooling refresher
Lipton. Like two bags of flavor in one
Lipton Instant Tea. The natural refresher
Bubbly, bubbly, bubbly Aero Bars
Chocolatey, chewy, long-lasting Tootsie Rolls
Captain Crunch is made crunchy to stay crunchy
Sugar Frosted cereal has a secret toasted-in sugar frosting

Sugar Pops . . . all puffed up with the good taste of sugar-toasted corn

EXPLOITATION

Rheingold natural beer
Korbel truly is a work of love
Cora. With a taste as delicate as love
Yago Sangria, the natural wine drink
Canada Dry Ginger Ale tastes like love

CATCH PHRASES

Colt 45 Malt Liquor: a completely unique experience
Michelob: the unexpected beer
Richard's Wild Irish Rosé Wine. It's the big one
Korbel . . . the first cold duck with a family tree
Share the wine. Italian Swiss Colony wine
Take life easy with Italian Swiss Colony wine
Cold Bear Wine. For a roaring good time
Wild Irish Rosé Wine. A whole new thing
7-Up, the Uncola
When you eat your Smartees, do you eat the red ones last?
Certs Gum is the kissing gum
Trix in the red box are still for kids
Sugar Smacks. A powerful breakfast food, Indian style
Buc Wheats . . . helps you feel like a million bucks

FOR DISCUSSION AND REVIEW

1. What are "weasel words"? Why do advertisers find them useful? Why is it important for the average American to know about weasel words? What are "qualifiers"?

2. As Stevens suggests, "tonight when you plop down in front of the boob tube for your customary three and a half hours of violence and/or situation comedies, take a pad and pencil, and keep score." Count the number of weasels that come up during the commercials. Make a list of ten or twelve of these and compare your list with those made by others in the class.

3. When an advertiser uses the word "like," he often creates a simile—"Ajax cleans *like* a white tornado." What, according to Stevens, is the advertiser's intent in using the simile?

4. What is a "Weasel of Omission"? Why is it difficult to detect? Cite several examples of this type of distortion from your own experience.

5. Why do you suppose that fruit images have such popular appeal in advertising? Consider, for example, the "BIC Banana." In this context discuss Stevens' suggestions or predictions about what will be fad trends in future advertising. Add some suggestions of your own.

6. What do you think a "buzz word" is? In addition to "lemon" what are some current "buzz words"? Discuss them.

NICHOLAS JOHNSON 2

The Corporate Censor

Nicholas Johnson, a former FCC commissioner, directs our attention to censorship in America—to the deliberate withholding of information from the public. While the government has been responsible for much censorship in the past, Johnson exposes another area of censorship—that by large, politically influential corporations. Since certain information is "inconsistent with corporate profits," it is often suppressed. Moreover, too often the public's airwaves are so thoroughly clogged with "intellectual pabulum" that no time remains for first-rate entertainment, social commentary, or coverage of public affairs. Citing the Dutch Television Network as a model, Johnson calls for television programming that will satisfy the full range of needs, tastes, and interests of the American people.

JULIAN GOODMAN, PRESIDENT OF NBC, BELIEVES THAT TELEVISION "is now under threat of restriction and control." Frank Stanton, president of CBS, says that "attempts are being made to block us." Elmer Lower, president of ABC News, thinks we may "face the prospect of some form of censorship."

I agree. Censorship *is* a serious problem in our country. My only dispute with these network officials involves just *who* is doing the censoring. They apparently believe it's the government. I disagree.

NBC recently cut Robert Montgomery's statements off the air when, during the Johnny Carson show, he mentioned a CBS station being investigated by the Federal Communications Commission. Folk singer Joan Baez was silenced by CBS when she wished to express her views about the Selective Service System on the Smothers Brothers show. Now, of course, the entire show has been canceled—notwithstanding the high ratings and its writers' recent Emmy. Sure there's censorship. But let's not be fooled into mistaking its source.

For at the same time that network officials are keeping off your television screens anything they find inconsistent with their corporate profits or personal philosophies, the FCC has been repeatedly defending their First Amendment rights against government censorship. Just recently, for example, the FCC ruled—over strong protests—that the networks' coverage of the Chicago Democratic Convention was protected by the Constitution's "freedom of the press" clause. In other decisions, the Commission refused to penalize radio station WBAI in New York for broadcasting an allegedly anti-Semitic poem, or a CBS-owned station for televising a "pot party."

Many broadcasters are fighting, not for *free* speech, but for *profitable* speech. In the WBAI case, for example, one of the industry's leading spokesmen, *Broadcasting* magazine, actually urged that WBAI be *punished* by the FCC—and on the same editorial page professed outrage that stations might not have an unlimited right to broadcast profitable commercials for cigarettes which may result in illness or death.

This country is a great experiment. For close to 200 years we have been testing whether it is possible for an educated and informed people to govern themselves. All considered, the experiment has worked pretty well. We've had our frustrations and disappointments as a nation, but no one has been able to come up with a better system, and most of the newer nations still look to us as a model.

Central to our system, however, is the concept of an educated and an informed people. As Thomas Jefferson said: "The way to prevent error is to give the people full information of their affairs." Our founding fathers were familiar with censorship by the King of England. They were going to replace a king with a representative Congress. But they were concerned lest any American institution become powerful enough to impede the flow of information to the people. So they provided in the First Amendment that *"Congress* shall make no law . . . abridging the freedom of speech. . . ." Why "Congress"? I believe they assumed Congress would be the only body powerful enough to abridge free speech. They were wrong.

A lot has happened to the creation and control of information in this country since 1789. That was an age of town meetings and handbills. Today most information comes from the three broadcasting networks, ABC, CBS, and NBC, and the two wire services, Associated Press and United Press International. As Professor John Kenneth Galbraith has reminded us in *The New Industrial State,* 70 years ago the large corporation confined itself to mass production in heavy industry. "Now," he writes, "it also sells groceries, mills grain, publishes newspapers, and provides public entertainment, all activities that were once the province of the individual proprietor or the insignificant firm."

It is easy for us to forget how large, profitable, and politically powerful some corporations have become. In 1948 about half of all manufacturing assets in the United States were controlled by 200 corporations; today a mere 100 corporations hold that power. A single corporation such as American Telephone and Telegraph (one of the FCC's many regulated companies) controls the wages and working conditions of 870,000 employees, purchases each year some $3.5 billion in goods and services, has assets of $37 billion, and has annual gross revenues in excess of $14 billion. This gross revenue is several times larger than the combined budgets of all the federal regulatory commissions, the federal court system, and the U.S. Congress; larger than the budget of each of the 50 states; a larger operation, indeed, than all but very few foreign governments.

I am not suggesting that large corporations are inherently evil. Not at all. They have created much of our wealth. I am merely urging that we be aware of the fact that large corporations have the incentive and the power to control the information reaching the citizenry of our free society.

Sometimes corporate pressures to control what you see on television are just plain silly. For example, in his book *TV—The Big Picture,* Stan Opotowsky reports that "Ford deleted a shot of the New York skyline because it showed the Chrysler building. . . . A breakfast-food sponsor deleted the line 'She eats too much' from a play because, as far as the breakfast-food company was concerned, nobody could ever eat too much." Often, however, corporate tampering with the product of honest and capable journalists and creative writers and performers can be quite serious. Sometimes there is a deliberate alteration of content; sometimes needed information is squeezed out by more profitable "entertainment" programming.

On February 10, 1966, the Senate was conducting hearings on the Vietnam war. Fred Friendly, who was president of CBS News at the time, wanted you to be able to watch those hearings. His network management did not permit you to watch. If you were watching CBS that day you saw, instead of George Kennan's views opposing the Vietnam war, the fifth rerun of *I Love Lucy.* Fred Friendly quit CBS because of this decision, and subsequently wrote *Due to Circumstances Beyond Our Control* to tell the story. He began his book with the quotation, "What the American people don't know can kill them." Indeed it can. In Vietnam, about 35,000 so far. We have been shown miles of film from Vietnam, it's true. But how much has television told you about the multibillion-dollar corporate profits from that war?

There are many other situations in which censorship exists side-by-side with large profits—and disease or death. The tobacco industry spends about $250 million a year on radio and television commercials designed to associate cigarette smoking, especially by the young, with fishing, football, the fresh air of the great outdoors, sexual prowess, and all other desirable attributes of a fun-packed adult world. In exchange for this investment, the industry sells on the order of $9 billion worth of cigarettes a year. Would it really surprise you to learn that the broadcasting industry has been less than eager to tell you about the health hazards of cigarette smoking? It shouldn't. Just recently, for example, a United States congressman alleged that the president of the National Association of Broadcasters had suppressed from Congress and the American public revealing information about the "substantial appeal to youth" of radio and television cigarette commercials. The relation of this forgetfulness to profits is clear: cigarette advertising provides the largest single source of television's revenue, about 8 percent.

The FCC has ruled that broadcasters can't present one point of view on a controversial issue and censor all others just to serve their own beliefs and profits. The "Fairness Doctrine" requires that all viewpoints be presented. The FCC applied this doctrine to cigarette commercials. And what was the response of the broadcasting industry? It fought the decision with all the economic and political strength at its command. It has finally gone all the way to the Supreme Court to argue that a doctrine which limits its power to keep *all* information about the health hazards of cigarette smoking from the American people is a violation of broadcasters' First Amendment rights!

Or how about the 50,000 people who die each year on our highways? Their deaths are due to many causes, of course, including their own intoxication and carelessness. But how many television stations told you—either before or after Ralph Nader came along—

that most auto-safety engineers agree virtually *all* those lives could be saved if our cars were designed properly? Nader, in *Unsafe at Any Speed,* speculates about the "impact which the massive sums spent ($361,060,000 in 1964 on auto advertising alone) have on the communications media's attention to vehicle safety design."

Television certainly didn't take the lead in telling us about the unfit meat, fish, and poultry. (Chet Huntley was found to have been editorializing *against* the Wholesome Meat Act at a time when he and his business partners were heavy investors in the cattle and meat business!) Bryce Rucker, in *The First Freedom,* notes that:

> Networks generally have underplayed or ignored events and statements unfavorable to food processors and soap manufacturers. Recent examples are the short shrift given Senate subcommittee hearings on, and comments favorable to, the 1966 "truth in packaging" bill and the high cost of food processing. Could it be that such behavior reflects concern for the best interests of, say, the top-50 grocery-products advertisers, who spent $1,314,893,000 in TV in 1965, 52.3 percent of TV's total advertising income?

What could be more essential than information about potentially harmful food and drugs?

All Americans are concerned about "the crime problem." Have you ever stopped to wonder why the only crimes most of us hear about are, in the words of the Presidential Commission on Law Enforcement and Administration of Justice, "the crimes that are the easiest for the poor and the disadvantaged to commit . . ."? What we haven't been told is that much of the crime in the United States is "white collar" crime; that the rich steal as much as or more than the poor. As the Crime Commission report defined it:

> The "white collar" criminal is the broker who distributes fraudulent securities, the builder who deliberately uses defective material, the corporation executive who conspires to fix prices, the legislator who peddles his influence and vote for private gain, or the banker who misappropriates funds. . . .

Did you ever find out from television, for example, that a *single* recent price-fixing case involved a "robbery" from the American people of more money than was taken in *all* the country's robberies, burglaries, and larcenies during the years of that criminal price fixing? The crime commission declared that "it is essential that the public become aware of the seriousness of business crime." Why is it the news media do not tell you about *these* threats to "law and order"?

One could go on and on. The inherent dangers in cyclamates (the artificial sweeteners in soft drinks) have been so widely discussed in Sweden that the government is considering prohibiting their use. The danger is scarcely known to the average American. Most of the nation's 160,000 coal miners have "black lung" disease (the disintegration of the lung from coal dust) in one form or another. Mine operators may refuse to pay for fresh-air masks—or support workmen's compensation legislation. Some television stations in coal-mining areas have, until recently, refused to televise programs offered them by doctors about this serious health hazard. Reports differ, and no one knows for sure, but one current sampling showed that 20 percent of the color-TV sets studied were emitting excess X-ray radiation. Natural-gas pipelines are exploding as predicted. And did you know that the life expectancy of the average American adult male has been *declining* in recent years? The list goes on almost without end.

Note what each of these items has in common: (1) human death, disease, dismemberment or degradation, (2) great profit for manufacturers, advertisers, and broadcasters, and (3) the deliberate withholding of needed information from the public.

Many pressures produce such censorship. Some are deliberate, some come about through default. But all have come, not from government, but from private corporations with something to sell. Charles Tower, chairman of the National Association of Broadcasters Television Board, recently wrote a letter to *The New York Times* criticizing its attack on CBS for "censoring" the social commentary on the Smothers Brothers show. He said,

> There is a world of difference between the deletion of program material by Government command and the deletion by a private party [such as a broadcaster]. . . . Deletion by Government command is censorship. . . . Deletion of material by private parties . . . is not censorship.

Another *Times* reader wrote in answer to Mr. Tower: "Mr. Tower's distinction . . . is spurious. The essence of censorship is the suppression of a particular point of view . . . over the channels of the mass media, and the question of who does the censoring is one of form only. . . ."

He's right. The results *are* the same. You and I are equally kept in ignorance, ill-prepared to "prevent error," and to engage in the process of self-governing which Thomas Jefferson envisioned—regardless of *who* does the censoring.

A number of talented people *within* the broadcasting industry recognize its failings. One of the nation's leading black announcers told me of his first job as a disc jockey. He was handed a stack of records, but forbidden to read any news over the air. Said his boss: "You're not going to educate the Negroes of this community at my expense." A high ABC network executive was recently quoted in the pages of *TV Guide* as saying, "There are many vital issues that we won't go near. We censor ourselves." Eric Sevareid has said of the pressures involved in putting together a network news show: "The ultimate sensation is that of being bitten to death by ducks." And the executive editor of the San Francisco *Chronicle* has warned: "The press is in danger. Not the exciting kind of Hollywood danger, but of dissolving into a gray mass of nonideas." For it is also a form of censorship to so completely clog the public's airwaves with tasteless gruel that there is no time left for quality entertainment and social commentary, no time "to give the people full information of their affairs." Mason Williams, the multitalented one-time writer for the Smothers Brothers, has left television in disgust and written a poem about his experiences with "The Censor," who, he says in conclusion,

Snips out
The rough talk
The unpopular opinion
Or anything with teeth
And renders
A pattern of ideas
Full of holes
A doily
For your mind

Your mind. My mind. The mind of America.

The Rolling Stones said it long ago:

When I'm drivin' in my car,
When the man comes on the radio,
He's tellin' me more and more
About some useless information . . .
Supposed to fire my imagination? . . .
*I can't get no satisfaction!**

Many Americans are trying to say something to each other. But the media haven't been listening. And you haven't been told. So some have turned to violence as a means of being heard. All you've been shown are the dramatic pictures; you know there's "something happening." But, like the Everyman of Bob Dylan's song, "You don't know what it is, do you, Mr. Jones?" The "silent screen" of television has left you in ignorance as to what it's all about.

The time may soon come when the media will have to listen. From many directions come suggestions for change. Law professor Jerome Barron says the courts should recognize a "public right of access to the mass media." Free speech in this age of television, he believes, requires that citizens with something to say be permitted to say it over radio and television. Suppose you approach a television station with a "commercial" you have prepared either supporting or protesting the President's conduct of the Vietnamese war. It may no longer be sufficient for the station to say to you, "Sorry, we don't like your views, so we won't broadcast your announcement"—as a San Francisco station did last year to those trying to express their point of view regarding a *ballot proposition!* As the U.S. Supreme Court said a few days ago in the Red Lion case, upholding the constitutionality of the FCC's Fairness Doctrine:

> There is no sanctuary in the First Amendment for unlimited private censorship operating in a medium not open to all. Freedom of the press from governmental interference under the First Amendment does not sanction repression of that freedom by private interests.

It is too early to know the full, ultimate impact of this decision.

In Holland, any group that can get 15,000 persons to support its list of proposed programs is awarded free time on the Dutch Television Network for a monthly program. There is even an organization for tiny and often eccentric splinter groups without 15,000 supporters. If a similar experiment were conducted in this country, groups interested in electronic music, drag racing, handicrafts, camping, as well as the League of Women Voters, the National Association for the Advancement of Colored People, local school boards, theater and drama associations, the Young Republicans (and, who knows, even the Smothers Brothers), could obtain television time to broadcast programs prepared under their supervision.

Or each network might devote a full one-third of its prime time (6 P.M. to 11 P.M.) programming to something other than entertainment or sports. It could be nonsponsored cultural, educational, and public-affairs programming; if the networks were required to stagger such fare, then at any given time during the 6 P.M. to 11 P.M. period of greatest audiences the American viewer would have an alternative, a *choice*. There would still be at all times *two* networks with the commercial-laden, lowest-common-denominator mass entertainment of situation comedies, Westerns, quiz shows and old movies. The third, however, would have something else.

It would be wholly inappropriate for me as an FCC Commissioner to insist that broadcasters present only the information, ideas, and entertainment that I personally find compatible. The FCC does not have, and would not want, the responsibility of selecting your television programs. But it would be equally irresponsible for me to sit idly by and watch the corporate censors keep from your TV screen the full range of needs, tastes, and interests of the American people.

The television-station owner, not the network, has ultimate responsibility for his programming. But somebody has to select his programs, you say; nobody's perfect. You're right. And all I'm urging is that, when in doubt, all of us—audience, networks, and government—ought to listen a little more carefully to the talented voices of those who are crying out to be heard. In short, I would far rather leave the heady responsibility for the inventory in America's "marketplace of ideas" to talented and uncensored *individuals*—creative writers, performers, and journalists from *all* sections of this great country—than to the *committees* of frightened financiers in New York City. Wouldn't you? I think so.

FOR DISCUSSION AND REVIEW

1. Since television cannot possibly report on everything that happens in the world, just as no single individual can experience everything, what, then, constitutes censorship? How does it differ from selectivity? Why is it undesirable?

2. By Johnson's definition, does not the FCC itself act as a "censor"? Are there important differences between the censorship practiced by the FCC and that practiced by large corporations? If so, what are these differences?

3. Public school teachers experience a great deal of pressure from various groups to exclude books from classroom use. Some of the most frequently assailed books are *The Catcher in the Rye, The Inner City Mother Goose, Soul on Ice, Huckleberry Finn, 1984, The Grapes of Wrath, Gulliver's Travels,* and, more recently, *Jonathan Livingston Seagull.* Probably some of these books have been read by members of your class. Discuss why these books might have been attacked. How justified are the attacks?

4. The following note, first published in *Time* (December 11, 1972), is another example of censorship, this time from an unexpected quarter:

Bowdler in Oregon

Some American place names have a unique resonance about them—places like Maggie's Nipples, Wyo., or Greasy Creek, Ark., Lickskillet, Ky., or Scroungeout, Ala. Collectors of Americana also savor Braggadocio, Mo., the Humptulips River in Washington, Hen Scratch, Fla., Dead Irishman Gulch, S. Dak., Cut 'N Shoot, Texas, Helpmejack Creek, Ark., Bastard Peak, Wyo., Goon Dip Mountain, Ark., Tenstrike, Minn., Laughing Pig, Wyo., Two Teats, Calif., or Aswaguscawadic, Me.

Not the least flavorsome was a sylvan place called Whorehouse Meadows, outside of Ontario, Ore. The meadow was named, with admirable directness, for some local women who once profitably entertained sheepherders there. But last week, the Oregon Geographic Names Board filed an official objection to a bit of bowdlerization by the Federal Bureau of Land Management. It discovered that the bureau, in drawing up a map of the area, had changed the name from Whorehouse Meadows to Naughty Girl Meadows. The bureau also cleaned up a nearby spot, deftly retitling it Bullshirt Springs, a change so small that the natives see no reason to contest it.

How are places and landmarks named? Why are some names more colorful than others? What is lost in the name changes mentioned in the *Time* article?

ALFRED F. ROSA AND PAUL A. ESCHHOLZ 3

Bunkerisms: Archie's Suppository Remarks in "All in the Family"

No recent television show has had a greater impact on the American public than the CBS situation comedy "All in the Family." Hardly a day passes without a writer commenting on the possible effects of the bigotry that is the major theme of the series. Archie's bigotry, like most prejudice, is embodied and manifested in his language. His persistent use of terms of ethnic abuse and his subconsciously motivated plays on words have become hallmarks of "All in The Family."

ON JANUARY 12, 1971, AMERICAN TELEVISION VIEWERS WERE FIRST introduced to "All in the Family." Now, at the end of its second highly successful year, the Bunker family is an American institution. This award-winning show reaches an estimated fifty to one hundred million viewers weekly. It has spawned a huge commercial enterprise offering such items as sweatshirts, T-shirts, posters, ashtrays, beer mugs, and "Bunker Stickers"; many of these items have a "Bunker for President" motif. The latest addition to this commercial bonanza is *The Wit & Wisdom of Archie Bunker,* a book containing the most humorous lines and sequences from the show. Indeed, the book indicates that the humor of the show derives not only from the fact that it is a situational comedy but also from Archie's use of language.

Archie's command of the language is legendary; viewers have witnessed him criticize Mike for reacting "on the sperm of the moment," castigate Edith for taking things "out of contest," and tell his family that his prejudice is a "pigment of their imaginations." Archie's use of malapropisms, spoonerisms, and "Bunkerisms" is one aspect of the show that deserves to be examined. These word formations are a major element in distinguishing "All in the Family" from other television situational comedies.

The manipulation of language for comic purposes is not a recent development. Shakespeare's Mistress Quickly in *Henry IV Parts I* and *II* and *Henry V* and Dogberry in *Much Ado About Nothing* are notorious for their comic misuse of the language. Mistress Quickly in *Henry V* claims that she is sure that Falstaff's is "in Arthur's bosom" and Dogberry states his belief that "comparisons are odorous." It is, however, Richard Sheridan's infamous Mrs. Malaprop who lends her name to this type of inappropriate usage. One recalls that in *The Rivals* she implores Lydia to "promise to forget this fellow—to illiterate him quite from [her] memory." The malapropism, in short, is the misapplication of a word; malapropisms indicate not only the ignorance but also the vanity and affectation of their speakers and in "All in the Family" Archie uses many of these malapropisms:[1]

What is this, the United Nations? We gotta have a whole addenda?
I come home and tell you one o' the great antidotes of all times, an item of real human interest, and you sit there like you're in a comma.
You sound like a regular Billie Sol Graham!
"Sorry" ain't gonna clench my thirst.
. . . as one of your faithful constitutionals.
You're taking it out of contest.
. . . you gotta grab the bull by the corns and heave-ho.
. . . this nation under God shall not diminish from the earth.
I don't need their whole Dun and Broadstreet.
We got a regular Edna St. Louis Millet here.
If he don't yell "pig" or none of them other epaulets, . . .
Ain't he took the exercise tax offa cars?
No, Edith. I was out expectin' the street lights.
How'd I know you had extensions to bein' an egghead.
. . . we don't want people thinking we live in no pig's eye.
Let's take a look here and see what new subversion you got fermentin' here.
. . . he's comin' over to claim his pound of fish.
It's the survivor of the fitness!
Them eggs are starting to foment.

[1] Examples used in this paper have been taken from *The Wit & Wisdom of Archie Bunker* (Popular Library), the record "All in the Family" (Atlantic), and the television show itself.

I received your leaflet at my home residence and the words "substantial profit" fought my eye.
It ain't German to this conversation.
It's like looking for a needle in a hayride!
Call it a father's intermission . . . but I smell a rat.
You're invading the issue.
No doubt about it there's somethin' broken off in there and it's ledged between the nervous system and the brain. . . .
Looking like it's straight outta Missile Impossible, . . .
Cold enough to freeze a witch's mitt.
It's some of that Morgan David wine.
You been standing on that phone like a pillow of salt.
. . . 'cause Cousin Oscar is leavin' here, in post and haste.
Rudy and me was as close as two peas in a pot.
I give ya the biggest build-up since Grant took Richard.
. . . right outta Science Friction.
For better or for worse, in secrets and in health till death do us part?
. . . on the sperm of the moment.
It's like trying to make a sow's purse outta silk!
We can suspense with the hellos, Edith.
Whoever sent 'em obviously wanted to remain unanimous.
I'll believe that when hell freezes under.

Several of the mistakes that Archie makes such as confusing *antidote* and *anecdote* and *ferment* and *foment* excite nervous laughter because we have all fallen into the trap at one time or another. Archie's pendant for name dropping betrays his ignorance and his inner desire to be more than the average American breadwinner. Although he is very funny, much of his humor is the product of dramatic irony; his use of clichés, humorous because of their inaccuracies, displays his lack of true wit and imagination.

Some of Archie's slips produce made-up or nonsense words which are akin to the spoonerism, an unintentional transposition of sounds, especially prefixes and suffixes, in spoken language. These bloopers are spontaneous and are not the product of ignorance or vanity. Some that Archie has used are:

What am I, a clairavoyage or somethin'?
. . . what you call, connubible difficulties . . .
It's gonna take a lotta thinkin' and it's gonna take all my consecretion.
One of these days I will probably de-head myself.
It was said under dupress.
. . . making you an excessity after the fact!
It's a regular facsamile of the Apollo 14.
Like the Presidential, the Senatorial, the Governororial, the Mayororial . . .
These things ain't exactly hairlooms, you know.

'Cause *that* evening is indeniably etched in my heart along with other strong memories of the past—. . .
It's inedibly etched in my mind.
He had the infrontery to imply that . . .
. . . what you might call a certain lack of drive—you know, personal inititianative.
Make this meathead take the literaracy test.
I remember some of the beauties you hung around with, and they wasn't exactly no "Madonises."
Now lay off the social menuneties.
He's a morphidite.
. . . nothin' but out in out *porna*graphy.
. . . some ground rules and some priorororities.
And then write yourself a little note—you know, like a reminder-andum.
. . . you'd be layin' on that floor waitin' for Rigor Morris to set in.
I ain't saying' it's largesse, smallesse or no' kinda esse.
Redeeming socialness is where they do the same old pornagraphs but they give ya some four-dollar words while they're doin' it.
. . . a kind of special stanima . . .
You didn't go and do something unlegal, you big dumb Polack?
You've got a warfed sense of humor.

Two techniques that the show's writers use in the creation of these nonsense words are the use of mnemonic devices and analogies. Archie remembers *accessory* because it is "something extra," *facsimile* because it is the "same as," and *memorandum* because it "reminds." The analogy process, *dehead, Governororial, smallesse, socialness,* and *unlegal,* is commonly found among children who are trying to cope with the complexities of the English language. These usages are laughable since Archie is trying to apply logic where tradition holds sway.

As humorous as Archie's malapropisms and made-up words are, the comedy of "All in the Family" relies heavily on a special variety of these two—the Bunkerism. Expressions such as "distinguished incrumbent," "Englebum Hunkerdunk," "dem bamboons," "like the immaculate connection," "pushy imported ricans," "Welfare incipients," and "A regular Marco Polish" are Bunkerisms. In addition to showing Archie's ignorance and pretentiousness, they illustrate his prejudicial nature. It is Archie's narrow-mindedness that is the essence of the Bunkerism. In *The Wit & Wisdom of Archie Bunker,* Archie's comic usages of the language are referred to as "Archie-isms." While this label recognizes the unique quality of Archie's speech, it does not effectively label his coinages. After all, Archie is the arch-conservative and arch-debunker, and all his remarks are in one way or another "suppository." In a conversation with Edith, Archie says:

You think he's a nice boy after he did what he did? Comin' in here, makin' suppository remarks about our country. And calling me prejudiced, while I was singin' "God Bless America," a song written by a well-known and respected Jewish guy. Milton Berlin.

Although Archie objects to someone else's derogatory remarks, the comment in this context says more about Archie's bigoted attitude.

Certain types of situations within the show give rise to the Bunkerism. When Archie is trapped by logic, usually by Mike, has an audience and wishes to appear as a "know-it-all," is embarrassed by or impatient with Edith, is nervous when confronted by a member of a minority group, or is forced to talk about taboo subjects, he loses control of the language and produces Bunkerisms, either proper words in the wrong context or made-up words, both of which have pejorative connotations. Some of the Bunkerisms of the first category include:

Why don't you write a letter to dear Abie?
And who are you supposed to be—Blackberry Finn?
Yeah, well, we can't help bunkin' into each other now and then. . . .
I personally don't agree with all the conflagration on the college campuses. . . .
Just who in hell are we entertaining here tonight? The Count of Monte Crisco?
Throwin' debriss at officers of the law . . . Desecrating on the American flag.
It's a proven fact that Capital Punishment is a known detergent for crime.
And you don't need to draw me any diaphragms neither!
. . . who weren't fortunate enough to be born with the same natural endorsements.
If tampering with the United States mail is a federal offense, so is excitement to riot.
It's for when you get one of them hot flushes.
We've got the world's grossest national product.
You coming here, a priest, hiding behind your hassock—. . .
I'll let you know when I—in my intimate wisdom—decide that the time has ripened.
You and that Reverend Bleedin' Heart Felcher up there in his ivory shower.
Don't take everything so liberally.
Look I know you'se kids go by what you call this new mortality—. . .
This political percussion is over as of here and now.
In them days Notre Dame was playing hardknocks football! No fat scholarships, none of them pet parties—. . .
Until then *I'm* king, the princess is upstairs, and you're the pheasant that has to keep her here!
It's just a pigment of your imagination.

And position is nine-tenths of the law, right?
Smells like a house of ill refute if ya ask me.
I call Chinese food chinks 'cause that what it is . . . chinks.
There was no slurp intended against the Chinese.
Lady, you wanna stoop this conversation down to the gutter level, that's your derogative.
The sexual submissiveness? It don't matter whatever time of day or night—well, that's your dimissive society.
He takes that for granted. It's a tactic understanding.

Bunkerisms akin to spoonerisms are:

She's hangin' around my neck like an Albacross.
Comin' in here full of ascusations . . .
. . . and wouldn't be related to me for complexionary reasons.
One religion. Until they started splitting 'em up 'til all them other denumerations.
'Cause if I hadda face that bum on a full stomach, I'd detergerate . . .
It ain't a very fancy theory, but it's all mine. Lionel—Familyarity breeds content!
Your mother-in-law and me don't make no fatish over birthdays.
What you see here is a frigment of your imagination.
He comes from the gretto.
Back to the groinocologist!
. . . the worst hypochondrijerk in the neighborhood . . .
. . . infilterating into our own house, Edith.
Which is just an excuse for Commie infliteration!
What do you mean by that insinuendo?
. . . insurruption of the campuses.
If you two malinjerers want anything . . .
Your mother ain't got no preconscrewed ideas.
. . . and confirm the Bunkers is goin' to Florida as prederanged.
You ain't gonna sell me none of your pregressive pinko welfare ideas . . .
The man don't have one regleaming feature.
He's got some big move up his sleeve that he can't revulge yet!
Well, goodbye and good ribbons.
People like your mother gotta be unpartial 'cause they got no subconceived notions.
The statements I made were supposed to be sub-rosy.
In my day we used to keep things in their proper suspective.
Don't you never read the papers about all them unflocked priests running around?

Laura Hobson in an article for the *New York Times* entitled "As I Listened to Archie Say 'Hebe' . . ." criticizes the show for its implicit claims of complete and honest bigotry and what to her appears to be a very subtle manipulation of language. She claims that the show's producers have managed to make a distinction between "acceptable" terms of ethnic abuse and those which would be truly offensive. This, she contends, falsely permits Archie to be a lovable bigot and bigotry itself to be not so bad after all. Although Miss Hobson recognizes the subtlety of the ethnic terms used on the show, she fails to see the full import of the self-debunking Bunkerism. There is a general impression that Archie is only "done out" in the waning moments of the show; however, the unintentional self-deprecating nature of the Bunkerism serves to undermine Archie's bigotry throughout the whole show. The writers have successfully employed an age-old comic device in a contemporary setting to fulfill their satiric intentions.

FOR DISCUSSION AND REVIEW

1. What is a malapropism? What is a Spoonerism? How do they differ?

2. What is a Bunkerism, and how is it related to both malapropisms and Spoonerisms?

3. In the concluding paragraph, the authors point out that Laura Hobson contends that Archie's language is subtly manipulated to make bigotry seem, in their words, "not so bad after all." Rosa and Eschholz, however, argue that "the unintentional self-deprecating nature of the Bunkerism serves to undermine Archie's bigotry throughout the whole show." Do you agree with Hobson or with Rosa and Eschholz, or with neither? Explain.

RUSSELL BAKER 4

Politigabble

How many times have you heard political campaign speeches and wondered what was really being said? How often have you listened to speeches that sound alike from politicians with completely different philosophies? Russell Baker's satiric translations of political jargon, reprinted from Poor Russell's Almanac, *indicate why voting often turns into a guessing game.*

IN A PRESIDENTIAL ELECTION YEAR, THE POLITICIANS ARE HIP DEEP in New Hampshire snow at this season, and it is time to start listening to them.

Following are some translations into English from that strange tongue, Politigabble:

"My fellow Americans"—"Anybody who switches to the channel showing the movie is unpatriotic."

"It's wonderful to be back here in the American heartland"—"What's the name of this dump?"

"Let's look at the record"—"Let's not."

"Peace with honor"—"War."

"Never has the threat to democratic government been graver . . ."

—"My polls show I am likely to get beaten."

"Let us never heed extremists from both sides"—"What's wrong with taking a little money from the oil industry?"

"Without regard to race, creed or color"—"Ho hum."

"Many people have asked me to spell out my position on American policy toward subsidies for the rectified juice industry"—"My ghost writer thinks there's some political mileage in this, so I agreed to try it."

"Let us remember that these wonderful young people are our citizens of tomorrow"—"At present, however, they are still just punks."

"On the way over here a little girl came up to me and said . . ."—"This isn't really true, of course, but my television adviser says it is good for my image to tell absurd anecdotes like this."

"I shall never stoop to smear and innuendo"—"The polls show I have it won if I play it cool."

"Let us not judge a man by the way he cuts his hair"—"I trust everyone has noticed that my opponent has not cut his for more than a year."

"My opponent's religion should not be an issue in this campaign, and I will never heed the advice of those who are urging me to make it an issue"—"In case it has not been generally observed here, I would like to point out that he adheres to a minority sect with extremely odd views on transsubstantiation."

"And standing there in that kibbutz, I said . . ."—"No Arab, I."

"My opponent has sought to sell himself as though he were a powder for the relief of acid indigestion through the use of the most expensive campaign of television huckstering in the history of American government. This crass commerical cheapening of public office is a vice in which I shall never indulge."—"I am in truly desperate need of funds to purchase television time."

"As Walter Bagehot once said of politics . . ."—"Will any intellectuals in the audience please note that I have a ghost writer who knows who Walter Bagehot is, and will tell me if I want to know?"

"The disgruntled young must learn to work effectively within the system for the reforms they so ardently desire"—"Do as I say, and in time you may be elected to public office to do as I don't, and have no intention of doing."

". . . *and I pledge myself to the defense of the Constitution of the United States"*—"Upon being elected, I shall immediately offer six amendments to the Constitution to do away with certain unconstitutional provisions now embedded in that document, and to make constitutional certain practices which it now, unfortunately, forbids."

"How wonderful it is to get away from Washington and be back

here with the people!"—"At least it gives my liver that rest the doctor ordered."

"Now, I am going to be perfectly honest about this"—"Oh no, I'm not."

FOR DISCUSSION AND REVIEW

1. Do any of the specific phrases in Baker's list remind you of contemporary personalities? Explain.

2. From your analysis of the statements and translations that Baker offers, is it possible to make any generalizations about the relationships among length and clarity and precision? Explain.

3. Make a list of current "politigabble" expressions and provide a translation for each phrase.

OTTO FRIEDRICH 5

A Vivacious Blonde Was Fatally Shot Today or How to Read a Tabloid

Because newspapers are primarily business enterprises, newspaper editors must always be conscious of their audience—the readers. Tabloid newspapers are certainly no exception. In this article, which appeared in The American Scholar, *Otto Friedrich, an editor at* Time *and a journalist for more than twenty years, takes an inside look at the world of the tabloid. He examines tabloid prose ("the art of exaggerating without actually lying"), editorial policies, and the product—a newspaper that creates a kind of Shangri-la for the reader.*

THERE IS A JOKE AMONG NEWSPAPERMEN THAT IF A WOMAN IS pretty, she is called "beautiful"; if she is plain, she is called "attractive"; and if she is hideous, she is called "vivacious." Half the joke is the exaggeration; the other half is that this is no exaggeration at all. In describing a woman involved in a murder or a robbery or a divorce case, the same technique is generally applied to every aspect of her appearance. If she is tall, she is "statuesque." If she is short, the word is "petite." Thin women are "slender," while fat ones are "curvaceous." Physical appearance is not so important in a man, and the emphasis shifts to financial appearance. "Socially prominent" is a popular description of any man who is murdered by his wife.

Bookies and gigolos may be identified as "sportsmen." And one connoisseur has defined "socialite" as "a tabloid term meaning human being."

This form of wordmanship—the art of exaggerating without actually lying—is so common in tabloid newspapers that it may be termed tabloid prose, but it is by no means restricted to tabloids. Indeed, most newspapers and most wire services use it much of the time. Tabloid prose is not merely a corruption of the English language, however. Literary critics tell us that form cannot be disassociated from content, and since many writers of tabloid prose are intelligent and cultivated people, the reason for the use of a word such as "curvaceous" may be found in the mentality of the person for whom it is written. More accurately, the reason lies in the editor's concept of the mentality of the person who can be enticed by such words into surrendering his five or ten cents.

Despite all its pretenses of representing the public, the average newspaper is simply a business enterprise that sells news and uses that lure to sell advertising space. It is scarcely different from enterprises selling shoes or grass seed. Like any other business, a newspaper obeys the law of supply and demand, and most newspapers have discovered that a sex murder attracts more readers than does a French cabinet crisis. Murder, however, is a fairly commonplace event—one a day is the average in New York alone—and the tabloid editor therefore makes distinctions between what are known as "classy cases" and "cheap cases."

It is commonly believed that a reader's interest is attracted by a case with which he can identify himself—there but for the grace of God, et cetera. But if the average tabloid reader were murdered, his misfortune would not receive much coverage in the average tabloid. He would be a "cheap case." Essentially, a cheap case involves what tabloid editors consider to be cheap people. This includes all working-class people, such as factory hands, waitresses and the unemployed. It also includes farmers, usually brushed aside as "hillbilly stuff." Alcoholics, whose antics are sometimes extremely entertaining, come under the same ban. So do Negroes, Mexicans, Puerto Ricans and other "lesser breeds without the law." This causes some difficulties for the wire services since the current fashion is to delete any references to a criminal's race as "irrelevant." Thus an editor who might begin by showing great interest in a murder would cut the story down to a few paragraphs after learning that it involved a "Jig," but he would not publicly divulge the dread word that motivated his editing—and, of course, his editorial columns would continue to clamor for civil rights.

There is another subdivision of the cheap case that the editor generally describes as "too gruesome." Onto his spike go the stories, more common than the average newspaper reader realizes, of children being raped or chopped to pieces, stories of burglars torturing their victims to make them reveal their cache. Both cheap and gruesome, in the minds of most editors, is the subject of homosexuality. A traveling salesman strangled by a boy he brought up to his room at the Y.M.C.A. would never deserve one-tenth the tabloid attention that he would attain if his assassin had been a girl.

Sadism, sodomy, tortures, drunken stabbings, certain adulteries—these things happen every day, but in a kind of nether world that lies beneath what the tabloids like to consider their dignity. In contrast to all this, there is the "classy case." What gives a murder "class"? Rich men, beautiful women, yachts, racing stables—everything, in short, that forms part of the dreamworld of the gum-chewing tabloid reader. For the secret of the whole tabloid formula is that the "classy" murder case is not one with which the reader *can* identify himself but one with which he *would like* to identify himself. The *New York Times* and the *Herald Tribune* provide society pages for social climbers to read; the tabloids provide society columns for daydreaming shopgirls. The concept of class, in other words, represents the Hollywood-fed all-American fantasy, and yet the "news" about this dreamworld is always at least implicitly disastrous. The stockbroker is discovered in his "love nest"; the heiress is a "love slave"; the playboy is sued for "heart balm." Thus the lower orders, in buying the news about the upper ones, are given satisfying accounts of their objects of envy committing depravities and defalcations, of their imminent descent to the readers' own level. Although reader-criminal identification may seem farfetched here, one can assume that the tabloid reader would like to be in a position to *have* a "love nest," even if it meant eventually being "exposed."

Once in a decade there is a case like the shooting of Jim Fisk or the kidnapping of the Lindbergh baby, a case in which all the rules of the tabloid form fit into place and a famous story virtually writes itself. But the tabloids are printed every day, and every day the readers are hungry for a new taste of high-class sensations. That is why the homely waitress strangled on the beach becomes a "shapely blonde" (the favored term "blonde" can apply to almost any color of hair, although obviously unblonde women are often exoticized by terms such as "flame-haired" or "raven-tressed"). This is why the seedy sawbones who pinches his patients becomes a "distinguished physician" living in "a luxurious home in the fashionable suburb of Blank." Indeed, tabloid prose often reads like the same newspaper's real estate section for the simple reason that both the tabloid writer and the advertising writer are trying to make the shabby reality conform to the fantasy. Homes, in both cases, if not luxurious, are then spacious. Suburbs are always fashionable.

And houses are always "homes," for all the idealizing forces behind the tabloid writer require him to use the genteel euphemism in every case where the unidiomatic word will provide "class." Thus sons become heirs or scions. Doctors become physicians, carpenters become contracting executives, and even the lowest of the species may be "socially prominent."

The tabloid distortions represent so ubiquitous a fantasy that the tabloid writer occasionally discovers one of his subjects really acting out the transformation of human being into socialite. A few years ago, a New York millionaire was shot to death by his wife, and the tabloids set up a hue and cry for every detail of the story. One of the gaps was the background of the wife, who had been generally thought to be the orphaned daughter of a colonel. It took a tabloid reporter a considerable amount of time to determine that the colonel had never existed, and that the actual father was still very much alive as a streetcar motorman in Detroit. When the father was finally interviewed about his daughter's misfortunes, he expressed surprise that she had married a New York millionaire. He remembered that she had changed her name to become a model, but for many years he had been under the impression that his daughter was a well-known Hollywood actress with a similar *nom de guerre*. Here is a tabloid creation in the flesh.

Sex, as is well known, combines with crime to provide the tabloids with their huge circulations. But sex is as strangely distorted as crime, as strangely twisted to fit the American fantasies. The same bans apply—drunks, Negroes, workers, homosexuals, all these have no sex life of any news value. And yet the lowest "starlet" in Hollywood has her casual affairs broadcast to millions under such wonderful disguises as "friends wonder if so-and-so is secretly married to so-and-so." Disguise is the essence of sex chronicles, for although sex sells newspapers, even the most lurid tabloid schizophrenically considers itself a "family newspaper." Although it may seem strange to a casual reader, the tabloid editor's desire to stimulate sales is handcuffed by a criterion known as "good taste." This criterion is so mysterious, so much a matter of "feel," that it can best be illustrated by an example.

An enterprising young lady once tried to achieve fame by going to a Cannes film festival, accosting a popular actor, stripping off all her clothes above the waist, and embracing the rather embarrassed actor while photographers frantically took pictures that could never be printed. From reporters' accounts of the scene, the girl achieved a certain small notoriety, enough to get her to Hollywood, where her misfortunes were usually reported as an excuse to run pictures of her. One day, this aspiring actress—or could it have been some other specimen of the familiar type?—appeared in a two-column picture, wearing a tiny crucifix that dangled down into a resting place between her luxurious breasts. The editor, who had been out of the office when the picture was first printed, returned to his desk and cried out in horror. At considerable expense, the picture was treated with an airbrush, which sprayed flesh-colored paint over the crucifix, so that a new engraving of the voluptuous bosom could be portrayed in the next edition without violating "good taste."

Perhaps one more incident would illustrate this strange concept further. A few years ago, a teen-age youth in a suburb of Boston murdered a girl with whom he had just had sexual intercourse on the front seat of an automobile. When the youth confessed to the police, he proudly repeated over and over the details of how he had become a man in the parked car, and the words he used to express that experience were: "Then I scored and then I scored again, that's where I scored." The childish boast embarrassed the same editors who normally want to emphasize every implication of sex, and when the story was finally printed the youth was quoted as saying that "intimacies had occurred" in the spotted front seat of the car.

Intimacies. This is the tabloid word for sex. It turns up over and over again. If any ingenuous tabloid writer tries to use a word like "sex," on the theory that an accurate term is always in better taste than a euphemism, the more experienced copy desk will change it to "intimacies." The reason for this involves the same fantasies that dominate Hollywood: Miss Blank, who has had three husbands, is cast as an ingénue stranded overnight on a mountain top with Mr. Blank, who has had three wives. There is much giggling as they pitch their separate tents, but at the end they will get married. The movie will be advertised with twenty-foot-high posters of Miss Blank lying panting on the mountain top in her chemise while Mr. Blank crouches nearby in the attitude of a neurotic gorilla. The movie-goer knows that he will not be actually shown anything that could offend the local archbishop, but he will be allowed his snicker. The snicker, the leer, that nervous substitute for the thwarted need, is the American emotional response to the so-called "popular culture."

Although the tabloids and the movies provide much the same outlet for the need to snicker, the tabloids push the whole process one step further than is possible in the movies. With an almost baroque stylization, the tabloids would take Mr. Blank and Miss Blank to the mountain top, and then, instead of fading out like a discreet movie camera, they would quote Miss Blank as saying that "intimacies occurred." Nor is that the only dainty disguise. Mr. Blank may also be said to have been "dallying" with Miss Blank, or maybe he was "romancing" her. He is her "sweetheart." No, says she, they are "just good friends," and everybody gets a good healthy snicker out of it.

Curiously enough, the chief trouble for the tabloid writer occurs in supposed sex cases where no sex has been enjoyed, as far as can be determined. The problem arises, for instance, in the periodic story of the "nice" teen-age girl running off with a boy. The tabloid editors enjoy a vicarious thrill at the prospect of a young girl's availability, but the writer finds that everything he can say about the errant couple has already been tinged with the implications of past cases. Were they just "close friends"? Were they "intimate friends"? Had there been, all virginally, a "romance"? Every word revives echoes of the old euphemisms and the old snickers. Denials are accepted as lies. The English language has been wrung out.

Are the tabloids hopeless? Perhaps, but not on the grounds of sensationalism. Having already become rich, they hunger nowadays after finer things, such as respectability and political influence. In New York, where the *Times* fills its half-size brothers with awe, the tabloids feel compelled to tell their uninterested readers about such portentous events as a Senate debate on farm parity, largely because the *Times* has or inevitably will do so. It is almost with shock that today's tabloid writer, looking back through clippings on the Lindbergh case, finds Damon Runyon reporting the execution of Bruno Hauptmann in terms of near-hysteria: "The Wolf-man is dead." What amazement he feels, then, in looking at the old *Graphic*'s faked pictures of Peaches Browning in the bedroom with her aged husband, at the balloon that issues from Daddy's mouth and quotes him as quacking like a duck. To find such authentic trashiness now, one must leave America and take a look at the London *Mirror,* which is comparatively entertaining and consequently sells twice as many copies as its biggest New York counterpart. Although American tabloid circulations are in or near the millions, their sales are actually stagnant or declining, despite the increase in population. That is natural, however, when the popular touch has become the genteelism, when irreverence has given way to reverence, stuffiness, even pomposity.

One tabloid's saucy story about the preparations of a European princeling's long-anticipated marriage to a celebrated beauty was killed on the strength of a new managerial directive that the wedding had been handled too impertinently and was henceforth to be treated "with dignity." And so for one solid week, it printed fifteen "romantic" but "dignified" manuscript pages per day on one of the most laughable events of our time. The stories were laughable too, precisely because they accepted their subjects' social pretensions at face value. I wrote them myself.

FOR DISCUSSION AND REVIEW

1. What is a tabloid newspaper? How does it differ from such non-tabloids as the New York *Times,* the *Christian Science Monitor,* and the *Wall Street Journal?*

2. What, according to Friedrich, characterizes "tabloid prose"? What reasons does he suggest for its use?

3. Explain the distinction Friedrich draws between a "cheap [murder] case" and a "classy murder case." What do the "classy murder case" and society pages in papers such as the New York *Times* have in common in terms of audience appeal? Cite some comparable phenomena from TV and movies.

4. The tabloid editor, Friedrich says, is restricted by a mysterious code of "good taste." On the basis of the examples he gives in the article, try to explain what is involved here. What is the connection between the diminishing popularity of the tabloids and this code of good taste?

WALKER GIBSON 6

Dullness and Dishonesty: The Rhetoric of Newswriting

Must a great newspaper be dull?

In this essay from Tough, Sweet and Stuffy, *Walker Gibson, Professor of English at the University of Massachusetts, analyzes newspaper reporting and confronts the question "Must a great newspaper be dull?" While he grants the relative impossibility of "straight" reporting, Gibson points to the inherent dangers in trying not to be dull. By looking at a single incident as reported by the New York* Times, *the New York* Herald Tribune, *and* Time *magazine, Gibson compares and contrasts the various stylistic alternatives available to the reporter.*

THIS [ESSAY] CONSIDERS SOME EXAMPLES OF HOW THE NEWS OF THE day is expressed for us, and how, in some of its expressions, a bastard form of the Tough Talker[1] can be detected.

[1] *Ed. note:* Earlier in *Tough, Sweet and Stuffy* Gibson defines the Tough Talker: "What I mean by Tough Talk is most easily discovered in works of fiction where a narrator-hero identifies himself as a hard man who has been around. . . . His rhetoric . . . shows its limitations openly: short sentences, 'crude' repetitions of words, simple grammatical structures with little subordinating. (I have no use for elegant variation, for the worn-out gentilities of traditional prose.) His tense intimacy with his assumed reader, another man who has been around, is implied by colloquial patterns from oral speech and by a high frequency of the definite article. He lets his reader make logical and other connections between elements. (You know what I mean; I don't have to spell

We begin with a conventional sample of "straight" reporting, though concerning events that lend themselves to excitable treatment. Here is a reporter for *The New York Times* (Claude Sitton) beginning his lead article on the race riots in Birmingham, Alabama, in the issue for May 8, 1963.

> The police and firemen drove hundreds of rioting Negroes off the streets today with high-pressure hoses and an armored car. The riot broke out after from 2,500 to 3,000 persons rampaged through the business district in two demonstrations and were driven back. The Negroes rained rocks, bottles and brickbats on the law-enforcement officials as they were slowly forced backward by the streams of water. The pressure was so high that the water skinned bark off trees in the parks and along sidewalks. Policemen from surrounding cities and members of the Alabama Highway Patrol rushed to a nine-block area near the business district to help quell the riot. An undetermined number of persons were injured in the demonstrations against segregation. They included the Rev. Fred L. Shuttlesworth, a prominent Negro leader, and two city policemen and a Jefferson County deputy sheriff.
>
> (The National Association for the Advancement of Colored People called for peaceful picketing in 100 cities around the country to protest the actions of the Birmingham officials. In Greenfield Park, N.Y., a group of Conservative rabbis left for Birmingham in a "testimony on behalf of the human rights and dignity" of Negroes.)

I have called this an example of "straight" reporting, and my quotation marks are intended to suggest, of course, that straightness is as absolutely impossible in writing as it is in higher mathematics. Readers of a semantic turn of mind, looking for loaded language in that introduction, might easily challenge some of it. The Negroes "rampaged" through the business district, and "rained" missiles on the police. The sentence about the velocity of the fire hoses would not have been composed by a Southern reporter. But on the whole it is hard to see how the job could have been done much straighter than it has been done here. A little dull, considering the circumstances? Unfeeling? Perhaps a little Stuffy? Or is the horror the more vivid because of the writer's very restraint? At any rate, taking this account as a base of operations, let us look at some alternative ways of reporting that day's events in Birmingham.

At the time when these events took place, the *New York Herald Tribune* was conducting a publicity campaign directed a little desperately at an obvious front-running competitor. MUST A GREAT

---

it all out for *you*.) He prefers naming things to describing them, and avoids modification, especially when suggestive of value. All these habits of behavior suggest that he is self-conscious about his language—even about language generally. He is close-lipped, he watches his words." (pp. ix, 41).

NEWSPAPER BE DULL?, the billboards were asking, and the answer, in the negative, was presumably to be found in the style of the *Tribune's* own pages. On the same day when the *Times* piece appeared, the *Tribune's* story, under the byline of Charles Portis, began as follows:

> Three times during the day, waves of shouting, rock-throwing Negroes had poured into the downtown business district, to be scattered and driven back by battering streams of water from high-pressure hoses and swinging clubs of policemen and highway patrolmen. Now the deserted streets were littered with sodden debris. Here in the shabby streets of the Negro section one of the decisive clashes in the Negro battle against segregation was taking place. Last night a tense quiet settled over the riot-racked city after a day in which both sides altered their battle tactics. The Negro crowds, who for days have hurled themselves against police barriers, divided into small, shifting bands, darted around the police and poured hundreds of separate patrols into the downtown business districts. The police, who had crowded hundreds into the city's jails, abandoned efforts to arrest the demonstrators. They concentrated on herding the mobs toward the 16th Street Baptist Church, headquarters for these unprecedented demonstrations. By day's end, Gov. George Wallace had ordered some 250 state highway patrolmen in to aid beleaguered local police and had warned at an opening session of the Legislature that he would prosecute Negroes for murder if anyone died in the Birmingham riots.

As often, we may begin by asking just where in place and time the two assumed authors are situated. The *Times* man is not, as far as we can tell, anywhere in particular. He is sitting in his hotel room typing out an account of what he has seen or heard during the day just ended. Or he is at a telephone dictating this information to New York. Who knows? Little or no distinction has been made between speaker and assumed author. There is no pretense that the reporter is anywhere else but where, in realistic fact, we must assume he *is,* as a working journalist. But the *Tribune* man is far more complex in locating himself. He uses, first, two verb tenses in identifying the time of utterance. During the day waves of Negroes *had poured* (first sentence). When is now? Presumably at the end of the day, at the time of writing. Why, then, *were* littered; why not *are* littered? This particular posture, of using "now" for a time spoken of as already having happened, is common in fiction, where an *imagined* voice can use "now" in that curious and palpably made-up way. The assumed author pretends with one word (now) that he is really there at the moment, while with another word (were) he reminds us that he isn't. Third sentence: *Here* in the shabby streets of the Negro section. Where is here? Where is the speaker? Well, the speaker is apparently in the shabby streets, but the *writer* certainly isn't in the streets. Squatting on the sidewalk with typewriter or telephone? Scarcely. What the writer has done, then, is to invent an imagined speaker, *on the model of the novelist,* who, because he is imaginary, can speak of the situation more authoritatively than any mere hotel-bound reporter. And authoritative this speaker (or, better, narrator) certainly is. It follows, to take a minor example, that he can call the streams from the fire hoses "battering," almost as if he felt them himself. (Compare the *Times* man's sentence about the fire hoses and the bark of trees: evidence he presumably observed personally.), Or, to take a more conspicuous example, it follows that this narrator can label the riot as "one of the decisive clashes in the Negro battle against segregation." How does he know that? He knows it because he is a made-up man, because he is like a teller of a tale, and it is his privilege and his business to know.

Further manifestations of this narrator's free-swinging position can be found in a number of his words and phrases. His willingness to use metaphor (however unoriginally) is characteristic. "Hundreds of rioting Negroes" (*Times*) are "waves" in the *Tribune*. The crowds "hurled themselves" while the police were "herding" the mobs toward the church. Throughout the passage the writer's liberal use of modification is significant. . . . [W]e find here a perceptible difference between the two pieces of prose in the number of words used as modifiers—that is, considerably more in the *Tribune* article. . . . [I]t is the omniscient assumed author who takes the liberty of modifying his nouns with adjectives. Why not? He knows, and can well afford to give us the qualities of things, not just their names. And the difference in genre is of course the whole point: [in contrast to] writing a clear piece of fiction, the *Tribune* purports to express actual events.

By such language the day's news is transformed into a tale told by a fictitious teller. It may not be dull, but as anyone can see, it can be dangerous. What the *Tribune* writer has done is to impose on a real-life situation an omniscient narrator of the sort familiar to traditional fiction. Must a great newspaper be dull? In this case, at least, the avoidance of "dullness" has been accomplished at the cost of making Birmingham a fictitious place, the kind of place where someone "in charge" (the narrator) can truly know the score. I do not disguise my own moral indignation at this literary make-believe. For Birmingham and its troubles are not fiction; they are serious and complicated matters to be cautiously expressed. Furthermore, insofar as naive readers may not recognize the *Tribune's* fictitiousness, and may assume that this is a Real Birmingham being described, the damage done in the long run to people's minds may be serious.

There is a problem of *genre* here that has attracted some attention just recently. With the publication of Truman Capote's enormously popular *In Cold Blood* (1965), the issue was explicitly raised. Was this factual journalism, or was it fiction? Mr. Capote has made much of his "invention" of a new style, combining the two. The fictional omniscience of his narrating voice is supposed to be justified by years of research, note-taking, tape-recording, and all the industry of the cautious reporter. Nevertheless he feels free to enter the minds of his protagonists and give us their "thoughts." Where are we? This muddle has upset some of his critics, notably Mr. F. W. Dupee, who has complained that Capote is "exploiting the factual authority of journalism and the atmospheric license of fiction."

But the device of the omniscient narrator in newswriting, as an attempt to avoid dullness, has been with us for quite a while. It has been most conspicuous in *Time,* "the weekly news-magazine." The style of *Time* has irked a great many people, and has inspired parodies of considerable venom. *Time*'s style has also, obviously, impressed many readers favorably, as the magazine's success over the years must demonstrate. It has not generally been understood that both the outrage and the admiration originate in one pervasive device of style: the intrusion into the news of an omniscient narrator, on the model of works of fiction.

Any random sampling of *Time*'s pages will show this omniscient speaker at work. Such a speaker can, for example, know what is going on inside the minds of other people—a privilege open to the fictitious narrator alone.

> The cold war, the President felt, was a stalemate. He sensed a deepening international discouragement . . . .

He can *know* the true significance of the events he describes:

> To eye and ear, the desultory discussion in the Senate seemed like anything but what it actually was: one of the most . . . .

He can be in possession of the most vivid details concerning events no human could possibly know:

> Leaping from his bed one night last January, Dahomey's President Hubert Maga excitedly telephoned military headquarters to report that his residence was being shelled. He soon went back to sleep. As it turned out . . . .

He can temptingly throw out details about a character he is introducing, *as if* the reader already knew whom he was talking about—the suspense-building technique of the story-teller:

> They called him "Tawl Tawm." His flamboyant Senate oratory could drown an opponent in sweet molasses or hogtie him in barbed wire. He smoked ten 15¢ cigars a day and wore his white hair so long that it crested in curls at the nape of his neck. He dressed . . . .

This piece is not headlined at all—such as "Senator Connolly Dies." Instead it is *titled*—"Tawl Tawm"—in the slightly mysterious way that stories are conventionally titled.

In fact *Time*'s dependence on models of fiction shows up clearly in its headings, where puns and echoes based on actual titles of fiction are common. "Revolution in the Afternoon," "Sounds in the Night," "The Monkey's Pa," are examples from a single issue. These instances of semi-literary semi-sophistication have their bearing on the tone of the magazine, in which the reader is flattered by being in the know with respect to such little jokes. But tricks of title are only a minor weapon in *Time*'s arsenal for putting the reader (fictitiously) in the know. It is the consistent omniscience of the narrating voice that primarily does the job.

How did *Time* describe the events of May 7, 1963, in Birmingham, Alabama? As follows:

> The blaze of bombs, the flash of blades, the eerie glow of fire, the keening cries of hatred, the wild dance of terror at night—all this was Birmingham, Alabama.
>
> Birmingham's Negroes had always seemed a docile lot. Downtown at night, they slouched in gloomy huddles beneath street lamps talking softly or not at all. They knew their place: they were "niggers" in a Jim Crow town, and they bore their degradation in silence.
>
> But last week they smashed that image forever. The scenes in Birmingham were unforgettable. There was the Negro youth, sprawled on his back and spinning across the pavement while firemen battered him with streams of water so powerful that they could strip the bark off trees. There was the Negro woman, pinned to the ground by cops, one of them with his knee dug into her throat. There was the white man who watched hymn-singing Negroes burst from a sweltering church and growled: "We ought to shoot every damned one of them." And there was the little Negro girl, splendid in a newly starched dress, who marched out of a church, looked toward a massed line of pistol-packing cops, and called to a laggard friend: "Hurry up, Lucile. If you stay behind you won't get arrested with our group."

The postures of Knowing taken here are obvious enough and hardly need stressing. "All this was Birmingham." The narrator knows the past, for the Negroes "had always seemed" docile. He has seen them "in gloomy huddles" over a long period of time; this concrete description implies close personal knowledge. They knew their place, he says, echoing ironically the white man's cliché, of which again he seems to have an intimate knowledge. "But last week they smashed that image *forever"*: now he knows the future too. Is that the news? Or is it the kind of statement an all-knowing story-teller can make about a place he has invented? (Of course we have to say, for this writer, that subsequent events have justified some of his fictitious wisdom!)

The suspicion is tempting that the *real* author of this piece never left his air-conditioned office in Manhattan's Time-Life Building. What he may have done was to read a lot of other people's accounts of Birmingham, including the *Times* man's observation about fire hoses and tree bark, which he then paraphrased in the manner of the novelist. More accurately, I suppose, this prose is the work of several hands, one or two of whom may actually have been on the scene in Birmingham.

But omniscience is not the only thing to notice about this narrator's use of words. The reader who reacts to that barrage of definite articles in *Time*'s first sentence may be reminded of an old friend.

> The blaze of bombs, the flash of blades, the errie glow of fire, the keening cries of hatred, the wild dance of terror . . . .

Part of the speaker's relation with the reader is that of a shared knowledgeable awareness of just the sort of "blaze" and "flash" and "eerie glow" the speaker is talking about. *You* know what I mean. It is the familiar intimacy of the Tough Talker, who implies that he already knows his reader before the story opens.

Actually, once the first sentence is over with, the writer for *Time* uses somewhat fewer definite articles than the writers of our other two Birmingham passages. But he has additional rhetorical characteristics that, statistically at least, carry him much closer to Frederic Henry[2] than is the case with the other two. Most important is the sheer size of his words. A count of monosyllables in all three passages shows that whereas in the *Times* and *Tribune* a little over half of the words are of one syllable, over three-quarters of *Time*'s diction is monosyllabic. In a count of longer words, those of three syllables or more, the *Times* piece shows 15 percent, the *Tribune* 12 percent, and *Time* only 5 per cent. And even these are simple and repetitious; "Birmingham" appears three times. We recall that the Tough Talker is chary with modification. If we list the words in each passage being used to modify nouns (omitting articles and demonstrative and personal pronouns), we discover that the *Time* writer, for all his eerie

[2] *Ed. note:* The hero of Ernest Hemingway's *A Farewell to Arms.*

glows and keening cries, has the least modification of the three, while the *Tribune* piece has the most.

A chart of such information may be useful:

	Times	*Tribune*	*Time*
Total words in passage	193	201	214
Average sentence length	22	25	19
Monosyllables (% of total words)	55%	57%	78%
Longer words (3 syllables & over)	15%	12%	5%
Modifiers of nouns	15%	19%	11%

Do such figures prove anything? Probably not by themselves, unless we can feel, in the tone of the *Time* passage, that particular intensity and intimacy we noted in the introduction to *A Farewell to Arms*. Can we? For all the embarrassing bad writing in the *Time* passage, I hope it is clear that we can. The speaker, surely "a hard man who has been around in a violent world," expects of us intimacy of a special closeness. If we are to become the sympathetic assumed reader of these words (which I personally find most difficult), we share a world defined in tight-lipped simplicity of language. It is a world where policemen are always cops and violence is taken for granted, and where crude pathos (the little Negro girl at the end) is expected to move us deeply right through the toughness. Beneath that harsh voice (as often, even in Hemingway) there beats all too visibly a heart of sugar. In fact the triteness of the piece is such as to give us momentary pause about our whole response so far. Can this very triteness be intended? Those piled-up alliterative clichés at the start—the blaze of bombs, the keening cries—suggest possibly an even further intimacy with the reader that may conceivably run something like this: You and I know this is mostly a verbal game. You recognize as I do the familiar theatrical phrases from who-done-it literature with which I adorn this account, and you recognize that I'm not trying to *tell you* anything about Birmingham. I'm just wittily entertaining you for a few moments after a busy day. After all, you've already read last week's newspapers. This is decorative.

If there is anything to the suspicions I have just uttered (and I am truly doubtful), then Timestyle has to be seen as cynical in the extreme. For if, as seems remotely possible, the sophisticated reader is to see this writer's pose as after all not tough and intense, but mock-tough, then the two of them, reader and writer, are engaged in a most irresponsible game. These are not events to play games with. The real trouble is that I, as a reader, can't tell whether this is a game or not.

And if it is not, then we return to locate again one huge distinction between the Tough Talker we saw in Hemingway and the one we see here. It is true that some of the Tough Talker's rhetoric is here visible: short sentences, simplified diction, relatively low modification. But omniscience has been added! We have an intense, human-sounding, tough-talking narrator *without* any human limitations. He knows. When, in other words, you invent a voice that asserts deep and violent feeling, and close intimacy with the reader, and omniscience, you have a public address system of formidable power. And when you apply that voice to the "reporting" of the *news,* you have committed an act of intellectual dishonesty.

In this comparison of three expressions of the news, the restraint of *The New York Times* has seemed to come off with highest marks. But let not the *Times* relax its vigil. The fact is that the charms of fiction-writing have beguiled the *Times* writers too, though usually without the rhetoric of the Tough Talker. We can see fictitious omniscience especially in the Sunday supplement called "The News of the Week in Review," where, in summarizing the week's news, it is apparently tempting to talk as if one knew what happened.

> THE COUP
> The time was just before 3 A.M. in Washington on Friday. In the "situation room" in the White House basement, a command center which receives diplomatic and intelligence reports from around the world, a message from the U.S. Embassy in Saigon clattered off one of the teletype machines. A watch officer phoned.

Without belaboring the point one can certainly make out in these lines the suspenseful devices of the novelist, from the mysterious title and *in-medias-res* beginning to the teletype machine that clattered off a message. Who heard it clatter? This is a case of the *Times* man having read his *Time* too well and too often rather than the other way around.

One appreciates any effort by journalists to make the reading of the news less of a chore and a bore. Nobody wants to be dull. But if the alternative to dullness is dishonesty, it may be better to be dull. On the other hand there are surely other alternatives. Without trying to tell the newswriter his business, I should suppose that a concrete and sober account of what a reporter *did* during his day's work would be, in many cases, neither dull nor dishonest. Such an account would not, to be sure, leave us with the satisfied feeling of knowing the Real Scoop on Birmingham, or the White House, or the Wide World. But as I have already said too often, this is not a feeling to be encouraged anyway.

FOR DISCUSSION AND REVIEW

1. Gibson states that "straightness is as absolutely impossible in writing as it is in higher mathematics." Discuss the characteristics of English that contribute to this situation. Go back through The New York *Times* paragraph and discuss examples not cited by Gibson. Should a writer nevertheless aim at "straight" reporting? Under what circumstances?

2. Discuss the importance of a writer's stance, the point Gibson makes by asking "just where in place and time" The New York *Times* and the New York *Herald Tribune* writers are located. What can a writer use to reveal his location and, by implication, his point of view?

3. What is the effect of the *Tribune* writer's extensive use of metaphor and modification? Compare Gibson's comments on the use of adjectives with Stevens' statement concerning "adjectival puffery" (p. 166).

4. Explain what an "omniscient narrator" is. What other points of view are used by writers? How do they differ? What circumstances are best suited for each?

5. What "pervasive device of style" is responsible for much of both the outrage and admiration directed at *Time?* Describe other devices mentioned by Gibson characteristic of "Timestyle." Can you add to Gibson's list? What effects do you think each has?

6. Discuss the question with which Gibson prefaces his selection: "Must a great newspaper be dull?"

WRITING

1. You are preparing for an upcoming school vacation and you are short of cash. You have decided to sell some of your possessions. Write an ad for the dorm bulletin board or school newspaper (75-word limit) that will bring you the best possible price for one of the following: stereo amp, guitar, bicycle, skis, '54 Ford.

2. Select a brief news item from a newspaper or magazine. Without changing the facts given, rewrite it so that it makes a different impression on the reader. Hand in the original article with your rewritten version.

3. Imagine that you are away at school. Recently you were caught

in a radar speed trap—you were doing 40 in a 25-mile zone—and have just lost your license. Because you have lost your license, you will not be able to go home this coming weekend, as you had planned. Write two letters in which you explain why you will not be able to get home, one to your parents and the other to your best friend.

4. Some of the most commonly used tricks and techniques of the propagandist include:

Term	*Example*
Name calling	My liberal opponent (*liberal* is an emotionally charged word and an objectionable concept for certain audiences)
Sweeping statement	We are all true Americans (a meaningless statement because we do not know what *true* or *American* means)
Bifurcation	Love America or Leave It (implies that there are no possibilities between these extremes)
Association	This document is the Magna Carta of the Women's Movement (elevates the document by comparing it to the great charter for English liberties)
Bandwagon	Join the Pepsi Generation (implies that there actually is a movement and that you will benefit from joining it)
Appeal to illegitimate authority	Johnny Cash endorses Amoco (because a person is an authority or personality in one field does not mean that he is an authority in another)

Write a paper in which you support a cause to which you are emotionally bound. Try to use as many as you can of the propaganda devices discussed above.

5. Real estate advertisements are often deliberately designed to manipulate potential buyers. For example, one language analyst noted that in his home town "adorable" meant "small," "eat-in kitchen" meant "no dining room," "handyman's special" meant "portion of building still standing," "by appointment only" meant "ex-

pensive," and "starter home" meant "cheap." Analyze the language used in the real estate advertisements in your local newspaper. Does the real estate that one company offers sound better to you than that offered by another company? Do any realtors have their own special vocabulary?

6. You have just been hired by a local real estate firm as an advertising copy writer. Your first assignment is to describe this house:

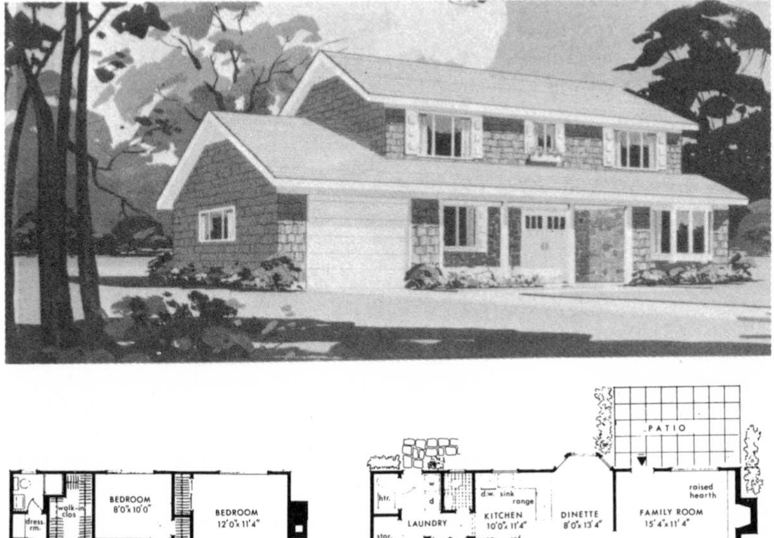

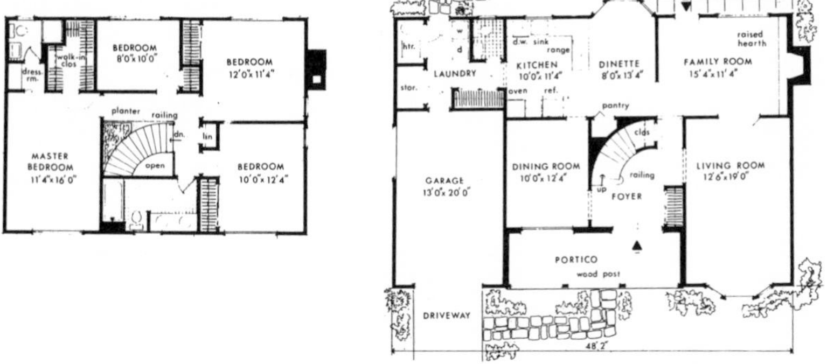

Using the same house, describe it as though you were a bank appraiser evaluating the house for a possible mortgage loan.

Your family is being transferred and you are in the new location looking at houses. You don't like this one. Describe it in such a way as to persuade your family to agree with you.

7. You work as a writer for a company employing 45,000 people. It is estimated that there are about 30,000 cars in the parking lots daily. In an effort to help ease the energy crisis, the company has directed you to prepare a bulletin for distribution to all employees

encouraging the formation of car pools. You feel that your position in the company will depend largely on the success of this bulletin. Use persuasive language.

8. Many advertisers seem to believe that by manipulating language and reality they can make any product appeal to consumers. Here is how a very common item might be made to appear desirable by means of advertising.

NEW! CONVENIENT!

STRIKE-UPS

The latest scientific advance for smokers since the cigarette lighter. Inexpensive and lightweight, you'll never want to be caught without Strike-Ups.

Why tolerate heavy, expensive cigarette lighters? Why run the risk of soiling your clothes with dangerous lighter fluid? Why be hassled by the technicalities of replacing flints? Why be embarrassed by a lighter that fails when it means everything to you?

STRIKE-UPS HAS A BETTER WAY

Lightweight, 100% reliable, Strike-Ups gives 20, that's right 20, or more lights. Each booklet has its own handy striking surface, right where you need it—up front. A striking surface so large you'll be able to get quick and easy lights even in the darkest places. Strike-Ups comes with a handsome decorator cover. An added feature, at no extra cost, is the plain white surface inside the cover useful for phone numbers or doodling.

Once you use Strike-Ups, you'll agree, as many Americans have, that you simply can't do without them. With Strike-Ups you can't help but smoke more.

ASK FOR STRIKE-UPS AT ALL STORES WHERE QUALITY SMOKING ACCESSORIES ARE SOLD.

Write an advertisement for any one of the items listed below; use as many of the advertiser's tricks or persuasive techniques as you can in order to sell your product.

paper clips
dental floss
toothpicks
rubber bands
salt shakers
staples
bottle caps

9. All advertising attempts to create an image for a product. In addition, the product and its image are designed to appeal to a certain segment of the buying public. For example,

Product	*Symbol*	*Audience*
Pepsi-Cola	Sociability	Youth
Ivory Snow	Softness	Mothers
Haley's M.O.	Youthfulness	Middle-aged
Ultra Brite	Sex appeal	Youth
Lincoln Continental	Elegance	Wealthy
Volkswagen	Economy	Thrifty and independent

Write an essay in which you explain how you would revise the established product symbol of one of the items listed above and redirect it to another audience. How, for example, would you sell Pepsi to senior citizens?

10. Americans of all ages, but especially the young, are bombarded with popular music. They are involved with songs almost from birth, songs that reach them from car radios, transistor go-everywhere radios, stereo sets, rock concerts, and even Muzak. Most of these popular songs have lyrics, and we hear the lyrics even without intending to listen to them. Yet we usually disregard their enormous impact on our view of what life is, an impact that is increased by their repetition. Analysis of popular song lyrics can reveal some surprising assumptions about such different aspects of American life as friendship, love, marriage, the proper roles for men and women, the value of material possessions. Drawing examples from the lyrics of songs currently popular, write an essay in which you construct and describe a value system for a young person today. Consider attitudes toward such things as love, friendship, responsibility, country, money, religion.

11. Many Americans express deep concern about government censorship. What they do not realize, however, is that they have been subjected to censorship in their education and communications systems, and have themselves used censorship on their children. Write an essay in which you argue *for* one of the following positions: (1) parents and school board members have an obligation to censor materials used in public schools; (2) teachers should have the right to use in their classrooms whatever material they consider appropriate.

12. Governments and the news media are prone to using euphemisms and connotatively "loaded" words for propaganda purposes. Depending on your position, for example, a "terrorist" and a "resistance fighter" are two very different things. To refer to a group as "self-styled" or as "calling themselves . . . ," to world leaders as "intransigent," "belligerent," "stern," and "forceful" is to use language that embodies very serious value judgments. Examine a recent news-

paper or news magazine article on world events for examples of "loaded" words and then write an analysis of how the news media attempt to alter attitudes through biased language.

13. Think of a product that you like and want to use but that has one dissatisfying or annoying feature. Write and send a letter to the company explaining your complaint and offering constructive criticism.

NOTABLE QUOTATIONS

"Adjectives are used so freely these days that we feel almost naked, robbed, if we don't get at least a couple." *Stevens*

"[In advertising] there is a direct, inverse proportion between the number of adjectives and the number of facts." *Stevens*

"Many broadcasters are fighting, not for *free* speech, but for *profitable* speech." *Johnson*

"I believe [our founding fathers] assumed Congress would be the only body powerful enough to abridge free speech. They were wrong." *Johnson*

"For it is also a form of censorship to so completely clog the public's air waves with tasteless gruel that there is no time left for quality entertainment and social commentary, no time to give the people full information of their affairs." *Johnson*

"Despite all its pretenses of representing the public, the average newspaper is simply a business enterprise that sells news and uses that lure to sell advertising space." *Friedrich*

"It is the omniscient assumed author who takes the liberty of modifying his nouns with adjectives." *Gibson*

"Nobody wants to be dull. But if the alternative to dullness is dishonesty, it may be better to be dull." *Gibson*

PROSPECTS V

The future exists only in language.
S. I. Hayakawa

THE COMPUTER'S FIRST CHRISTMAS CARD

JOLLYMERRY
HOLLYBERRY
JOLLYBERRY
MERRYHOLLY
HAPPYJOLLY
JOLLYJELLY
JELLYBELLY
BELLYMERRY
HOLLYHEPPY
JOLLYMOLLY
MARRYJERRY
MERRYHARRY
HOPPYBARRY
HEPPYJARRY
BOPPYHEPPY
BERRYJORRY
JORRYJOLLY
MOPPYJELLY
MOLLYMERRY
JERRYJOLLY
BELLYBOPPY
JORRYHOPPY
HOLLYMOPPY
BARRYMERRY
JARRYHAPPY
HAPPYBOPPY
BOPPYJOLLY
JOLLYMERRY
MERRYMERRY
MERRYMERRY
MERRYCHRIS
AMMERRYASA
CHRISMERRY
ASMERRYCHR
YSANTHEMUM

Edwin Morgan

JACOB ORNSTEIN AND WILLIAM W. GAGE 1

The Dream of a World Language

Discouraged by the confusion and misunderstandings that have resulted from language barriers, people have always dreamed of the possibility of a world language, and more than six hundred schemes for a universal language have been proposed. Jacob Ornstein, a lecturer at the Institute for Languages and Linguistics at Georgetown University, and William Gage, a research linguist at the Center for Applied Linguistics, survey several of the most prominent: Volapük, Esperanto, and Interlingua. In addition to pointing out the needs for a world language, the authors indicate some of the obstacles that are likely to prohibit the adoption of one.

The Language Barrier

THE OLD TESTAMENT DESCRIBED THE MULTIPLICITY OF LANGUAGES as an affliction visited on mankind, and history is replete with confusions resulting from language barriers. Modern examples are at hand:

A Venezuelan shipper sends an order for automobile spare parts to Italy—and is shipped tractor parts instead. The British Foreign Office uses the word *requérir* ("to demand") incorrectly—and an incensed French general demands an apology. American tourists in a

Far Eastern metropolis attempt to communicate in sign language—and are severely mauled because their signs are interpreted as insults. People drown unnecessarily in a sea disaster (the *Andrea Doria*) because they cannot understand rescue directions given in a tongue other than their own.

Surely we were better off during the Middle Ages, when everything of international importance was expressed in Latin. Can't we appreciate the advantages of a universal language and devise one? A world language has been one of the most persistent dreams of man from ages immemorial. No less than six hundred schemes for a universal language have been proposed by men and women seeking a solution to this knottiest of communication problems. The parade of language planners has been a colorful and varied one and has included learned scholars and dilettantes, scientists and crackpots.

Descartes, for example, speculated about a language so perfect in its symbolism that it would be impossible for human beings to err in it. In the nineteenth century a man named Sodre invented Solresol, a universal language based on the musical scale. More recently some scholars have devised Translingua Script, which makes use of numerical codes. For example, a tree would be known in every country by the number 31 and a man by 10 and so on.

Several billion earth dwellers have, however, remained blissfully unaffected by the hundreds of schemes which have been dreamed up to pull them out of their linguistic imbroglio. Most of the languages which have been offered have never gone much farther than the walls of the inventor's own study or beyond a handful of devotees. Only three languages have made some sort of dent in the field.

Volapük

The first artificial medium to enjoy mass appeal was Volapük, devised in 1879 by a German Monsignor named Johann Martin Schleyer, a man whose linguistic prowess became legendary—he was reputed to speak over seventy languages. Schleyer—arbitrarily it would seem by modern scientific linguistic standards—created his Volapük (meaning "world speech") out of English, French, German, and the Romance languages, with heaviest emphasis on Germanic as a source of roots. The Lord's Prayer in Volapük appeared as follows:

> "O Fat obas, kel binol in süls, paisaludomöz nem ola! Kömomöd monargän ola! Jenomöz vil olik, as in sül i su tal! Bodi obsik vädeliki givolös obes adelo! E pardolos obes debis obsik, äs id obs aipardobs debeles obas. E no obis nindukoläs in tentadi; sed aidalivolös obis de bad. Jenosöd!

Volapük came along at a time when the atmosphere was particularly receptive to an idea of this sort. It became the rage of Europe, from 1879 to 1889, and societies were formed in which pastry cooks hobnobbed with archdukes in a fraternal effort to master the new "world" language. In the United States, the American Philosophical Society (founded by Benjamin Franklin) considered supporting the language, but finally decided that it was too difficult. Some Parisian department stores even gave their sales personnel lessons in the new idiom.

The success of Volapük was, however, shortlived, largely because of the unnecessary difficulty of its grammar with complicated case-endings and a sound system which included umlauts such as the German *ü* and *ö*. Amusingly enough, it collapsed entirely in 1889 at an international conference of Volapük speakers when enthusiasts, trying to deliver speeches in the language, found it too cumbersome to use.

Esperanto

Before Volapük was decently buried, a new contender appeared. This was Esperanto, brain-child of Dr. Ludwik Zamenhof, a Polish doctor reared in the city of Bialystok where Poles, Lithuanians, Ukrainians, Germans, Russians, and Jews lived together in uneasy hostility. The idealistic doctor came to feel that at the base of tension among peoples was the language problem, and believed that a universal language would bring peace and understanding.

The Polish doctor fashioned his international language out of English, German, and the Romance tongues, with the heaviest representation from the latter group. Profiting from the experience of Volapük, Zamenhof aimed—quite successfully—at utmost simplicity in designing his Esperanto.

The basic grammar, consisting of only sixteen rules, is simplicity itself and can actually be learned in a few hours. However, to learn to write and speak the language is quite another matter. The sound system is simple for most Europeans although it might not necessarily be so for persons speaking certain Oriental tongues.

Here is a sample of Esperanto:

Esperanto	*English*
La astronomo, per speciala teleskopo fotografas la sunon, la lunon, kaj la planedojn.	The astronomer, by means of a special telescope, photographs the sun, the moon, and the planets.
Modernaj delikataj instrumentoj	Modern, delicate instruments per-

permesas la detalan ekzamenon de la strukturo de la atomo.	mit the detailed examination of the structure of the atom.
La teorio de Einstein, la nova principo de relativeco, presentas komplikan problemon.	The Einstein theory, the new principle of relativity, presents a complex problem.

Today, almost seventy-five years since its origination and fifty-seven years after the first Esperanto World Congress, which ushered in the period of its practical use, the artificial tongue is still quite alive. But many students consider that Esperanto is more of an idealistic movement than it is a language. Each year, Esperantists hold a Universal Congress. A wide range of programs in cultural and social activities is offered, as well as several score specialized conferences, all in the *internacia lingvo*. At many places in the world, the wearer of the Esperantists' green badge (green for hope) can rely upon fellow members for assistance in getting around. At the World's Fair in Brussels, for instance, Esperanto interpreters were available along with those in principal languages.

According to Dr. William Solzbacher, one of the leading Esperantists in the United States, more than fifty scholarly publications in fifteen countries publish articles or summaries in Esperanto, and about 145 periodicals are printed entirely in the tongue. Fifteen radio stations in Rome, Paris, Vienna, Warsaw, Sofia, Valencia, Caracas, Pyongyang, and other cities broadcast programs in Esperanto. The Voice of America has used the language in four series of shortwave programs in the past two years and has received almost two thousand letters in Esperanto from ninety-one countries, including every Iron Curtain country except Albania. Esperanto is taught by about seven hundred schools in forty countries. When the University of Leningrad, breaking a long-standing ban, announced after-hours classes in Esperanto, there was a rush by applicants. Although the Esperanto organizations number only about 110,000 actual members, roughly one million persons make some use of the language. There now are even some native speakers, raised in homes where Esperanto was used as the household language. It is the only interlanguage that can claim a considerable literature, with some 8,400 titles that include original works as well as translations of the Bible, *The Divine Comedy,* and other classics.

Interlingua

As inevitably occurs, one splinter group after another has broken away from Esperanto to form rival offshoots, such as Ido, Novial, and Occidental. Nevertheless none of these has ever made much headway.

The only language which has seriously challenged Esperanto's preeminence is Interlingua, presented to the world by the American linguist Dr. Alexander Gode, whose work over a period of twenty years was supported by a wealthy "angel," Mrs. Alice Vanderbilt Morris, who was converted to the idea of a world language.

Interlingua is what its founders call an extracted rather than a derived language. This means that a given word is generally taken in toto and subjected to little or no modification. Other artificial languages have generally altered considerably to conform to prescribed patterns. The Interlingua vocabulary is taken from French, Italian, Spanish, English and, to a much lesser extent, German and Russian. Only words that appear in at least three of these tongues are adopted. When no term meets these requirements, a word is usually taken from Latin. The developers made attempts to construct the language as scientifically as possible in an effort to arrive at what the architects of Interlingua term "standard average European." The Interlinguists claim that it can be read with little or no previous study by persons familiar with higher education. Its grammatical structure is of the same order as Esperanto and can be learned in a few hours. A book recently appeared comparing the difficulties of these two languages. It was done by an Esperantist, and the findings were favorable to Esperanto.

Here is an example of Interlingua:

INTERLINGUA	ENGLISH
Professor H. Oberth, un del pioneros in le campo del rochetteria scientific in Germania e plus recentemente un associato de Dr. W. von Braun in su recercas de roccheteria al arsenal Redstone in Alabama, ha elaborate un vehiculo adoptate al exploration del luna. Un tal vehiculo debe esser capace a superar le difficultates extraordinari del terreno e del ambiente del luna que es characterisate per le absentia de omne atmosphere, per un gravitate reducite, per extrememente acute alterationes de temperatura, e per un superficie plus pulverose que ullo cognoscite in terra.	Professor H. Oberth, one of the pioneers in the field of scientific rocketry in Germany and more recently an associate of Dr. W. von Braun in his research on rocketry at the Redstone Arsenal in Alabama, has elaborated plans for a vehicle adapted for lunar exploration. Such a vehicle must be capable of overcoming the extraordinary difficulties of the terrain and surroundings of the moon, characterized by the absence of any atmosphere, by reduced gravity, by extremely sharp changes of temperature, and by a more dusty surface than any known on earth.

For the present at least, the aims of Interlingua are more modest than those of Esperanto. No real attempt has been made to promote it as a spoken language, although one of the writers heard and understood a talk given in it at a meeting of the Modern Language Association of America. Its first objective is to secure acceptance as a medium of scientific and scholarly communication. It has done quite well in the dozen years of its existence, and by now, some twenty journals make use of Interlingua, mostly for summaries. The Interlingua Division of Science Service, Inc., Washington, D.C., attempts to promote Interlingua by offering to provide summaries and abstracts in that language for specialized journals and resumés for conferences of international research significance. (This organization also publishes an Interlingua version of *Science News Letter.*) By now there are in Interlingua several newsletters for sub-disciplines in which no specific periodicals are available. According to Dr. Alexander Gode, "The community of those who can be reached through Interlingua includes anyone with fair or full qualifications to grasp the technical import of the same message if presented in either French, Italian, Spanish, English, Greek, or Latin. In many scientific disciplines this makes for the possibility of complete and world-wide coverage through Interlingua . . . on the basis of what the reader knows and has known all along by virtue of his professional training."

Other Approaches

The trouble with artificial languages is that, although arousing tremendous enthusiasm among their devotees, they do not attract enough mass support to achieve their objectives. And yet they have proved that they are fully capable of performing the written and spoken communication tasks of modern technological societies.

One more method of arriving at an artificial international auxiliary language has been suggested. The Russian linguist N. D. Andreyev believes that intermediary languages containing most of the features shared by the major natural languages will necessarily be developed in work on machine translation done by electronic computers. When the ideal intermediate language has been hammered out, Andreyev feels, it will be usable for human international communication. This amounts to saying that since people have botched the job, machines will do it for them.

Another school of thought recommends the simplification of existing languages. The best known of these attempts has been Basic English, devised by the British philosopher, C. K. Ogden, and promoted in America by Harvard Professor I.A. Richards. With its vocabulary of some eight hundred words and about sixteen general-purpose verbs, "Basic" sounds terribly easy. In reality, however, it requires skill to manipulate this small stock of words so that complex concepts can be expressed in it. An Esperantist has pointed out that to render "The watermelon tastes good," one must say something like, "The large round, sweet vegetable has a good taste." Basic English reached its peak during World War II when it received a strong endorsement from Sir Winston Churchill and the British Government. This, of course, caused the charge of "imperialism" to be leveled against it.

Here is a sample of Basic English:

BASIC ENGLISH (NEW TESTAMENT)	KING JAMES BIBLE (ACTS 4:32)
And all those who were of the faith were one in heart and soul: and not one of them said that any of the things which he had was his property only; but they had all things in common. . . . And no one among them was in need; for everyone who had land or houses, exchanging them for money, took the price of them, and put it at the feet of the Apostles for distribution to everyone as he had need.	And the multitude of them that believed were of one heart and one soul: neither said any of them that ought of the things which he possessed was his own; but they had all things common. . . . Neither was there any among them that lacked: for as many as were possessors of lands or houses sold them, and brought the prices of the things that were sold, and laid them down at the apostles' feet: and distribution was made unto every man according as he had need.

Another school of thought vigorously opposes "made" or "simplified" languages, preferring to take their languages "straight." A large number of natural languages have been advocated as world auxiliaries, including French, English, German, Russian, Spanish, Italian, Greek, Chinese, Latin, Hebrew, and even Yiddish. Only French and English have any real chance of acceptance in the Western world, because these two languages are actually functioning as auxiliaries in almost every continent of the globe.

India and Pakistan, which had hoped to establish Hindi and Urdu respectively as their number one tongues by 1960, have realized that they cannot do so and will have to rely on English for some time to come. Ironically enough, at the bitterly anti-Western Bandung conference—to which Britain and the United States were not invited—English, which was familiar to the largest number of delegates, had to be used as the working language. Today, in fact, the use of English as a language of wider communication is expanding rapidly all over the world. In almost any country of Africa, Latin America, or Asia outside Communist China, there is a tremendous demand for teachers of English as a second language.

Some observers even advise adoption of a multiple system of languages, according to which the world would be divided into a number of zones and a different combination of natural languages used in each. This would mean, for instance, that each country in the "zone of the Far East" would use the native language plus English and Chinese. The trouble with this sort of plan is that it would perpetuate the very thing which it tries to combat, at the same time placing an enormous burden of language learning on children in areas speaking little-known tongues.

With such conflict and partisan feelings about one or another proposed "interlanguage," it is more encouraging to turn to the growing trend toward adopting limited international codes in a variety of fields. One might well call these "sublanguages."

A language of written symbols has been one of the most persistent schemes for improving international communication. Recently, Rudolf Modley, Ford Foundation consultant, speaking at the New York Conference of Communication Arts, pleaded for the development of an international science of "symbology." He provided strong evidence of how this symbology can be helpful in such specialized areas as machine tool design. For example, control panels would be lettered in internationally recognizable symbols.

Another triumph for touring motorists was achieved not long ago when some forty road symbols were adopted by most Western nations as official traffic and driving directions.

The universality of numbers has persistently suggested their use as an international code. Most recently, Professor Erich Funke of the University of Iowa devised his Translingua Script, based on arabic numerals. Dictionaries in all the important languages would carry Translingua Script word equivalents.

Progress has been made by the Federal Aviation Agency with Basic English for international aviation communication, since its short vocabulary is useful for limited conversations such as occur between air and ground. Unfortunately, the use of English in any form presents problems. Certain sounds, such as those for *f* and *s,* do not transmit well and can be confused. Monosyllables, as in the case of *five* and *nine,* can be confused also. Moreover, there is scarcely an English sound that is not difficult to pronounce for one nationality or another. Scandinavians have trouble with *j*'s and the Japanese with *l* and *r*.

Additional codes are being devised in other fields. Specialists in documentation, here concerned with the world-wide collection and retrieval of information, have made increasing use of data processing machines and have developed international codes and symbols to control greater amounts of information than ever before.

One of the challenging by-products of "intelligent machine" research is the development of an international computer language. According to Bell Telephone Research scientist John R. Pierce, this would really consist of various forms of an "artificial, unambiguous, logical mathematical language" understandable to all computer experts.

And so the controversy rages on. Esperanto and Interlingua enthusiasts argue that these languages, which are perfectly regular, take about one twentieth the time to learn that is required for, say, a West European language. They point out that since these are not identified with any specific nation, they are free of any political taint, or the charge of imperialism, which makes such languages as English and French unacceptable to some countries, particularly the small, emergent nations. Their opponents retort by alleging that for most people the artificiality of these tongues gives them the feeling that they are not learning real languages. The fact that languages like Esperanto are not rooted in a specific nation deprives their learners of access to the rich cultural heritage which the major languages afford. They argue that the extra effort to learn a natural language is well worth while when one considers the millions who can be reached in the Romance languages, German, or for that matter Arabic, Russian, or Chinese.

In the Communist world, of course, it is Russian which is being promoted as the "world language of communism." Its teaching is compulsory in the schools of most of the satellites, and "friendship societies" attempt to interest adults in this Slavic tongue. Although Russian is definitely making inroads, its grammatical complexity and longer learning time put it at a disadvantage except among fellow Slavs. The curtain on artificial languages has lifted a bit, and announcements of after-hours teaching of Esperanto brought long lines of applicants in Leningrad. Eastern Europe's greatest activity is in Poland, home of the Esperanto movement. An Esperanto exhibition in the summer of 1959 brought visitors from many parts of the globe to Warsaw.

What are the prospects for a universally acceptable auxiliary language? Mario Pei's *One Language for the World,* published in 1958, said the answer would not come through creating new, artificial languages, since some that exist are adequate already. The only real solution must be reached by joint agreement of all nations. Pei proposed that an international conference be called to discuss the merits of a number of languages and that one be adopted by majority vote. Following this, each nation would pledge itself to teach that language from kindergarten up. Dr. Pei believes that the world could become bilingual within a generation, sweeping away many of the barriers that beset international communication today.

Since such an international language would be taught mainly to children, the difficulties that adults might experience in learning it should not be a consideration in selecting it. Under Professor Pei's rules, Mandarin Chinese—written in a Latin alphabet—would be the logical choice, however unlikely it might seem in today's political situation.

Dr. Pei sent copies of his book to the heads of sovereign states. From all indications there has been no wholesale movement to take concerted action on this matter.

FOR DISCUSSION AND REVIEW

1. Non-native speakers of a language often have difficulty with idiomatic phrases; for example, "raining cats and dogs," "clean as a whistle," "ticklish problem," and "step on the gas" might perplex a foreigner. List other idioms in your own speech that would be difficult to translate literally into another language. If you are currently enrolled in a foreign language course, make a list of idioms for that language and explain them to your class.

2. What do Ornstein and Gage mean when they say Interlingua is "an extracted rather than a derived language"?

3. Most attempts at a world language have ended in failure. What accounts for the continued popularity and relative success of Esperanto?

4. Would it be more realistic to hope for one universal language or several world languages that are designed for specific purposes?

5. A recent attempt to create a new language is found in Anthony Burgess' *A Clockwork Orange,* a futuristic novel set in England. Here is how the novel begins:

> "What's it going to be then, eh?" There was me, that is Alex, and my three droogs, that is Pete, Georgie, and Dim, Dim being really dim, and we sat in the Korova Milkbar making up our rassoodocks what to do with the evening, a flip dark chill winter bastard though dry. The Korova Milkbar was a milk-plus mesto, and you may, O my brothers,

have forgotten what these mestos were like, things changing so skorry these days and everybody very quick to forget, newspapers not being read much neither. Well, what they sold there was milk plus something else. They had no license for selling liquor, but there was no law yet against prodding some of the new veshches which they used to put into the old moloko, so you could peet it with vellocet or synthemesc or drencrom or one or two other veshches which would give you a nice quiet horrorshow fifteen minutes admiring Bog And All His Holy Angels And Saints in your left shoe with lights bursting all over your mozg. Or you could peet milk with knives in it, as we used to say, and this would sharpen you up and make you ready for a bit of dirty twenty-to-one, and that was what we were peeting this evening I'm starting off the story with.

How would you describe the language in this passage? What impressions does it create? Is it unintelligible?

MELVIN MADDOCKS 2

The Limitations of Language

In this recent article from Time, *essayist Melvin Maddocks reports on the epidemic proportions in the United States of an old disease. "Semantic aphasia," or "that numbness of ear, mind, and heart—that tone deafness to the very meaning of language," is something more than the pollution of language that Orwell warned us about in the 1940's. Semantic aphasia results from the overloading and consequent jamming of our individual communication networks. Although he offers some hope for the prevention of semantic aphasia, Maddocks is not very optimistic about its elimination.*

IN J. M. G. LE CLÉZIO'S NOVEL *The Flood,* THE ANTI-HERO IS A young man suffering from a unique malady. Words—the deluge of daily words—have overloaded his circuits. Even when he is strolling down the street, minding his own business, his poor brain jerks under the impact of instructions (WALK—DON'T WALK), threats (TRESPASSERS WILL BE PROSECUTED), and newsstand alarms (PLANE CRASH AT TEL AVIV). Finally, Le Clézio's Everyman goes numb—nature's last defense. Spoken words become mere sounds, a meaningless buzz in the ears. The most urgent printed words—a poem by Baudelaire, a proclamation of war—have no more profound effect than the advice he reads (without really reading) on a book of matches: PLEASE CLOSE COVER BEFORE STRIKING.

If one must give a name to Le Clézio's disease, perhaps semantic aphasia will do. Semantic aphasia is that numbness of ear, mind and heart—that tone deafness to the very meaning of language—which results from the habitual and prolonged abuse of words. As an isolated phenomenon, it can be amusing if not downright irritating. But when it becomes epidemic, it signals a disastrous decline in the skills of communication, to that mumbling low point where language does almost the opposite of what it was created for. With frightening perversity—the evidence mounts daily—words now seem to cut off and isolate, to cause more misunderstanding than they prevent.

Semantic aphasia is the monstrous insensitivity that allows generals to call war "pacification," union leaders to describe strikes or slowdowns as "job actions," and politicians to applaud even moderately progressive programs as "revolutions." Semantic aphasia is also the near-pathological blitheness that permits three different advertisers in the same women's magazine to call a wig and two dress lines "liberated."

So far, so familiar. Whenever the ravishing of the English language comes up for perfunctory headshaking, politicians, journalists, and ad writers almost invariably get cast as Three Horsemen of the Apocalypse. The perennially identified culprits are guilty as charged, God knows. At their worst—and how often they are!—they seem to address the world through a bad PA system. Does it matter what they actually say? They capture your attention, right? They are word manipulators—the carnival barkers of life who misuse language to pitch and con and make the quick kill.

So let's hear all the old boos, all the dirty sneers. Paste a sticker proclaiming Stamp Out Agnewspeak on every bumper. Take the ribbons out of the typewriters of all reporters and rewritemen. Force six packs a day on the guy who wrote "Winston tastes good *like* . . ." Would that the cure for semantic aphasia were that simple.

What about, for example, the aphasics of the counterculture? The ad writer may dingdong catch phrases like Pavlov's bells in order to produce saliva. The Movement propagandist rings his chimes ("Fascist!" "Pig!" "Honky!" "Male chauvinist!") to produce spit. More stammer than grammar, as Dwight Macdonald put it, the counterculture makes inarticulateness an ideal, debasing words into clenched fists ("Right on!") and exclamation points ("Oh, wow!"). Semantic aphasia on the right, semantic aphasia on the left. Between the excesses of square and hip rhetoric the language is in the way of being torn apart.

The semantic aphasia examined so far might be diagnosed as a hysterical compulsion to simplify. Whether pushing fluoride toothpaste or Women's Lib, the rhetoric tends to begin, rather than end, at an extreme. But there is a second, quite different variety of the disease: overcomplication. It damages the language less spectacularly but no less fatally than oversimplification. Its practitioners are commonly known as specialists. Instead of unjustified clarity they offer unjustified obscurity. Whether his discipline is biophysics or medieval Latin, the specialist jealously guards trade secrets by writing and speaking a private jargon that bears only marginal resemblances to English. Cult words encrust his sentences like barnacles, slowing progress, affecting the steering. And the awful truth is that everybody is a specialist at something.

If the oversimplifier fakes being a poet, the overcomplicator fakes being a scientist. Perhaps it is unfair to pick on economists rather than anybody else—except that they are, after all, talking about money. And as often as not it turns out to be our money. Here is a master clarifier-by-smokescreen discussing the recruiting possibilities of a volunteer army if wages, military (W_m) are nudged seductively in the direction of wages, civilian (W_c): "However, when one considers that a military aversion factor must be added to W_c or subtracted from W_m, assuming average aversion is positive, and that only a portion of military wages are perceived, the wage ratio is certainly less than unity and our observations could easily lie on the increasing elasticity segment of the supply curve." All clear, everyone?

The ultimate criticism of the overcomplicator is not that he fuzzes but that he fudges. If the cardinal sin of the oversimplifier is to inflate the trivial, the cardinal sin of the overcomplicator is to flatten the magnificent—or just pretend that it is not there. In the vocabulary of the '70s, there is an adequate language for fanaticism, but none for ordinary quiet conviction. And there are almost no words left to express the concerns of honor, duty or piety.

For the noble idea leveled with a thud, see your nearest modern Bible. "Vanity of vanities, saith the Preacher . . ." In one new version his words become, "A vapor of vapors! Thinnest of vapors! All is vapor!"—turning the most passionate cry in the literature of nihilism into a spiritual weather report. The new rendition may be a more literal expression of the Hebrew original, but at what a cost in grace and power.

Who will protect the language from all those oversimplifiers and overcomplicators who kill meaning with shouts or smother it with cautious mumbles? In theory, certain professions should serve as a sort of palace guard sworn to defend the mother tongue with their lives. Alas, the enemy is within the gates. Educators talk gobbledygook about "non-abrasive systems intervention" and "low structure-low consideration teaching style." Another profession guilty of non-defense is lexicography. With proud humility today's dictionary editor abdicates even as arbiter, refusing to recognize any standards but usage. If enough people misuse *disinterested* as a synonym for *uninterested,* Webster's will honor it as a synonym. If enough people say *infer* when they mean *imply,* then that becomes its meaning in the eyes of a dictionary editor.

Con Edison can be fined for contaminating the Hudson. Legislation can force Detroit to clean up automobile exhausts. What can one do to punish the semantic aphasics for polluting their native language? None of man's specialties of self-destruction—despoliation of the environment, overpopulation, even war—appears more ingrained than his gift for fouling his mother tongue. Yet nobody dies of semantic aphasia, and by and large it gets complained about with a low-priority tut-tut.

The reason we rate semantic aphasia so low—somewhere between athlete's foot and the common cold on the scale of national perils—is that we don't understand the deeper implications of the disease. In his classic essay, *Politics and the English Language,* George Orwell pointed out what should be obvious—that sloppy language makes for sloppy thought. Emerson went so far as to suggest that bad rhetoric meant bad men. Semantic aphasia, both men recognized, kills after all. "And the Lord said: 'Go to, let us go down, and there confound their language, that they may not understand one another's speech.' " Is there a more ominous curse in the Bible? It breathes hard upon us at this time of frantic change, when old purposes slip out from under the words that used to cover them, leaving the words like tombstones over empty graves.

How, then, does one rescue language? How are words repaired, put back in shape, restored to accuracy and eloquence, made faithful again to the commands of the mind and the heart? There is, sadly enough, no easy answer. Sincerity is of little help to clichés, even in a suicide note, as Aldous Huxley once remarked. Read, if you can, the Latinized techno-pieties of most ecologists. Good intentions are not likely to produce another Shakespeare or a Bible translation equivalent to that produced by King James' bench of learned men. They wrote when English was young, vital and untutored. English in [the 1970s] is an old, overworked language, freshened sporadically only by foreign borrowings or the flickering, vulgar piquancy of slang. All of us—from the admen with their jingles to the tin-eared scholars with their jargon—are victims as well as victimizers of the language we have inherited.

Concerning aphasia, the sole source of optimism is the logic of necessity. No matter how carelessly or how viciously man abuses the language he has inherited, he simply cannot live without it. Even Woodstock Nation cannot survive on an oral diet of grunts and expletives. Mankind craves definition as he craves lost innocence. He simply does not know what his life means until he says it. Until the day he dies he will grapple with mystery by trying to find the word for it. "The limits of my language," Ludwig Wittgenstein observed, "are the limits of my world." Man's purifying motive is that he cannot let go of the Adam urge to name things—and finally, out of his unbearable solitude, to pronounce to others his own identity.

FOR DISCUSSION AND REVIEW

1. Politicians, journalists, and ad writers suffer from semantic aphasia. Who else suffers from this disease? Give some examples of semantic aphasia.

2. Maddocks identifies two varieties of semantic aphasia: oversimplification and overcomplication. Explain his statement: "If the oversimplifier fakes being a poet, the overcomplicator fakes being a scientist."

3. What assumptions does Maddocks make about the proper role of the lexicographer?

4. Why are people so indifferent to semantic aphasia? Are its effects harmless?

5. What hope does Maddocks offer for the rescue of language?

ALVIN TOFFLER 3

The Semi-Literate Shakespeare

Alvin Toffler's best-selling Future Shock *has had a tremendous influence on many Americans. It documents the acceleration of all aspects of contemporary life, an acceleration that appalls many people. In this passage from his book, Toffler, a former editor at* Fortune *magazine, turns his attention to the remarkable increase in our vocabulary, the transiency of many of our words, and other changes that are "convulsing" our language.*

IF OUR IMAGES OF REALITY ARE CHANGING MORE RAPIDLY, AND THE machinery of image-transmission is being speeded up, a parallel change is altering the very codes we use. For language, too, is convulsing. According to lexicographer Stuart Berg Flexner, senior editor of the *Random House Dictionary of the English Language,* "The words we use are changing faster today—and not merely on the slang level, but on every level. The rapidity with which words come and go is vastly accelerated. This seems to be true not only of English, but of French, Russian and Japanese as well."

Flexner illustrated this with the arresting suggestion that, of the estimated 450,000 "usable" words in the English language today, only perhaps 250,000 would be comprehensible to William Shakespeare. Were Shakespeare suddenly to materialize in London or New York today, he would be able to understand, on the average, only five out of every nine words in our vocabulary. The Bard would be a semi-literate.

This implies that if the language had the same number of words in Shakespeare's time as it does today, at least 200,000 words—perhaps several times that many—have dropped out and been replaced in the intervening four centuries. Moreover, Flexner conjectures that a full third of this turnover has occurred within the last fifty years alone. This, if correct, would mean that words are now dropping out of the language and being replaced at a rate at least three times faster than during the base period 1564 to 1914.

This high turnover rate reflects changes in things, processes, and qualities in the environment. Some new words come directly from the world of consumer products and technology. Thus, for example, words like "fast-back," "wash-and-wear" or "flashcube" were all propelled into the language by advertising in recent years. Other words come from the headlines. "Sit-in" and "swim-in" are recent products of the civil rights movement; "teach-in" a product of the campaign against the Vietnam war; "be-in" and "love-in" products of the hippie subculture. The LSD cult has brought with it a profusion of new words—"acidhead," "psychedelic," etc.

At the level of slang, the turnover rate is so rapid that it has forced dictionary makers to change their criteria for word inclusion. "In 1954," says Flexner, "when I started work on the *Dictionary of American Slang,* I would not consider a word for inclusion unless I could find three uses of the word over a five-year period. Today such a criterion would be impossible. Language, like art, is increasingly becoming a fad proposition. The slang terms 'fab' and 'gear,' for example, didn't last a single year. They entered the teen-age vocabulary in about 1966; by 1967 they were out. You cannot use a time criterion for slang any more."

One fact contributing to the rapid introduction and obsolescence of words is the incredible speed with which a new word can be injected into wide usage. In the late 1950's and early sixties one could actually trace the way in which certain scholarly jargon words such as "rubric" or "subsumed" were picked up from academic journals, used in small-circulation periodicals like the *New York Review of Books* or *Commentary,* then adopted by *Esquire* with its then circulation of 800,000 to 1,000,000, and finally diffused through the larger society by *Time, Newsweek* and the larger mass magazines. Today the process has been telescoped. The editors of mass magazines no longer pick up vocabulary from the intermediate intellectual publications alone; they, too, lift directly from the scholarly press in their hurry to be "on top of things."

When Susan Sontag disinterred the word "camp" and used it as the basis of an essay in *Partisan Review* in the fall of 1964, *Time* waited only a few weeks before devoting an article to the word and its rejuvenator. Within a matter of a few additional weeks, the term was cropping up in newspapers and other mass media. Today the word has virtually dropped out of usage. "Teenybopper" is another word that came and went with blinding speed.

A more significant example of language turnover can be seen in the sudden shift of meaning associated with the ethnic term "black." For years, dark-skinned Americans regarded the term as racist. Liberal whites dutifully taught their children to use the term "Negro" and to capitalize the "N." Shortly after Stokely Carmichael proclaimed the doctrine of Black Power in Greenwood, Mississippi in June, 1966, however, "black" became a term of pride among both blacks and whites in the movement for racial justice. Caught off guard, liberal whites went through a period of confusion, uncertain as to whether to use Negro or black. Black was quickly legitimated when the mass media adopted the new meaning. Within a few months, black was "in," Negro "out."

Even faster cases of diffusion are on record. "The Beatles," says lexicographer Flexner, "at the height of their fame could make up any word they like, slip it into a record, and within a month it would be part of the language. At one time perhaps no more than fifty people in NASA used the word 'A-OK.' But when an astronaut used it during a televised flight, the word became part of the language in a single day. The same has been true of other space terms, too—like 'sputnik' or 'all systems go.' "

As new words sweep in, old words vanish. A picture of a nude girl nowadays is no longer a "pin-up" or a "cheesecake shot," but a "playmate." "Hep" has given way to "hip"; "hipster" to "hippie." "Go-go" rushed eagerly into the language at breakneck speed, but it is already gone-gone among those who are truly "with it."

The turnover of language would even appear to involve non-verbal forms of communication as well. We have slang gestures, just as we have slang words—thumbs up or down, thumb to nose, the "shame on you" gesture used by children, the hand moving across the neck to suggest a throat-slitting. Professionals who watch the development of the gestural language suggest that it, too, may be changing more rapidly.

Some gestures that were regarded as semi-obscene have become somewhat more acceptable as sexual values have changed in the society. Others that were used only by a few have achieved wider usage. An example of diffusion, Flexner observes, is the wider use today of that gesture of contempt and defiance—the fist raised and screwed about. The invasion of Italian movies that hit the United States in the fifties and sixties probably contributed to this. Similarly, the upraised finger—the "up yours" gesture—appears to be gaining greater respectability and currency than it once had. At the same time, other gestures have virtually vanished or been endowed with radically changed meaning. The circle formed by the thumb and forefinger to suggest that all goes well appears to be fading out; Churchill's "V for Victory" sign is now used by protesters to signify something emphatically different: "peace" *not* "victory."

There was a time when a man learned the language of his society and made use of it, with little change, throughout his lifetime. His "relationship" with each learned word or gesture was durable. Today, to an astonishing degree, it is not.

FOR DISCUSSION AND REVIEW

1. How does Toffler explain the rapidity with which a word can gain popularity and then become obsolescent? In what areas of our vocabulary is this process particularly rapid?

2. "A-OK" and "camp" are two examples cited by Toffler of words that have spread very rapidly. Add some other examples from your own experience. Give some examples of once-popular words that are now little used.

3. Toffler suggests that gestural language is also changing. Give several examples of gestures that have changed in meaning.

4. Have certain *kinds* of words changed more extensively than others? In answering this question, consider nouns, verbs, prepositions, and articles. What are the implications of your answer in terms of Toffler's assertion that if Shakespeare were reincarnated today, he "would be a semi-literate"?

ARTHUR BERGER 4
Hot Language and Cool Lives

Have you ever wondered just how big "Giant King Size" actually is or what "groovy" actually means? These are examples of what Arthur Berger, pop culture expert at San Francisco State College, calls "hot" language, a mode of speech that he feels is increasingly being used to mask, even from ourselves, the "cool" or less-than-exciting lives most of us lead.

THERE IS A FISH THAT ALWAYS DELIGHTS ME WHENEVER I TAKE MY children to the aquarium. It is a slender rather trivial thing that has the ability to puff itself up into a big ball and scare off (hopefully) other fish that might wish to attack it. It is literally a big windbag, yet this defense mechanism works—well enough, at least, for other windbags to be born and survive.

The whole business is quite absurd except that it does work, and what is more fantastic, with people as well as with fishes. A lot of people are leading rather luke-warm lives, if not cool (and not in the sense of "good" as some use the term) or tepid lives, yet they describe themselves and their actions in terms of what might be called "hot" language.

I can recall once overhearing two bored youths at a tennis court.

Said one of them, "Let's split," a phrase much in usage these days, in fitting with the schizophrenic nature of the times. Somehow "splitting" from a place is much more exciting than "going someplace else" or "leaving."

Is it not possible that there is a direct correlation between a growing sense of powerlessness and futility in our lives and the jazzed-up language we use? The more you feel yourself diminished the more you "build yourself up" by using hot language, showing that you are in some kind of an "in" group, and know what's going on. It is only natural to try to represent oneself in the best possible light, but if we study the way people do this, we find that this hot or inflated language is somewhat self-defeating.

As everything becomes inflated and *tremendous,* the word loses its currency. What is normal becomes tremendous. What then do we say about something that really is tremendous? It seems that the more we use hot language to add color to our otherwise colorless lives, the less utility the hot language has; it becomes devalued, and we have to work harder for less, so to speak. What used to be large is now "giant king size," and we have reached the point of no return.

Perhaps there is some kind of a searching for the infinite at work. In a recent advertisement from a humane society, various kinds of memberships were announced: Annual $5, Patron $10, Life $100, Perpetual $250. A lifetime is no longer enough. We must have a rate for those who would be immortal. On the opposite side of the fence death must be made more final, somehow. Thus we find ads for insecticides claiming that they "kill bugs *dead!*"

It may be that we can now think of killing without death—for as everything grows out of control and the fantastic becomes the commonplace (men on the moon on prime-time television), the old words like the old lifestyle become, somehow, inadequate. We need more and more emphasis and must be told that when something is killed it will be dead.

Television commercials have bred within the average American a skepticism that must somehow be overcome. We find all about us claims that are obviously absurd: on menus, travel brochures, bookjackets, etc. The law of diminishing returns is at work. Since people now believe less and less, you have to promise more and more to come out even. In this sense advertising is self-defeating for it (more than anything else) has created this skepticism, which it keeps attacking and forcing at the same time.

The use of this hot language is symptomatic of a certain malaise affecting people, which leads them to believe that life must at all times be exciting, vital, dazzling, full of "fabulous" experiences. This is nonsense, obviously. Everyone—even "world historical figures" such as leaders of great nations or movie celebrities—spends a great deal of his time doing routine, ordinary things. Thus, the use of hot language makes us *devalue* our lives, since we take a rather absurd conception of what is normal, measure our lives against this false norm, and find ourselves wanting. We all want to lead Giant King Size lives in an age when there are few giants or kings. Since we cannot, we then define ourselves as leading lives of quiet desperation, describe life as absurd and meaningless, and try to escape from all this by consumerism, drugs, or some other kind of narcoticism.

A distinguished sociologist, Leo Lowenthal, has discussed a form of hot language, the use of "superlatives," in the following manner:

> This wholesale distribution of highest ratings defeats its own purpose. Everything is presented as something unique, unheard of, outstanding. Thus nothing is unique, unheard of, outstanding. Totality of the superlative means totality of the mediocre. It levels the presentation of human life to the presentation of merchandise.

He wrote this in reference to the tendency of contemporary writers to use superlatives in biographies done for popular magazines. Lowenthal noticed that there was a change from early biographies that didn't use superlatives and dealt with heroes of production to recent biographies (around 1940) that used superlatives and were about heroes of consumption. On first sight the superlatives didn't seem very significant, until their real function was discovered. This was, Lowenthal suggested, to create "a reign of psychic terror, where the masses have to realize the pettiness and insignificance of their everyday life. The already weakened consciousness of being an individual is struck another heavy blow by the pseudo-individualizing forces of the superlative."

This was written in the forties, when we had "stars." How does the ordinary man feel in the seventies, in an era when being a "star" is no longer significant, since we now have *"superstars"*? When the star is relegated to mediocrity, what do we say about the average citizen? The fact is significant that we now use terms such as the "little guy"; his stature and significance are diminishing greatly, and he is on the verge of becoming a "forgotten" American.

Author's postscript: It is curious but behind such terms as "groovy," "my bag," and "heavy," there is a suggestion of containment and control. Could it be that many of the "now" generation are really seeking a bit of guidance and direction?

FOR DISCUSSION AND REVIEW

1. Berger suggests that the verb "split" is appropriate for the "schizophrenic nature of the times." In general, does slang reflect the culture of which it is a product?

2. How might Stevens (pp. 155–172) react to Berger's statement that "since people now believe less and less, you have to promise more and more to come out even"? Is advertising really "self-defeating"? Explain.

3. Discuss the implications of Lowenthal's statement about "superlatives" for students' grades, job evaluations, reviews of movies and books, and personal compliments.

4. Berger points to the power of language in shaping reality. Can "hot" language make a dull, boring existence exciting? Explain.

GEORGE ORWELL 5
The Principles of Newspeak

George Orwell's 1984, *his terrifying vision of life in the future, was published in 1949. Both the novel and the movie based upon it continue to fascinate audiences, who recognize all too clearly the similarities between the contemporary world and the imaginary future world that Orwell describes. In Orwell's Oceania, all the media are completely controlled by the government, and even people's thoughts are shaped by those in power, primarily through the deliberate introduction of a new language, Newspeak. "Newspeak," Orwell explains, "was designed not to extend but to* diminish *the range of thought. . . ." Here Orwell demonstrates how language controls thought and how those who control language can control people's minds.*

NEWSPEAK WAS THE OFFICIAL LANGUAGE OF OCEANIA AND HAD BEEN devised to meet the ideological needs of Ingsoc, or English Socialism. In the year 1984 there was not as yet anyone who used Newspeak as his sole means of communication, either in speech or writing. The leading articles in the *Times* were written in it, but this was a tour de force which could only be carried out by a specialist. It was expected that Newspeak would have finally superseded Oldspeak (or Standard English, as we should call it) by about the year 2050. Meanwhile it gained ground steadily, all Party members tending to use Newspeak words and grammatical constructions more and more in their everyday speech. The version in use in 1984, and embodied in the Ninth and Tenth Editions of the Newspeak dictionary, was a provisional one, and contained many superfluous words and archaic formations which were due to be suppressed later. It is with the final, perfected version, as embodied in the Eleventh Edition of the dictionary, that we are concerned here.

The purpose of Newspeak was not only to provide a medium of expression for the world-view and mental habits proper to the devotees of Ingsoc, but to make all other modes of thought impossible. It was intended that when Newspeak had been adopted once and for all and Oldspeak forgotten, a heretical thought—that is, a thought diverging from the principles of Ingsoc—should be literally unthinkable, at least so far as thought is dependent on words. Its vocabulary was so constructed as to give exact and often very subtle expression to every meaning that a Party member could properly wish to express, while excluding all other meanings and also the possibility of arriving at them by indirect methods. This was done partly by the invention of new words, but chiefly by eliminating undesirable words and by stripping such words as remained of unorthodox meanings, and so far as possible of all secondary meanings whatever. To give a single example. The word *free* still existed in Newspeak, but it could only be used in such statements as "This dog is free from lice" or "This field is free from weeds." It could not be used in its old sense of "politically free" or "intellectually free," since political and intellectual freedom no longer existed even as concepts, and were therefore of necessity nameless. Quite apart from the suppression of definitely heretical words, reduction of vocabulary was regarded as an end in itself, and no word that could be dispensed with was allowed to survive. Newspeak was designed not to extend but to *diminish* the range of thought, and this purpose was indirectly assisted by cutting the choice of words down to a minimum.

Newspeak was founded on the English language as we now know it, though many Newspeak sentences, even when not containing newly created words, would be barely intelligible to an English-speaker of our own day. Newspeak words were divided into three distinct classes, known as the A vocabulary, the B vocabulary (also called compound words), and the C vocabulary. It will be simpler to discuss each class separately, but the grammatical peculiarities of the language can be dealt with in the section devoted to the A vocabulary, since the same rules held good for all three categories.

The A Vocabulary

The A vocabulary consisted of the words needed for the business of everyday life—for such things as eating, drinking, working, putting on one's clothes, going up and down stairs, riding in vehicles, gardening, cooking, and the like. It was composed almost entirely of words that we already possess—words like *hit, run, dog, tree, sugar, house, field*—but in comparison with the present-day English vocabulary, their number was extremely small, while their meanings were far more rigidly defined. All ambiguities and shades of meaning had been purged out of them. So far as it could be achieved, a Newspeak word of this class was simply a staccato sound expressing *one* clearly understood concept. It would have been quite impossible to use the A vocabulary for literary purposes or for political or philosophical discussion. It was intended only to express simple, purposive thoughts, usually involving concrete objects or physical actions.

The grammar of Newspeak had two outstanding peculiarities. The first of these was an almost complete interchangeability between different parts of speech. Any word in the language (in principle this applied even to very abstract words such as *if* or *when*) could be used either as verb, noun, adjective, or adverb. Between the verb and the noun form, when they were of the same root, there was never any variation, this rule of itself involving the destruction of many archaic forms. The word *thought,* for example, did not exist in Newspeak. Its place was taken by *think,* which did duty for both noun and verb. No etymological principle was followed here; in some cases it was the original noun that was chosen for retention, in other cases the verb. Even where a noun and verb of kindred meaning were not etymologically connected, one or other of them was frequently suppressed. There was, for example, no such word as *cut,* its meaning being sufficiently covered by the noun-verb *knife*. Adjectives were formed by adding the suffix *-ful* to the noun-verb, and adverbs by adding *-wise*. Thus, for example, *speedful* meant "rapid" and *speedwise* meant "quickly." Certain of our present-day adjectives, such as *good, strong, big, black, soft,* were retained, but their total number was very small. There was little need for them, since almost any adjectival meaning could be arrived at by adding *-ful* to a noun-verb. None of the now-existing adverbs was retained, except for a very few already ending in *-wise;* the *-wise* termination was invariable. The word *well,* for example, was replaced by *goodwise*.

In addition, any word—this again applied in principle to every word in the language—could be negatived by adding the affix *un-,* or could be strengthened by the affix *plus-,* or, for still greater emphasis, *doubleplus-.* Thus, for example, *uncold* meant "warm," while *pluscold* and *doublepluscold* meant, respectively, "very cold" and "superlatively cold." It was also possible, as in present-day English, to modify the meaning of almost any word by prepositional affixes such as *ante-, post-, up-, down-,* etc. By such methods it was found possible to bring about an enormous diminution of vocabulary. Given, for instance, the word *good,* there was no need for such a word as *bad,* since the required meaning was equally well—indeed, better—expressed by *ungood.* All that was necessary, in any case where two words formed a natural pair of opposites, was to decide which of them to suppress. *Dark,* for example, could be replaced by *unlight,* or *light* by *undark,* according to preference.

The second distinguishing mark of Newspeak grammar was its regularity. Subject to a few exceptions which are mentioned below, all inflections followed the same rules. Thus, in all verbs the preterite and the past participle were the same and ended in *-ed.* The preterite of *steal* was *stealed,* the preterite of *think* was *thinked,* and so on throughout the language, all such forms as *swam, gave, brought, spoke, taken,* etc., being abolished. All plurals were made by adding *-s* or *-es* as the case might be. The plurals of *man, ox, life* were *mans, oxes, lifes.* Comparison of adjectives was invariably made by adding *-er, -est* (*good, gooder, goodest*), irregular forms and the *more, most* formation being suppressed.

The only classes of words that were still allowed to inflect irregularly were the pronouns, the relatives, the demonstrative adjectives, and the auxiliary verbs. All of these followed their ancient usage, except that *whom* had been scrapped as unnecessary, and the *shall, should* tenses had been dropped, all their uses being covered by *will* and *would.* There were also certain irregularities in word-formation arising out of the need for rapid and easy speech. A word which was difficult to utter, or was liable to be incorrectly heard, was held to be ipso facto a bad word; occasionally therefore, for the sake of euphony, extra letters were inserted into a word or an archaic formation was retained. But this need made itself felt chiefly in connection with the B vocabulary. *Why* so great an importance was attached to ease of pronunciation will be made clear later in this essay.

The B Vocabulary

The B vocabulary consisted of words which had been deliberately constructed for political purposes: words, that is to say, which not only had in every case a political implication, but were intended to impose a desirable mental attitude upon the person using them. Without a full understanding of the principles of Ingsoc it was difficult to use these words correctly. In some cases they could be translated into Oldspeak, or even into words taken from the A vocabulary, but this usually demanded a long paraphrase and always involved the loss of certain overtones. The B words were a sort of verbal shorthand, often packing whole ranges of ideas into a few syllables, and at the same time more accurate and forcible than ordinary language.

The B words were in all cases compound words.* They consisted of two or more words, or portions of words, welded together in an easily pronounceable form. The resulting amalgam was always a noun-verb, and inflected according to the ordinary rules. To take a single example: the word *goodthink,* meaning, very roughly, "orthodoxy," or, if one chose to regard it as a verb, "to think in an orthodox manner." This inflected as follows: noun-verb, *goodthink;* past tense and past participle, *goodthinked;* present participle, *goodthinking;* adjective, *goodthinkful;* adverb, *goodthinkwise;* verbal noun, *goodthinker.*

The B words were not constructed on any etymological plan. The words of which they were made up could be any parts of speech, and could be placed in any order and mutilated in any way which made them easy to pronounce while indicating their derivation. In the word *crimethink* (thoughtcrime), for instance, the *think* came second, whereas in *thinkpol* (Thought Police) it came first, and in the latter word *police* had lost its second syllable. Because of the greater difficulty in securing euphony, irregular formations were commoner in the B vocabulary than in the A vocabulary. For example, the adjectival forms of *Minitrue, Minipax,* and *Miniluv* were, respectively *Minitruthful, Minipeaceful,* and *Minilovely,* simply because *-trueful, -paxful,* and *-loveful* were slightly awkward to pronounce. In principle, however, all B words could inflect, and all inflected in exactly the same way.

Some of the B words had highly subtilized meanings, barely intelligible to anyone who had not mastered the language as a whole. Consider, for example, such a typical sentence from a *Times* leading article as *Oldthinkers unbellyfeel Ingsoc.* The shortest rendering that one could make of this in Oldspeak would be: "Those whose ideas were formed before the Revolution cannot have a full emotional understanding of the principles of English Socialism." But this is not an adequate translation. To begin with, in order to grasp the full mean-

* Compound words, such as *speakwrite,* were of course to be found in the A vocabulary, but these were merely convenient abbreviations and had no special ideological color.

ing of the Newspeak sentence quoted above, one would have to have a clear idea of what is meant by *Ingsoc*. And, in addition, only a person thoroughly grounded in Ingsoc could appreciate the full force of the word *bellyfeel,* which implied a blind, enthusiastic acceptance difficult to imagine today; or of the word *oldthink,* which was inextricably mixed up with the idea of wickedness and decadence. But the special function of certain Newspeak words, of which *oldthink* was one, was not so much to express meanings as to destroy them. These words, necessarily few in number, had had their meanings extended until they contained within themselves whole batteries of words which, as they were sufficiently covered by a single comprehensive term, could now be scrapped and forgotten. The greatest difficulty facing the compilers of the Newspeak dictionary was not to invent new words, but, having invented them, to make sure what they meant: to make sure, that is to say, what ranges of words they canceled by their existence.

As we have already seen in the case of the word *free,* words which had once borne a heretical meaning were sometimes retained for the sake of convenience, but only with the undesirable meanings purged out of them. Countless other words such as *honor, justice, morality, internationalism, democracy, science,* and *religion* had simply ceased to exist. A few blanket words covered them, and, in covering them, abolished them. All words grouping themselves round the concepts of liberty and equality, for instance, were contained in the single word *crimethink,* while all words grouping themselves round the concepts of objectivity and rationalism were contained in the single word *oldthink*. Greater precision would have been dangerous. What was required in a Party member was an outlook similar to that of the ancient Hebrew who knew, without knowing much else, that all nations other than his own worshiped "false gods." He did not need to know that these gods were called Baal, Osiris, Moloch, Ashtaroth, and the like; probably the less he knew about them the better for his orthodoxy. He knew Jehovah and the commandments of Jehovah; he knew, therefore, that all gods with other names or other attributes were false gods. In somewhat the same way, the Party member knew what constituted right conduct, and in exceedingly vague, generalized terms he knew what kinds of departure from it were possible. His sexual life, for example, was entirely regulated by the two Newspeak words *sexcrime* (sexual immorality) and *goodsex* (chastity). *Sexcrime* covered all sexual misdeeds whatever. It covered fornication, adultery, homosexuality, and other perversions, and, in addition, normal intercourse practiced for its own sake. There was no need to enumerate them separately, since they were all equally culpable, and, in principle, all punishable by death. In the C vocabulary, which consisted of scientific and technical words, it might be necessary to give specialized names to certain sexual aberrations, but the ordinary citizen had no need of them. He knew what was meant by *goodsex*—that is to say, normal intercourse between man and wife, for the sole purpose of begetting children, and without physical pleasure on the part of the woman; all else was *sexcrime*. In Newspeak it was seldom possible to follow a heretical thought further than the perception that it *was* heretical; beyond that point the necessary words were nonexistent.

No word in the B vocabulary was ideologically neutral. A great many were euphemisms. Such words, for instance, as *joycamp* (forced-labor camp) or *Minipax* (Ministry of Peace, i.e., Ministry of War) meant almost the exact opposite of what they appeared to mean. Some words, on the other hand, displayed a frank and contemptuous understanding of the real nature of Oceanic society. An example was *prolefeed,* meaning the rubbishy entertainment and spurious news which the Party handed out to the masses. Other words, again, were ambivalent, having the connotation "good" when applied to the Party and "bad" when applied to its enemies. But in addition there were great numbers of words which at first sight appeared to be mere abbreviations and which derived their ideological color not from their meaning but from their structure.

So far as it could be contrived, everything that had or might have political significance of any kind was fitted into the B vocabulary. The name of every organization, or body of people, or doctrine, or country, or institution, or public building, was invariably cut down into the familiar shape; that is, a single easily pronounced word with the smallest number of syllables that would preserve the original derivation. In the Ministry of Truth, for example, the Records Department, in which Winston Smith worked, was called *Recdep,* the Fiction Department was called *Ficdep,* the Teleprograms Department was called *Teledep,* and so on. This was not done solely with the object of saving time. Even in the early decades of the twentieth century, telescoped words and phrases had been one of the characteristic features of political language; and it had been noticed that the tendency to use abbreviations of this kind was most marked in totalitarian countries and totalitarian organizations. Examples were such words as *Nazi, Gestapo, Comintern, Inprecorr, Agitprop*. In the beginning the practice had been adopted as it were instinctively, but in Newspeak it was used with a conscious purpose. It was perceived that in thus abbreviating a name one narrowed and subtly altered its meaning, by cutting out most of the associations that would otherwise cling to it. The words *Communist International,* for instance, call up a composite picture of universal human brotherhood, red flags, barricades, Karl Marx, and the Paris Commune. The word *Comintern,* on the other hand, suggests merely a tightly knit organization and a well-defined body of doctrine. It refers to something almost as easily recognized, and as limited in purpose, as a chair or a table. *Comintern* is a word that can be uttered almost without taking thought, whereas *Communist International* is a phrase over which one is obliged to linger at least momentarily. In the same way, the associations called up by a word like *Minitrue* are fewer and more controllable than those called up by *Ministry of Truth.* This accounted not only for the habit of abbreviating whenever possible, but also for the almost exaggerated care that was taken to make every word easily pronounceable.

In Newspeak, euphony outweighed every consideration other than exactitude of meaning. Regularity of grammar was always sacrificed to it when it seemed necessary. And rightly so, since what was required, above all for political purposes, were short clipped words of unmistakable meaning which could be uttered rapidly and which roused the minimum of echoes in the speaker's mind. The words of the B vocabulary even gained in force from the fact that nearly all of them were very much alike. Almost invariably these words—*goodthink, Minipax, prolefeed, sexcrime, joycamp, Ingsoc, bellyfeel, thinkpol,* and countless others—were words of two or three syllables, with the stress distributed equally between the first syllable and the last. The use of them encouraged a gabbling style of speech, at once staccato and monotonous. And this was exactly what was aimed at. The intention was to make speech, and especially speech on any subject not ideologically neutral, as nearly as possible independent of consciousness. For the purposes of everyday life it was no doubt necessary, or sometimes necessary, to reflect before speaking, but a Party member called upon to make a political or ethical judgment should be able to spray forth the correct opinions as automatically as a machine gun spraying forth bullets. His training fitted him to do this, the language gave him an almost foolproof instrument, and the texture of the words, with their harsh sound and a certain willful ugliness which was in accord with the spirit of Ingsoc, assisted the process still further.

So did the fact of having very few words to choose from. Relative to our own, the Newspeak vocabulary was tiny, and new ways of reducing it were constantly being devised. Newspeak, indeed, differed from almost all other languages in that its vocabulary grew smaller instead of larger every year. Each reduction was a gain, since the smaller the area of choice, the smaller the temptation to take thought. Ultimately it was hoped to make articulate speech issue from the larynx without involving the higher brain centers at all. This aim was frankly admitted in the Newspeak word *duckspeak,* meaning "to quack like a duck." Like various other words in the B vocabulary, *duckspeak* was ambivalent in meaning. Provided that the opinions which were quacked out were orthodox ones, it implied nothing but praise, and when the *Times* referred to one of the orators of the Party as a *doubleplusgood duckspeaker* it was paying a warm and valued compliment.

The C Vocabulary

The C vocabulary was supplementary to the others and consisted entirely of scientific and technical terms. These resembled the scientific terms in use today, and were constructed from the same roots, but the usual care was taken to define them rigidly and strip them of undesirable meanings. They followed the same grammatical rules as the words in the other two vocabularies. Very few of the C words had any currency either in everyday speech or in political speech. Any scientific worker or technician could find all the words he needed in the list devoted to his own speciality, but he seldom had more than a smattering of the words occurring in the other lists. Only a very few words were common to all lists, and there was no vocabulary expressing the function of Science as a habit of mind, or a method of thought, irrespective of its particular branches. There was, indeed, no word for "Science," any meaning that it could possibly bear being already sufficiently covered by the word *Ingsoc.*

From the foregoing account it will be seen that in Newspeak the expression of unorthodox opinions, above a very low level, was well-nigh impossible. It was of course possible to utter heresies of a very crude kind, a species of blasphemy. It would have been possible, for example, to say *Big Brother is ungood.* But this statement, which to an orthodox ear merely conveyed a self-evident absurdity, could not have been sustained by reasoned argument, because the necessary words were not available. Ideas inimical to Ingsoc could only be entertained in a vague wordless form, and could only be named in very broad terms which lumped together and condemned whole groups of heresies without defining them in doing so. One could, in fact, only use Newspeak for unorthodox purposes by illegitimately translating some of the words back into Oldspeak. For example, *All mans are equal* was a possible Newspeak sentence, but only in the same sense in which *All men are redhaired* is a possible Oldspeak sentence. It did not contain a grammatical error, but it expressed a palpable untruth, i.e., that all men are of equal size, weight, or strength. The concept of political equality no longer existed, and this secondary meaning had accordingly been purged out of the word *equal.* In 1984, when Oldspeak was still the normal means of communication, the danger theoretically existed that in using Newspeak words one might remember their original meanings. In practice it was not difficult for any person well grounded in *doublethink* to avoid doing this, but within a couple of generations even the possibility of such a lapse would have vanished. A person growing up with Newspeak as his sole language would no more know that *equal* had once had the secondary meaning of "politically equal," or that *free* had once meant "intellectually free," than, for instance, a person who had never heard of chess would be aware of the secondary meanings attaching to *queen* and *rook*. There would be many crimes and errors which it would be beyond his power to commit, simply because they were nameless and therefore unimaginable. And it was to be foreseen that with the passage of time the distinguishing characteristics of Newspeak would become more and more pronounced—its words growing fewer and fewer, their meanings more and more rigid, and the chance of putting them to improper uses always diminishing.

When Oldspeak had been once and for all superseded, the last link with the past would have been severed. History had already been rewritten, but fragments of the literature of the past survived here and there, imperfectly censored, and so long as one retained one's knowledge of Oldspeak it was possible to read them. In the future such fragments, even if they chanced to survive, would be unintelligible and untranslatable. It was impossible to translate any passage of Oldspeak into Newspeak unless it either referred to some technical process or some very simple everyday action, or was already orthodox (*goodthinkful* would be the Newspeak expression) in tendency. In practice this meant that no book written before approximately 1960 could be translated as a whole. Prerevolutionary literature could only be subjected to ideological translation—that is, alteration in sense as well as language. Take for example the well-known passage from the Declaration of Independence:

> We hold these truths to be self-evident, that all men are created equal, that they are endowed by their Creator with certain inalienable rights, that among these are life, liberty and the pursuit of happiness. That to secure these rights, Governments are instituted among men, deriving their powers from the consent of the governed. That whenever any form of Government becomes destructive of those ends, it is the right of the People to alter or abolish it, and to institute new Government. . . .

It would have been quite impossible to render this into Newspeak while keeping to the sense of the original. The nearest one could come to doing so would be to swallow the whole passage up in the single word *crimethink*. A full translation could only be an ideological translation, whereby Jefferson's words would be changed into a panegyric on absolute government.

A good deal of the literature of the past was, indeed, already being transformed in this way. Considerations of prestige made it desirable to preserve the memory of certain historical figures, while at the same time bringing their achievements into line with the philosophy of Ingsoc. Various writers, such as Shakespeare, Milton, Swift, Byron, Dickens, and some others were therefore in process of translation; when the task had been completed, their original writings, with all else that survived of the literature of the past, would be destroyed. These translations were a slow and difficult business, and it was not expected that they would be finished before the first or second decade of the twenty-first century. There were also large quantities of merely utilitarian literature—indispensable technical manuals and the like—that had to be treated in the same way. It was chiefly in order to allow time for the preliminary work of translation that the final adoption of Newspeak had been fixed for so late a date as 2050.

FOR DISCUSSION AND REVIEW

1. What are the purposes of Newspeak? Can Newspeak be used to solve the problems of language pollution today?

2. Orwell sees a connection between language and thought. What exactly is the nature of the relationship for him, and does his view of the relationship seem reasonable to you?

3. One "benefit" of Newspeak would be a tremendous reduction in our vocabulary. New words would be formed, but their meanings would be readily apparent. What, in your opinion, would be the advantage of such a limitation of vocabulary? Another "advantage" of Newspeak would be a uniform and consistent grammar. What goals would be achieved by such a remodeling of English grammar?

4. Orwell says that the purpose of some Newspeak words "was not so much to express meanings as to destroy them." Can you detect any such current attempts to destroy or obscure meanings in this way?

LINCOLN BARNETT 6

The Linguistic Wonder of the Modern World

For centuries men have dreamed of a universal language that would enable people all over the world to communicate with one another. Through historical accident, English today has come closer than any language in the past to fulfilling the role of a "world language." In this selection, the opening chapter in his book The Treasure of Our Tongue, *Lincoln Barnett, prolific author and winner of numerous writing awards, brings together examples demonstrating that everywhere "people of all classes now look to English as a window, a magic casement opening on every horizon of loquacious men."*

And who in time knows whither we may vent
The treasure of our tongue? To what strange shores
This gain of our best glory shall be sent,
To enrich unknowing nations with our stores?
What worlds in the yet unformed Occident
May come refined with the accents that are ours?
Samuel Daniel (1562–1619), English poet and historian

THE SIMPLE ANSWER TO SAMUEL DANIEL'S MULTIPLE QUESTION IS that the treasure of our tongue has been transported around the world. Strange shores and far-off nations have been enriched with the verbal stores, if not necessarily refined by the accents, that are ours. For, unbelievable as it might have seemed to a contemporary of Shakespeare, English has become the most widely spoken language on earth. Today 300 million people—nearly one in ten—employ English as their primary language; and 600 million—nearly one in four—can be reached by it in some degree.

Few events in man's turbulent history compare in scope or significance with this global linguistic conquest. When Daniel wrote his prophetic lines, he expressed a poet's vision conceived in the bright morning of the expanding British Empire. At the time of the Norman Conquest in 1066, English had no more than 1.5 million speakers. In the ensuing five centuries it evolved slowly into the rich, flexible medium of the Elizabethan poets who, while cherishing their language, never dreamed it might become a universal tongue. In 1582 Richard Mulcaster, the most famous English educator of his day, headmaster of the Merchant Taylors' School in London and later high master at St. Paul's, remarked: "The English tongue is of small reach, stretching no further than this island of ours, nay not there over all." Portia, in *The Merchant of Venice,* said regretfully of the young English Baron Falconbridge: "You know I say nothing to him, for he understands not me, nor I him: he hath neither Latin, French nor Italian." As recently as the eighteenth century, English was still outranked by French, Latin (for scholarship), German, Spanish, Russian, and Italian; and European academicians deplored the fact that English writers wrote only in English.

Today English is written, spoken, broadcast, and understood on every continent, and it can claim a wider geographical range than any other tongue. There are few civilized areas where it has any competition as the lingua franca—the international language of commerce, diplomacy, science, and scholarship. Its speakers cover one quarter of the globe, ranging from the fair-skinned people of the British Isles through every gradation of color and race the world around. It is spoken by Christians, Jews, Moslems, Buddhists, Hindus, and adherents of every major religious faith on earth.

The dominance of any language, however, rests not only on statistical superiority and geographical sweep, but on cultural prestige and the status of the people who use it. Voltaire expressed this notion when he observed: "The first among languages is that which possesses the largest number of excellent works." Of the nearly four thousand languages spoken by mankind on this planet today, only a dozen have international or cultural significance. As a primary language, Chinese can claim more speakers than English—an estimated

700 million. It can also boast a more ancient heritage than English and an imposing cultural tradition descending from Confucius and Lao-tse through twenty-five centuries down to the present time. But its alphabet and calligraphy present enormous difficulties. And so far as the spoken language is concerned, its four main regional varieties —each divided into numerous sub-dialects—are mutually unintelligible save to the educated ear. The differences between spoken Mandarin and spoken Cantonese, for example, are as formidable as those between Danish and Dutch. So, the use of Chinese is largely confined to those born to the tongue, and living for the most part in China or Taiwan.

After Chinese and English, the other great languages of the world are, in descending order of the number of speakers who employ them as a *primary* tongue: Spanish with 140 million speakers; Russian with 130 million; German with 100 million; Japanese, 95 milion; Arabic, 80 million; Bengali, Indonesian, and Portuguese, 75 million each; Urdu (spoken in Pakistan and parts of India), 70 million; French and Hindi, 65 million each; and Italian, 55 million.

Of these, French has been paramount in the Western world for centuries. It has been the international language of diplomacy since the reign of Louis XIV. It has been the language of culture, of the educated classes, of the aristocracy of all European nations from the Urals to the British Isles. But with the erosion of the French Empire in the last two decades, it has lost ground on every continent. Although its cultural prestige is undimmed and can never wane so long as its literary legacy is preserved for posterity to enjoy, French is no longer the principal language of diplomacy and trade. Even in such erstwhile French dominions as Laos, Vietnam, and Lebanon, English is now a competing tongue. It is noteworthy that in the United Nations, 53 member states now regularly receive transcripts of speeches and proceedings in English, as against 27 which request drafts in French.

Culturally, as well as from the standpoint of geographical radius and numerical status, Spanish ranks near the apex of the linguistic hierarchy. It has hegemony through Central and South America (save for Portuguese-speaking Brazil), and the numbers of its adherents are multiplying swiftly with the swelling populations of the Latin-American states. But it shows no signs at present of overflowing its existing domain. German and Italian are also largely encompassed by their respective national boundaries—although the former was the leading language of science until the Nazi extermination of intellect, and the latter is still mandatory in the higher realms of music and art. Arabic, despite its vast territorial range from Casablanca to

Baghdad, and notwithstanding the current hot fires of Arab nationalism, has disadvantages both in speech and writing that will probably preclude its passing very far beyond the limits of the Moslem world.

So far as Russian is concerned, its 130 million speakers are resident mostly within the Soviet Union, whose enormous spatial confines and total population of 224,700,000 also accommodate 148 other languages. Although Russian is the medium for some of the world's greatest literature—the works of Tolstoy, Dostoevsky, Turgenev, Gogol, Chekhov, Pushkin, Pasternak—and although the political and scientific dynamism of the Soviet Union presents the greatest challenge which the English-speaking nations face today, the Russian language is unlikely to win a linguistic war. It has a specialized alphabet, and its inflected grammar is far more difficult to master than the comparatively simple grammar of English. Like Chinese, Russian is currently limited to its geographical place of origin.

English, however, is spreading around the planet at a constantly accelerating tempo. Virtually every capital city in Asia and Africa (save for former French colonies) has an English-language daily. More than 70 percent of the world's mail is written and addressed in English. More than 60 percent of the world's radio programs are in English. It is noteworthy and ironical that among the leading disseminators of English are the Russians and Chinese in their attempt to woo friends and influence nations in uncommitted regions of the earth. The Russians use English for their propaganda broadcasts to the Far East. On African channels formerly dominated by programs from Cairo in Arabic and Swahili, listeners in Kenya, Malawi, and Zanzibar now receive clear loud broadcasts from Peiping Radio in Red China—all in English. Freight shipments of heavy machinery and other commodities from Russia to the Near East are stamped "Made in U.S.S.R."—in English. In many cities Russian cultural offices compete with British and American centers in advertising English courses. And of the 30 million books which the Russians annually distribute to former British colonies in Africa and Asia, a large proportion are in English—among them technical books, novels, and children's books, including *Goldilocks and the Three Bears,* by Leo Tolstoy (actual author: Robert Southey).

English is also the language of international aviation, spoken by pilots and airport control-tower operators on all the airways of the world. Besides its status as the official air language of NATO, it is increasingly employed by pilots of many countries on local flights within their own national boundaries. The West German Luftwaffe and even the flyers of East Germany use it. And the French, though ever jealous of their proud and beautiful language, find English far more efficient for air-ground communication. It takes less time, for example, to say *jet* than *avion à réaction,* or to talk of *flaps* rather than *volets de flexions*. And there are other areas of mankind's diverse activities within which English now reigns virtually supreme. It is the international language of sport in every country where people play *futbol* or *beisbol*. It is the international language of jazz, whose followers in all lands know the difference between *le bebop* and *buki-buki* (boogie-woogie) and can do the Twist. And it is the language of international youth—of teen-agers everywhere who wear *blue djins* and *pulova* sweaters, chew *gomma americana* (specifically bubble gum), smoke *Looky Strooky* cigarettes (as in Russia), and enjoy hot dogs and Coke (or, as in Japan, *Koka-Kora,* and its rival *Pepusi-kora*).

It is in the realm of statesmanship, however, that English has attained the status of a universal tongue to a degree never faintly approached by Latin in the heyday of the Roman Empire or by French in the eighteenth and nineteenth centuries. Of the various new sovereign states created since World War II, many have formally adopted English either as their official language or the recognized second language of the land. At the Bandung Conference of 1955, which represented 1.4 billion people from twenty-nine Asian and African countries (including Red China), the proceedings were conducted entirely in English—not for any love of England or the United States, but because it was the only means by which the multilingual delegates could communicate with one another. More recently, when Egypt and Indonesia drew up a cultural treaty, it was specified that the definitive version of the agreement between these two Moslem countries, neither one an ardent lover of the Western world, would be the English-language copy. By the same token, when a trade delegation from Ceylon journeyed to the Soviet Union for a conference, their Russian hosts, who met them in Kabul, Afghanistan, greeted them in English. And when the Dalai Lama fled down from his Tibetan highlands to seek sanctuary in India, he was welcomed by Prime Minister Nehru on the nothern frontier.

"How are you?" Nehru asked in English.

"Very nice," the Dalai Lama replied with perfect lucidity (though he was doubtless unaware that the word *nice* has a whole spectrum of meanings of which the original one was "foolish").

The most spectacular advances made by English are in the so-called underdeveloped areas of the world. The polyglot populations of Asia and Africa find it much easier to learn English than to try to comprehend the speech of their nearest neighbors. For contrary to popular supposition, languages evolve in the direction of simplicity.

English, being a highly evolved, cosmopolitan, sophisticated language, has been refined and revised, planed down and polished through centuries of use, so that today it is far less complicated than any primitive tongue. Some of the most difficult languages in the world are spoken by some of the world's most backward people—e.g. the Australian aborigines, the Eskimos, the Hottentots, and the Yahgan Indians of Tierra del Fuego. In West Africa alone, some 60 million tribesmen speak more than 400 different languages; hence wherever European influence has left its mark, Africans talk to each other in English or French when they leave their local language district—which in some towns may mean across the street.[1] Ghana has proclaimed English its official language and requires English instruction from primary school on. In East Africa, whose tribes have communicated for centuries in Swahili, a linguistic hybrid woven by Arab slavers a thousand years ago out of a mixture of Arabic and Bantu idiom, even rabid nationalists today favor English over Swahili as the common tongue.

English continues to be the lingua franca of the Middle East, despite the political ferment of Islam. From Cairo to Teheran, no traveler who speaks it is ever at a loss in finding lodging, food, or transport. Most Arab radio stations have English programs; and English-language newspapers, books, and magazines are sold in every major city. Despite recent attempts to employ Arabic more generally in education, most universities in Islam quietly concluded during 1963–4 that English had to be retained as the language both of instruction and of textbooks. Even at conservative El Azhar University in Cairo, ancient and orthodox seat of Moslem higher learning, English is compulsory at all levels (as well as in the prep schools which feed El Azhar). Cairo's *Egyptian Gazette,* addressing Arab nationalists, declared recently: "English is not the property of capitalist Americans, but of all the world."

The swift and astonishing spread of English around the globe has not taken place without opposition here and there. The French in particular, ever protective of their cultural heritage, have endeavored to hold the linguistic lines in their former colonies in Asia and Africa; while in metropolitan France, the Office du Vocabulaire Français continually exhorts newspapers and magazines to avoid the *snobisme* of using English words where French equivalents exist. Unfortunately, succinct French equivalents do not always exist, at least for such vivid contemporary terms as *call girl, snack bar, supermarket, missile*

[1] At a meeting of the foreign ministers of the Organization of African Unity early in 1964, the Egyptian delegate began an address in Arabic. From all sides of the hall came cries of "Speak English!" or *"Parlez français!"*

gap, gadget, gunman, parking, mixer, teen-ager, jukebox, job, flash, smash, and *boom.* Alarmed at the contamination of his native tongue by such vulgar neologisms, René Etiemble, a professor of comparative literature at the Sorbonne, launched a counterattack at the end of 1963 in the form of a best-selling book *Parlez-Vous Franglais?* in which he estimated that at least five thousand common Anglo-American words and thirty thousand technical terms had entered the French vernacular in the last decade. "If we do not take care now," he warned, "in forty years' time the French language will have ceased to exist." Proposing that fines be imposed on *Américano-latres,* Etiemble declared: "The French language is a treasure. To violate it is a crime. Persons were shot during the war for treason. They should be punished for degrading the language." The august Académie Française at once backed up Etiemble's campaign by announcing that its dictionary commission would start preparing a blacklist of "foreign words" that are *impropres à la langue.*

A few years earlier in Belgium, a bilingual country where rivalry between French and Flemish has long been a fact of national life, French-speaking Walloons were outraged when Henri Fayat, then Minister of Foreign Trade, addressed the 1958 Council of Europe Assembly in English. "A deliberate insult!" French-language newspapers expostulated. "A political gesture meant to snub a large section of the Belgian population!" But the Dutch-speaking Flemings, long jealous of French linguistic dominance, had not the slightest objection to the advent of English as Belgium's third and common tongue.

Like the French, the Spaniards are reluctant to let their ancient, romantic language suffer the incursions of a foreign idiom. Of all European countries, Spain has been the least receptive to English, partly because of its geographical isolation, partly because Spaniards historically profess little love for the homeland of Sir Francis Drake. In the spring of 1964 the Royal Spanish Academy at Madrid, not to be outdone by the Académie Française, initiated a campaign to defend the Spanish tongue from bastardization by Anglo-American idioms disseminated by the press, radio, television, and the cinema —especially Hollywood films that had been dubbed in Mexico. Many of the objectionable expressions derived, like those which aroused the ire of French purists, from the ever-enlarging glossaries of science, aviation, sports, and jazz, and were borrowed intact. Some, however, acquired a distinctly Spanish accent: e.g. *gangsterismo, columnista, cocktel* (for cocktail party), and *perrito caliente* (hot dog).

Even in Latin America, where English is now virtually mandatory for business and professional men, purists recurrently plead for the preservation of Spanish as "the most beautiful, majestic and sonorous language in the world." Argentina's Perón tried briefly (and unsuccessfully) to ban Hollywood movies in his country unless Spanish titles were superimposed; today in Buenos Aires, enrollment in English-language schools is increasing at the rate of more than 10 percent a year. In Peru more recently, the Ministry of Education ordered certain schools in Lima—the Abraham Lincoln High School, the John Dewey High School, the William Prescott High School, and others—to change their names. The order was obeyed; but the names soon reappeared, for they indicated that the schools specialized in English, a commodity in enormous demand.

Throughout Latin America, English is spoken and understood almost everywhere save in the remote hinterland. Wealthy families from Mexico to Chile who formerly sent their teen-age children abroad to school in France and Switzerland now tend to enroll them in prep schools and colleges in England and the United States. In Portuguese-speaking Brazil especially, English is acknowledged as a necessity for anyone who seeks economic advancement, and as such it is a required course in primary and secondary schools. "Portuguese is a tomb," a Brazilian educator said not long ago. "It is good only in Brazil and Portugal." (In Portugal too, English has made spectacular progress, joining French as a second tongue). Most of the countries in the Caribbean area are bilingual; American programs appear on television nightly; airport signs and menus are printed both in English and Spanish; many schools and colleges teach at least half their classes in English. And on the island of Hispaniola, uneasily shared by French-speaking Haiti and the Spanish-speaking Dominican Republic, government officials of the two countries use English for mutual interchange when circumstances make it necessary for them to talk to each other at all.

Perhaps the most notable victory of the English language over nationalistic resistance was recently won in India. In an effort to expunge relics of the British Raj, the Central Government had proclaimed in 1950 that the official language of India would henceforth be Hindi (the vernacular of northern India), and that the transition from English must be complete by 1965. Although this pleased the Hindu populations in the north, the reaction was quite different in the rest of the vast subcontinent, which encompasses 845 distinct languages and dialects. The Bengali-speakers in the east did not like the decree; and in the south the millions of speakers of Tamil and related Dravidian languages protested that fifteen years was too brief an interval in which to adopt a tongue as alien to them as any in the

Occidental world. For more than a century English has been the common tongue; and although not more than 3 percent of India's population of 461,300,000 employ it with any degree of fluency, they represent the ruling 3 percent—administrators, judges, legislators, and other educated groups. Moreover, the leading newspapers of India (as of Pakistan) are English-language dailies. If English were expunged, they pointed out, there would be no way for all the peoples of the huge land to communicate with one another. Months of argument ensued, marred recurrently by bloody riots. At the University of Lucknow, which switched at once from English to Hindi, levels of learning went into an alarming decline. Faculty members evolved a kind of Anglo-Hindi jargon, inventing hybrid words for technical terms in an attempt to comply with the government edict. The result was Babel.[2]

Finally the so-called "Save Hindi" campaign was called off. The announcement, significantly, was published in English. In Parliament, Prime Minister Nehru declared that for an indefinite period English would continue as an "associate official language." While Hindus listened in silence and non-Hindu-speaking legislators cheered, Nehru termed English "the major window for us to the outside world."

"We dare not close that window," he said. "And if we do, it will spell peril to our future."

In Nehru's words lies one explanation for the virtually unopposed diffusion of English around the globe. For not only in Asia and Africa, but in Europe, crisscrossed by linguistic frontiers and dissected by deep-rooted cultural loyalties, people of all classes now look to English as a window, a magic casement opening on every horizon of loquacious men. Smaller countries, whose national languages are encompassed by narrow boundaries, have been the most receptive, because experience has taught them that Anglo-Saxons seldom trouble to master the speech of other lands. When Eisenhower visited Norway some years ago in his role as commander-in-chief of NATO, he remarked: "I have the impression that every second Norwegian speaks the English language." Today in Norway—as in Sweden, Denmark, Finland, the Netherlands, Austria, Portugal, Greece, Turkey, and Japan—English is taught in all schools and colleges, usually as a required subject, but otherwise as the most popular choice among other elective language courses.

In West Germany, schools require six to nine years of English. The

[2] Similar efforts to make Urdu the language of education in West Pakistan met with no greater success. In a speech at Karachi on May 12, 1964, Pakistan's President Mohammed Ayub Khan said: "I doubt very much if we have reached a stage where we could afford to abandon English and make Urdu the medium of instruction for various sciences."

obligation meets with no emotional resistance, for unlike the French the Germans feel no sense of linguistic betrayal in studying English; they are eager to learn, and experience little difficulty in the process since English is more a Teutonic than a Romance language. "To a Frenchman," a Swiss journalist observed recently, "his language is a sacrosanct cultural endowment, almost a state of mind. If a German wants to enlarge his intellectual horizons he will take up another language. A Frenchman will read more French."

Even behind the Iron Curtain, English is expanding its enclaves without opposition. In East Germany (where Russian used to be, but is no longer, a compulsory subject), English now holds first place among optional language courses in secondary schools, with twelve applicants for every available departmental vacancy. English classes are equally in demand in Poland. In Yugoslavia, English replaced Russian as the country's second language several years ago. In 1960, for example, Yugoslav publishers issued 86 books in English, 57 in French, 49 in German, and only 31 in Russian. Within the Soviet Union itself, schools offer English from the fourth or fifth grades on; and in some of the larger cities, it is the one compulsory language in the curriculum. One of the best-sellers in the bookshops of Moscow is an English grammar.

The teaching of language in schools, however, represents only one of many channels through which the torrent of English is inundating all lands. A tremendously important source is the cinema—American and British movies are shown the world over. Other tributary freshets include radio and television, recordings of popular songs, English-language publications, adult education courses, language centers, mobile libraries and exchange fellowships sponsored by government agencies and private foundations; and, perhaps most important of all, the incomputable numbers of informal encounters that occur every hour of the day among businessmen, professional men, politicians, scientists, technicians, students, and just plain tourists linked together on a shrinking planet by the swift instrumentalities of the jet age.

Although the flood tide of English dates only from the end of World War II, its incipient stage actually began more than three centuries ago, when British adventurers first carried their speech to the far places of the earth, erecting the initial bastions of empire. In the wake of the conquerors came traders, and after them missionaries—who still exercise a potent force in Africa and Asia. But the major catalyst in the English-language explosion was war—especially the two great conflicts of this century. "War is perhaps the most rapidly effectual excitant of language," a British etymologist has observed.

The occupation troops that moved into defeated countries after World War I and on incomparably greater scale after World War II did more to spread English (particularly American English) than any other agency of dissemination. From the hundreds of thousands of soldiers and their dependents deployed throughout both hemispheres, English words and phrases filtered down to every level of the diverse populations in every nation and zone. No longer was English speech the limited possession of the educated, the wealthy, and the peripatetic social élite. It became the economically valuable property of all, from shopkeepers and salesgirls, bellboys and bartenders, down to barefoot urchins in the streets of Tokyo and Teheran, Berlin and Baghdad, who swiftly learned to chirp, "Hey Joe, gimme gum," or "Hey Joe, wanna some fun?"

The popular desire to learn English has increased each year as America's international interests and commercial commitments continue to radiate in widening circles across the seas. The desire has been met by a vast complex of organizations, both national and international, British and American, public and private. The United States Information Agency (USIA) maintains 239 cultural centers in 106 countries, ranging from small circulating libraries that offer English books and magazines to elaborate establishments like Amerika House in Berlin, which provides programs of lectures, concerts, dances, and language instruction to as many as 1,800 visitors a day. During the last few years an average of 30 million persons have annually used the facilities of USIA centers around the world. Of these more than one million have attended English-language seminars each year, among them 5,000 local teachers whose combined classes represented more than two million pupils. The network of the USIA is complemented by the British Council, an older organization of parallel purposes which maintains centers in all important cities as well as such exotic and far-away places as Tabriz, Addis Ababa, and Basra. The Council's teaching methods differ from those of the USIA in one detail; they devote more attention to reading, the USIA more to speech. Another United States agency in the field is AID—the Agency for International Development—which offers English lessons for technical-aid projects, and transports foreign businessmen and technicians to the United States, where they are taught English as a prelude to courses in industrial management, engineering, and such. The Voice of America broadcasts English-language programs five times daily, and the radio of the United States Armed Forces beams popular programs of music, news, and comment in English from the North Sea to the Sea of Japan. In addition, a 26-week television course of instruction in English, consisting of 130 half-hour lessons, has been recorded on film by the USIA for the free use of telecasting stations in all countries around the world. The film is supplemented by a textbook, *Let's Learn English,* and a vocabulary list, which stations may buy for five cents apiece and give free to participants. Local teachers speaking local languages preside over the telecast classes. Students who pass examinations at the conclusion of the course receive certificates of achievement; by that time they generally have a working knowledge of 1,000 to 1,300 English words, sufficient to enable them to read not-too-difficult books in English.

Along with the government agencies, many private organizations abet the educative process. American corporations with overseas affiliates or operating concessions provide English lessons to workers in oil fields, factories, and offices in other lands. The Ford and Rockefeller Foundations have granted millions of dollars to institutions both in foreign countries (the American University in Cairo, Robert College in Istanbul) and in the United States (the University of Michigan, the University of Texas, U.C.L.A., Columbia) which specialize in teaching English to foreign students. Organizations such as Language Service and Language Research, Inc., combine instruction with experimental studies aimed at the improvement of teaching techniques. Meanwhile, all around the globe, English lessons are proffered for varying fees by innumerable private teachers, by international language schools (like Berlitz), and by various home study systems (like Linguaphone), which employ a combination of phonographic recordings and the printed word.

Of vastly greater import than the scale and momentum of the English irruption from its wellsprings in the West is the fact that it came in response to a worldwide and seemingly insatiable demand. The agencies of dissemination are not engaged in force-feeding. Nor, as often implied in Congress and in the press, is the teaching of English merely a propaganda tactic in the Cold War or, worse, an expensive and visionary attempt to promote international understanding through the medium—generally deprecated by the tough-minded—of cultural interchange. No government agency created the demand for English; it was there. In the absence of the demand, no plethora of appropriations, no intensity of missionary zeal could induce millions of people to undertake the arduous chore of learning a foreign language. The eagerness with which these people, sundered from one another by all the great linguistic divisions of mankind, are now dedicating themselves to that chore stems from the realization that English is a gateway to opportunity in every land. For it is the language in which man can best communicate with his fellowman in a small, crowded, and interdependent world.

The universal hunger for English is manifested daily in all countries where it is now being taught. Some recent situations and episodes:

• In Athens, police were called out to control a crowd that descended on the USIA center following an announcement of registration for English classes.

• In Santos, Brazil, a local newspaper failed to print the text of a daily lesson accompanying a radio English course. More than 500 people called the newspaper, 100 called the United States Consulate, and several hundred called the radio station to ask what happened.

• In Baghdad, during the violent upheaval of 1958, the United States Embassy and the Consulate were forced to close, but the USIA language school remained open by request of the Iraqi government. The reason for the exception was that Iraqi officials were attending the school themselves.

• In Finland, where English classes are hopelessly overcrowded, a number of private corporations participate in what is known as the Teacher-Secretary Plan. They engage British secretaries to handle international correspondence during office hours and to give English lessons to staff employees and others at night.

• In Kabul, when English courses were announced, Afghans queued up in a driving snowstorm to wait their turn to enroll.

• In Tunisia, President Bourguiba deemed English so important for his newly created republic that he asked the United States government for aid in establishing a school. The Bourguiba School of Language at the University of Tunisia is now flourishing, under the joint auspices of the State Department, the USIA, and AID.

• In Teheran, no less than 122 private language schools give lessons in English to thousands of adults, at an average fee of 20 cents an hour. Their services are officially endorsed by the Iranian government with the slogan: "If you don't know English, you know nothing."

• In Peru, villagers and townspeople in many small communities foregather daily at noon in squares and plazas for English lessons via loudspeaker.

• In Japan, an American librarian in a town on the island of Nagoya, agreed to spend a little time conversing in English informally with a casual acquaintance. The next day the pupil returned with a friend. The day after that he returned with several friends. Within a few days the informal group had expanded into a full-fledged class, then into two classes, then three, then four. At this point the harried librarian called USIA headquarters in Washington to protest that she was not a professional teacher and to plead for reinforcements.

How can this worldwide and apparently insatiable demand for English be explained? None of the external factors—business motivations, the extended military and economic influence of the English-speaking people, circumglobal pathways of communication and travel —can adequately account for the phenomenon. The essential catalyst lies in the international anatomy of the language itself.

Ever since the events at Babel, when, according to Genesis, "the Lord did there confound the language of all the earth," man has lamented his linguistic fragmentation; and he has endeavored from time to time to construct an ideal, supranational language as a medium of intellectual exchange for all lands. None of these synthetic languages—Esperanto, Gloro, Ido, Interlingua, Langue Bleue, Novial, Nulange, Volapük, or any other of perhaps thirty such inventions—has ever won enough speakers to satisfy the zeal of their proponents. Today, through the accidents of history and entirely under its own momentum, English has become the fulfillment of this philological dream. Dr. Samuel Johnson would have rejoiced to witness its spread. For he cherished the treasure of his tongue. "Wondrous the English language," he once exclaimed, "language of live men!"

FOR DISCUSSION AND REVIEW

1. What factors account for the international importance of English?

2. Barnett argues that "the dominance of any language . . . rests not only on statistical superiority and geographical sweep, but on cultural prestige and the status of the people who use it." How have cultural prestige and the status of speakers of English contributed to its widespread use?

3. The leaders of some countries have tried to slow, if not curtail, the growing influence that English is having on their languages. On what grounds have arguments against the spread of English been based? How reasonable are the arguments, and how successful do you think their proponents will be?

4. Barnett claims that World War II had an influence on the spread of English throughout the world. Explain.

WRITING

1. Argue either that the euphemism is "a handy verbal tool to avoid

making enemies needlessly, or shocking friends," or that it is "a danger to thought and action, since its fundamental intent is to deceive." Be specific.

2. Write three paragraphs in which you describe the same incident, person, scene, or thing. In the first paragraph, use language that will produce a neutral impression; in the second, language that will produce a favorable impression; and in the third, language that will produce an unfavorable impression. Keep the factual content of each of your paragraphs constant; vary only the language.

3. Choose an editorial dealing with a controversial issue. Assume that you have been offered equal space in the newspaper in which to present the opposing viewpoint. Write an editorial in the form of a rebuttal. Hand in both your editorial and the original that stimulated it.

4. In his article on the spread of the English language, Lincoln Barnett discusses the attempts of the French to stop Franglais (pp. 259–60). Such snobbism, especially in the light of the long-standing relationships that England and America have had with France, seems appropriate for the satirist. Write a satire on the French purists, drawing upon examples of Franglais included in the following articles: "Le Come-Back de Savoir-Faire" (*Newsweek,* January 29, 1973) and "Franglais" (*Saturday Review of the Society,* April, 1973). You may also wish to check the *Reader's Guide to Periodical Literature* for additional articles.

5. The meanings of words are constantly changing in a number of ways. One interesting kind of change is that of a word such as "very." In the fourteenth century, Chaucer wrote, "He was a verray, parfit gentil knyght." Here "verray" means "genuine, true, real." Now, of course, it has lost that meaning and become instead an intensifier. The word "real" is undergoing similar change: it can mean "genuine," as in "That's a real diamond"; but by some speakers it is also used as an intensifier to mean "very," as in "I'm real tired."

After consulting the *Oxford English Dictionary,* give examples of words that have changed meaning and how they have changed. If possible, make some generalizations about word change. Then, write an essay on kinds of semantic change.

6. John Ciardi has argued that every culture needs its "taboo areas." Depending upon such taboos, what constitutes profanity in one culture may not be regarded as profane at all in another. For Chaucer, for example, profanity included the religious: "By Goddes precious herte!" and "By his nailes!" and "By the blood of Christ that is in Hailes" (all from "The Pardoner's Tale") and "by the crois which that Sainte Elaine foond" (from the "Epilogue" to "The Pardoner's Tale"). In America today, however, mention of sex and various

bodily functions is often taboo. Write an essay in which you discuss Ciardi's idea and its implications for the future of American English. Use specific details from contemporary language.

7. Each of the six articles in this final section presents a view of what the future holds for English. These views are very different from one another. Which of them do you find most plausible? If none of the possibilities seems convincing to you, describe your own vision of the future.

NOTABLE QUOTATIONS

"Semantic aphasia is that numbness of ear, mind and heart—that tone deafness to the very meaning of language—which results from the habitual and prolonged abuse of words." *Maddocks*

"Words now seem to cut off and isolate, to cause more misunderstanding than they prevent." *Maddocks*

"Whenever the ravishing of the English language comes up for perfunctory headshaking, politicians, journalists, and ad writers almost invariably get cast as Three Horsemen of the Apocalypse. . . . They are word manipulators—the carnival barkers of life who misuse language to pitch and con and make the quick kill." *Maddocks*

"What can one do to punish the semantic aphasics for polluting their native language?" *Maddocks*

"Few events in man's turbulent history compare in scope or significance with [English's] global linguistic conquest." *Barnett*

"The dominance of any language . . . rests not only on statistical superiority and geographical sweep, but on cultural prestige and the status of the people who use it." *Barnett*

"Is it not possible that there is a direct correlation between a growing sense of powerlessness and futility in our lives and the jazzed-up language we use?" *Berger*

"Surely we were better off during the Middle Ages, when everything of international importance was expressed in Latin." *Ornstein and Gage*

". . . A universal language [will] bring peace and understanding." *Ornstein and Gage*